# Soviet Theatre during the Thaw

CULTURAL HISTORIES OF THEATRE AND PERFORMANCE

The Bloomsbury series of Cultural Histories of Theatre and Performance recognizes that historical knowledge has always been contested and revised. Since the turn of the twenty-first century, the transformation of conventional understandings of culture created through new political realities and communication technologies, together with paradigm shifts in anthropology, psychology and other cognate fields, has challenged established methodologies and ways of thinking about how we do history. The series embraces volumes that take on those challenges, while enlarging notions of theatre and performance through the representation of the lived experience of past performance makers and spectators. The series' aim is to be both inclusive and expansive, including studies on topics that range temporally and spatially, from the locally specific to the intercultural and transnational.

**Series editors:**

Claire Cochrane (University of Worcester, UK)

Bruce McConachie (University of Pittsburgh, USA)

*George Farquhar: A Migrant Life Reversed*
David Roberts

*The Polish Theatre of the Holocaust*
Grzegorz Niziołek

*A Century of South African Theatre*
Loren Kruger

*Alternative Comedy: 1979 and the Reinvention of British Stand-Up*
Oliver Double

**Forthcoming titles**

*Theatre, Performance and Commemoration: Staging Crisis, Memory and Nationhood* Edited by Miriam Haughton, Alinne Balduino P. Fernandes and Pieter Verstraete

*Performing Modernity: Culture and Experiment in the Irish Free State, 1922-1937* Elaine Sisson

*Theatre with a Purpose: Amateur Drama in Britain 1919-1949*
Don Watson

*German Amateur Theatre and Social Change in the Early Nineteenth Century*
Meike Wagner

# Soviet Theatre during the Thaw

*Aesthetics, Politics and Performance*

Jesse Gardiner

methuen | drama
LONDON • NEW YORK • OXFORD • NEW DELHI • SYDNEY

METHUEN DRAMA
Bloomsbury Publishing Plc
50 Bedford Square, London, WC1B 3DP, UK
1385 Broadway, New York, NY 10018, USA
29 Earlsfort Terrace, Dublin 2, Ireland

BLOOMSBURY, METHUEN DRAMA and the Methuen Drama logo are trademarks of Bloomsbury Publishing Plc

First published in Great Britain 2023
This paperback edition published 2024

Copyright © Jesse Gardiner, 2023

Jesse Gardiner has asserted his right under the Copyright, Designs and Patents Act, 1988, to be identified as Author of this work.

For legal purposes the Acknowledgements on p. ix constitute an extension of this copyright page.

Series design by Adriana Brioso
Cover image: *Mystery Bouffe* at the Moscow Satire Theatre, 1957. Courtesy of the Museum of the Moscow Academic Satire Theatre

All rights reserved. No part of this publication may be reproduced or transmitted in any form or by any means, electronic or mechanical, including photocopying, recording, or any information storage or retrieval system, without prior permission in writing from the publishers.

Bloomsbury Publishing Plc does not have any control over, or responsibility for, any third-party websites referred to or in this book. All internet addresses given in this book were correct at the time of going to press. The author and publisher regret any inconvenience caused if addresses have changed or sites have ceased to exist, but can accept no responsibility for any such changes.

A catalogue record for this book is available from the British Library.

Library of Congress Cataloging-in-Publication Data.
Names: Gardiner, Jesse, author.
Title: Soviet theatre during the thaw: aesthetics, politics and performance / Jesse Gardiner.
Description: London; New York: Methuen Drama, 2022. | Series: Cultural histories of theatre and performance | Includes bibliographical references and index.
Identifiers: LCCN 2022017967 (print) | LCCN 2022017968 (ebook) |
ISBN 9781350150621 (hardback) | ISBN 9781350346017 (paperback) |
ISBN 9781350150638 (epub) | ISBN 9781350150645 (ebook)
Subjects: LCSH: Theater–Soviet Union–History.
Classification: LCC PN2724 .G37 2022 (print) | LCC PN2724 (ebook) |
DDC 792.0947090/45–dc23/eng/20220613
LC record available at https://lccn.loc.gov/2022017967
LC ebook record available at https://lccn.loc.gov/2022017968

ISBN: HB: 978-1-3501-5062-1
PB: 978-1-3503-4601-7
ePDF: 978-1-3501-5064-5
eBook: 978-1-3501-5063-8

Series: Cultural Histories of Theatre and Performance

Typeset by Deanta Global Publishing Services, Chennai, India

To find out more about our authors and books visit www.bloomsbury.com and sign up for our newsletters.

*For Stef*

# Contents

| | | |
|---|---|---|
| List of figures | | viii |
| Acknowledgements | | ix |
| Explanatory note | | x |
| | | |
| Introduction | | 1 |
| 1 | Soviet theatre under Stalin | 22 |
| 2 | Leningrad in the shadow of the Other: Akimov at the Lensovet Theatre, 1952–5 | 52 |
| 3 | Restaging Mayakovsky and remembering Meyerhold: The Moscow Satire Theatre productions, 1953–7 | 76 |
| 4 | Redefining socialist realism in the era of de-Stalinization: Tovstonogov and Okhlopkov revive the Soviet classics, 1955–6 | 102 |
| 5 | New writers for new times: Moscow realism at the Sovremennik Theatre-Studio, 1956–9 | 127 |
| 6 | The fairy tale that would not come true: Staging Evgenii Shvarts, 1960–3 | 149 |
| Epilogue | | 173 |
| | | |
| Notes | | 177 |
| Select Bibliography | | 203 |
| Index | | 206 |

# Figures

| | | |
|---|---|---|
| 1 | Valentin Lebedev and Galina Korotkevich in *Shadows* at the Lensovet Theatre in Leningrad, 1952 | 67 |
| 2 | The prologue in *The Case* at the Lensovet Theatre in Leningrad, 1954 | 70 |
| 3 | The Phosphorescent Woman looks down at Pobedonosikov in *The Bathhouse* at the Moscow Satire Theatre, 1953 | 83 |
| 4 | The hunt for the bedbug in *The Bedbug* at the Moscow Satire Theatre, 1955 | 89 |
| 5 | Vladimir Lepko in *The Bedbug* at the Moscow Satire Theatre, 1955 | 91 |
| 6 | Dancing devils in *Mystery Bouffe* at the Moscow Satire Theatre, 1957 | 96 |
| 7 | The finale of *Mystery Bouffe* at the Moscow Satire Theatre, 1957 | 98 |
| 8 | The Commissar leads the regiment with Vozhak following behind. *An Optimistic Tragedy* at the Aleksandrinskii Theatre, 1955 | 116 |
| 9 | Kapitolina Pugacheva as Lady Niurka in *Aristocrats* at the Mayakovsky Theatre, 1956 | 120 |
| 10 | Oleg Efremov and Viktor Rozov at the premiere of *Alive Forever* at the Sovremennik Theatre-Studio, 1956 | 133 |
| 11 | Zinaida Sharko and Efim Kopelian in *Five Evenings* at the Leningrad Bolshoi Dramatic Theatre, 1959 | 142 |
| 12 | Oleg Efremov and Lilia Tolmacheva in *Five Evenings* at the Sovremennik Theatre-Studio, 1959 | 144 |
| 13 | Evgenii Evstigneev and Igor Kvasha in *The Naked King* at the Sovremennik Theatre-Studio, 1960 | 159 |
| 14 | Evgenii Evstigneev in *The Naked King* at the Sovremennik Theatre-Studio, 1960 | 161 |
| 15 | Nelli Korneva and Lev Kolesov in *The Dragon* at the Leningrad Comedy Theatre, 1962 | 168 |

# Acknowledgements

This book could not have been written without the support, advice and expertise of many friends and colleagues. I must first thank my former PhD mentors Cynthia Marsh and Polly McMichael for their incredible knowledge and guidance. I am also indebted to the Arts and Humanities Research Council, which funded the doctoral project that led to this book and enabled me to carry out archival research in Moscow and St Petersburg. I would like to thank the University of St Andrews for providing a period of sabbatical leave and my brilliant colleagues past and present, in particular Claire Whitehead, Victoria Donovan and Laura Todd who read and commented on parts of the book. I am very grateful for the support of many Russian friends and associates. I am particularly indebted to Oleg and Tatiana Skorik, Anna Lipskaia, Margarita Vaysman, Kirill Arbuzov, Varvara Arbuzova-Kulish, Dmitrii Simukov, Liudmila Sidorenko, Alexander Chepurov, Marina Kalinina and Liza Spivakovskaia for their help with the researching of this book. I would like to thank my editors at Bloomsbury Mark Dudgeon and Ella Wilson for their help throughout the project and the series editors Bruce McConachie and Claire Cochrane for their constructive and insightful feedback. I owe an enormous debt of thanks to my parents for their unwavering support over the years. Finally, I would like to express my profound gratitude to my wife Stefanie Petschick for reading multiple drafts of the manuscript and without whose love and support none of this would have been possible.

# Explanatory note

To make it easier for the reader, I have used familiar anglicizations of the names of well-known figures like Stanislavsky, Meyerhold, Trotsky, Gorky, Tolstoy, Tchaikovsky and Ehrenburg. Where possible the names of theatres have been translated into English rather than transliterated. For other names I have used the standard transliteration model set by the Library of Congress, but without diacritics.

# Introduction

## Between the squares

If you walk north from Moscow's Red Square, on the eastern side of the Kremlin, and cross over Theatre Street you reach Theatre Square. Built in 1821, the square is flanked to the north by the neoclassical colonnades of the Bolshoi Theatre and to the east by the Malyi Theatre, with its yellow façade and white cornices. On the west side of the square sits the Russian Academic Youth Theatre, formerly known as the Central Children's Theatre, and just north of it lies the Moscow State Operetta Theatre. If you walk a few yards west from the Operetta Theatre down Kamergerskii Lane you reach the Chekhov Moscow Art Theatre. Sitting just a stone's throw from the seat of power, the academic theatres clustered around Theatre Square are some of the most prestigious and privileged cultural institutions in Russia. During the Soviet era, the Bolshoi, Malyi and in particular the Moscow Art Theatre became closely tied to the establishment: awarded generous subsidies and attended regularly by the Soviet elite. In turn, some of the most celebrated actors and actresses at these theatres were elected as deputies to the Supreme Soviet, the highest legislative body in the USSR.

But if you continue past the Moscow Art Theatre and walk north up Tverskaia Street for about a mile you reach another square, known informally as Moscow's second theatre square.[1] Triumfal'naia Square lies on the north side of the Moscow Garden-Ring, where Tverskaia Street meets Bolshaia-Sadovaia. At the end of the sixteenth century, this spot marked the city limits, the point at which the main gates led out onto the road to Tver. By the end of the eighteenth century, a small market square had appeared on the site next to where a triumphal arch had been built to commemorate the signing of the Treaty of Nystad in 1721, giving the square its original name Staraia Triumfal'naia.[2] In the 1930s the square was renamed after Vladimir Mayakovsky, as part of the poet's canonization under Stalin, but reverted to its former name in 1992 following the collapse of the Soviet Union. Since the beginning of the twentieth century, the history of Triumfal'naia Square has been intertwined with the history of the theatre, its perpetual openings and closures, its reconfigurations and reconstructions. But if Moscow's main Theatre Square tells the history of the distinguished, academic institutions, then Triumfal'naia Square tells a different history, a counter-history, of the less illustrious theatrical genres: the 'small forms' of variety revue, music hall, cabaret, satire, circus and puppet show.

This counter-history can be traced in the lives of the buildings surrounding Triumfal'naia Square, which housed many of the theatre companies featured in this book. The Al'kazar Variety Theatre on the west side of the square provided a home at one time for the Moscow Art Theatre's rebellious first studio, the Satire Theatre (from 1927 to 1954), the Moscow Estrada (variety) Theatre and the Sovremennik Theatre (from 1961 to 1974). In the north-east corner of the square, Nikolai Okhlopkov's Realistic Theatre, formerly the Moscow Art Theatre's Fourth Studio, made its home (from 1927 to 1937) before it was closed down and the building handed over to Sergei Obraztsov's Puppet Theatre. To the north-west of the square, the Pegasus Electro-Theatre housed one of Moscow's first cinema screens in the 1910s, while to the south-west the domed building of the Nikitin Brothers' Circus, built in 1911, was home to the Moscow Music Hall, the Theatre of Operetta and the Satire Theatre (from 1964 to the present). To the south-east corner of Triumfal'naia Square sits the Tchaikovsky Concert Hall which began life as the Omon Theatre of Buffonade and Miniatures in 1901. From 1920 it housed the State Meyerhold Theatre (initially known as the RSFSR Theatre No. 1) and became a centre of avant-garde innovation before closing for renovations in 1931. Vsevolod Meyerhold oversaw its reconstruction into a new three thousand-seat theatre designed by Sergei Vakhtangov and Mikhail Barkin. However, endless delays to the project meant that the building was only just approaching completion when the State Meyerhold Theatre was liquidated in January 1938. After Meyerhold's arrest and execution, the building was extensively modified with seats placed in the empty space where Meyerhold's revolutionary extended proscenium would have been. Built over and around the void of Meyerhold's discontinued future, the Tchaikovsky Concert Hall stands today as a monument to that rupture, as much as to Russia's musical heritage.

This book explores the dynamic intersection between the symbolic poles of Moscow's two theatre squares: the overlap and merger of officially patronized theatre with alternative and divergent forms of performance. It is interested in the sites and spaces where these cultures meet and the messy and muddled outcomes that arise when established norms, traditions and hierarchies are disrupted or inverted. One of the radical innovations of Soviet avant-garde theatre was its egalitarian mixing of 'high' and 'low' genres – combining ballet and circus, opera and cabaret, drama and farce. In doing so it broke with the system of conventions that tied specific artistic forms to specific subjects. Instead, the avant-garde embraced the potential of the stage to represent all experiences, through any expressive means and for every kind of spectator. It was a practice that dismantled the hierarchy of genres that had developed in the Russian theatre since 1756, when the first Russian-language theatre was established in St Petersburg for the performance of tragedies and comedies: a hierarchy that would continue to underpin official attitudes towards theatre in the Soviet Union from the Stalinist period onwards. An illustration of this hierarchy can be found in the theatre listings section on the back page of any Soviet edition of *Pravda* from the mid-1930s onwards. From this point in time, the order in which theatres were listed was fixed according to their status: at the top came the Bolshoi, followed by the Malyi and then the Moscow Art Theatre; at the bottom came the Music Hall, Puppet Theatre, Estrada Theatre and finally the Circus. It was also in the mid-1930s that avant-garde theatre (which sought to disturb this hierarchical order) became anathema to the Soviet cultural authorities and its practitioners denounced, ostracized and silenced. The persecution of the avant-garde was one of the defining features of Soviet theatre in the Stalinist period. But the Thaw following Stalin's death in 1953 brought with it a re-emergence of avant-garde styles, forms and techniques onto the stage, where they jostled and mixed with the dominant practices of the day. These disruptive and unruly interventions are the primary theme of this book.

In the following chapters we will examine how the revival of avant-garde theatre during the Thaw (1953–64) posed a challenge to certain normative ways of staging theatre productions, based on the Moscow Art Theatre model, and how this disruptive process influenced, and was in turn influenced by, the broader societal processes of de-Stalinization. De-Stalinization of society (rehabilitation of political victims, restructuring of the legal system, rewriting school textbooks, removing monuments, etc.) took place alongside the disruption of the Stalinist aesthetic system – its hierarchy of genres, its privileging of certain performance techniques over others and its linking of forms of patronage and reward to those preferred methods. The Thaw was a confusing and unsettling time when nostalgia for the pre-Stalinist 1920s mingled with optimism and hope for the future. This book explores both of these aspects: the revival of proscribed theatre styles and play texts from the past and the new theatre companies and playwrights that emerged in the few short years of the Thaw. By doing so it reveals a society in flux, cautiously negotiating its place in the world and the modes of visibility used to express that reality on the stage.

## The Thaw

The news of Stalin's death, recorded at ten minutes to ten on the evening of 5 March 1953, stunned the Soviet Union and led to outpourings of grief and anguish. Some, who were school children at the time, recalled their entire classroom weeping hysterically as the teacher tearfully announced the death of the man they looked up to as a father figure.[3] Others recalled a feeling of exhilaration, full of anticipation and the tantalizing hope that change might be on its way.[4] It was these feelings of exhilaration and hope, rather than of grief or sadness, that the writer Ilia Ehrenburg gave voice to in his novella, written in 1953 and first published in May 1954, which he called *The Thaw*.[5] Ehrenburg used this seasonal metaphor to convey a sense of optimism, of rebirth and of emancipation from the long Stalinist winter. Ehrenburg was not the first Russian writer to use the idea of the thaw to describe a change in the political climate. The romantic poet Fedor Tiutchev had used the same metaphor to capture the mood of anticipation among the Russian intelligentsia following the death of Tsar Nikolai I in 1855 and the succession to the throne of his son Aleksandr II, who would enact the abolition of serfdom and other liberal reforms in the 1860s. In both Tiutchev and Ehrenburg's writing, the thaw signified a particular atmosphere of hope and the prospect of new beginnings. Like all metaphors, however, it was imperfect – to critics of liberalization the thaw connoted slush, inconsistency and weakness: a retreat from firm and rigid principles. For others, the cyclical nature of the seasons added a fatalistic undertone to the thaw metaphor, with its promise of another winter to come after the spring.[6] Ehrenburg and his contemporaries were well aware of the unstable and unpredictable nature of thaws, which always carry the possibility of further frosts, both in the short and long term. But in some ways the very ambiguity of the thaw metaphor helped to ensure its enduring appeal both at the time and in the years and decades afterwards. While during the period itself the liberal intelligentsia was often frustrated by the failure to achieve lasting reforms, during the Brezhnev era that followed they would look back nostalgically on the Thaw with rose-tinted glasses.[7] That being said, many conservatives within the administration, who had been alarmed at the chaotic lurches in policy and messaging under Nikita Khrushchev, greeted the end of the Thaw and the stability of Brezhnev's 'gerontocracy' with relief.[8]

Since the 1960s, scholarship on the Thaw has interrogated both the viability of the metaphor and the chronological parameters that it demarcates.[9] Of course, much of Soviet society during the Thaw remained unchanged from the Stalinist era: the cultural values, beliefs and behaviours of people did not switch suddenly overnight. It is also widely acknowledged that the Thaw can trace at least some of its origins back to the late Stalin years – Gulag amnesties, for example, took place prior to 1953.[10] Scholarship has also rooted the willingness to embrace change during the Thaw in the heightened expectations of the war years, when censorship and restrictions were eased, and in the optimism that followed victory in 1945.[11] Although these hopes were ultimately frustrated in the post-war period, they nevertheless survived, awaiting another chance to bud. The cut-off date for the Thaw has also proved to be elusive. Khrushchev's fall from power in October 1964 is often cited as the end of the Thaw: however, a reaction against liberal reforms in the cultural sphere had already begun by early 1963. On the contrary, some particular cultural industries saw liberal freedoms extend beyond 1964: for example, Grigorii Chukhrai's experimental film studio continued to operate until 1967; while Iurii Liubimov's appointment at the Taganka Theatre in April 1964 led to ground-breaking productions of Brecht in 1966 and Molière in 1968.[12]

Despite these qualifications, the Thaw did see unprecedented social changes, distinctive in terms of their scale and speed, which were prompted or catalysed by Stalin's death. From the mass release and rehabilitation of Gulag prisoners to the development of a modern consumer culture, Soviet lived experience changed dramatically over the decade.[13] In cultural terms, the Thaw saw a greater diversity of voices contributing to the perennial debates on artistic matters, many of which questioned Stalinist paradigms that had up until then appeared fixed and intransigent. The shifting sands of censorship threw up certain unexpected discoveries and buried others which lay dormant, awaiting another tide. More assertively, the Thaw witnessed an opening up towards the West as foreign musicians, performers and exhibitions of art works were allowed into the country for the first time in over a decade. In the theatre, the Comédie-Française toured Moscow and Leningrad in 1954, Peter Brook brought his minimalist *Hamlet* to Moscow's Vakhtangov Theatre in 1955, and a New York Everyman Opera production of *Porgy and Bess* was staged in Moscow and Leningrad during the winter of 1956–7. The Everyman performances coincided with French crooner Yves Montand's concert tour of the USSR which delighted his many Soviet fans. In August 1959, the Ed Sullivan Show performed in Moscow and Leningrad, with performances by singer Rise Stevens, tap dancer Conrad Buckner and high-wire acrobat Hubert Castle, among others.

When discussing the Thaw it is commonplace to define the period in terms of a series of small thaws which were each followed by short reactionary freezes, creating a pattern of pendulum shifts in policy, messaging and cultural production.[14] The first thaw was precipitated by Stalin's death and lasted until mid-1954, the second began after Khrushchev's 'secret speech' at the Twentieth Party Congress in February 1956 and lasted until November of that year, while the third thaw followed the Twenty-Second Party Congress in October 1961 and ended in December 1962 with Khrushchev's attack on avant-garde art at the Manege exhibition in Moscow. Of course, one issue with this model is that it risks creating a sense of shifts between neat, self-contained binary positions (liberal and reactionary, thaw and frost), whereas in fact people's experiences throughout these years were inconsistent, unpredictable and highly variable.[15] It might, then, be more useful to define the Thaw in terms of a liminal state of uncertainty in which the behaviour and attitude of the party, state organs, the press and all the many thousands of individuals who worked for them could not be taken for granted, an environment of constant oscillations in that elusory figment known as the 'party line'. Each interaction between a writer and a publishing editor, each discussion between a theatre director and a censorship board was a micro-negotiation in a perpetual tug-of-war that could have varied and unpredictable outcomes. At different points in time and for sometimes spurious or unexplained reasons, decisions and actions could be taken that gave an appearance of greater liberalization, freedom of expression and the easing of restrictions. But just as quickly, a decision could be taken or an editorial published that seemed to erase any sense of change in overall direction and policy.

For example, in the heady months following the Twentieth Party Congress, Boris Pasternak felt sufficiently emboldened to send the manuscript of his novel *Dr Zhivago* to the journal *Novyi mir* for publication. Although the editor Konstantin Simonov rejected it, there was no further censure of Pasternak for having written the work. However, following the novel's release in Italian translation in November 1957 there was a swift and harsh backlash in the Soviet press, and Pasternak was expelled from the Writers' Union. By the summer of 1958, Khrushchev appeared to be on a charm offensive with the liberal intelligentsia once again, reinstating Aleksandr Tvardovskii as editor of *Novyi mir*, a position from which he had been sacked four years earlier. However, a few months later in October 1958, Pasternak was forced to reject the Nobel Prize for literature he had just been awarded and beg Khrushchev not to have him deported. The campaign against him was called off but the stress had taken its toll and he died two years later. What this sequence of events suggests is that the party's approach to cultural matters in these years was volatile and ambiguous, and that shifts in attitude and policy happened continuously whether the period was subsequently labelled one of thaw or one of frost. Nevertheless, the key events used to delineate the various thaws in the post-Stalin period remain useful markers and they undoubtedly created conditions in which certain outcomes became more likely than others.

## The Thaw in the Soviet theatre

The Thaw in the Soviet theatre began a few months prior to Stalin's death with a production of nineteenth-century Russian satirist Mikhail Saltykov-Shchedrin's play *Shadows* at the Lensovet Theatre in Leningrad (see Chapter 2). This production proved to be a bellwether for the direction of theatre during the Thaw, both in its critique of the corrupt state apparatus and in its combination of psychologically realist acting with a stylized mise en scène. *Shadows*, directed by Nikolai Akimov, set down a marker which other theatres quickly followed in the weeks and months after Stalin's death. This period saw drastic changes in government policy and tone: some actioned publicly, others expressed behind closed doors. The 27 March amnesty led to the release of 48 per cent of the Gulag population *en masse* (although not political prisoners), while the unpublished decree issued at the July Plenum of the Central Committee, kept secret for many years, committed to a programme of political and economic reform and criticized a 'cult of personality' (*kul't lichnosti*) which had operated at *every* level of the party hierarchy.[16] The most significant intervention in theatre criticism was an article published in *Pravda* on 27 November 1953, bearing only the cryptic signature – 'A spectator'.[17] In the article titled 'The Right and Duty of Theatre', the nameless spectator issued a clarion call for bold innovation, diverse creative styles and the 'right of the artist to independence'.[18] The author railed against 'homogenization' in the arts which 'erases individuality' and insisted that socialist realism creates space for new ideas and can incorporate 'the most varied genres, directions and styles'. Redefining the parameters of socialist realism to include a broad variety of methods and approaches would become a key concern during the Thaw, not only in the theatre but across the entire cultural spectrum. It was by reimagining the normative practices of the Soviet theatre as they had become entrenched under Stalinism that the avant-garde was able to reintegrate onto the stage. As if in answer to the anonymous spectator's call, a week later, on 5 December 1953, Vladimir Mayakovsky's play *The Bathhouse* opened at the Moscow Satire Theatre in a production that revived elements of Meyerhold's original avant-garde staging (see Chapter 3).

The most controversial new play written in this early phase of the Thaw was Leonid Zorin's *The Guests*, which was published in the journal *Teatr* in February 1954 and staged at the Moscow Ermolova Theatre by Andrei Lobanov on 2 May that year.[19] While writing the play in the summer of 1953, Zorin was undoubtedly influenced by the widespread calls in the press for greater 'legality' in the criminal justice system and the arrest of Lavrentii Beria who was denounced for having abused his power as minister of Internal Affairs. *The Guests* uses the motif of generational conflict between a father and son to attack corruption within the Ministry of Justice. The son is a high-ranking ministry official who has an expensive taste for luxury items and a desire to retain his position at all costs, even if it means covering up a miscarriage of justice. With his materialist outlook and self-serving corruption, Zorin's protagonist is the epitome of the Stalinist bureaucrat. In stark contrast, the minister's father is an old Bolshevik who embodies the lost ideals of the revolution. Nostalgia for 'Leninist norms' would become a prevailing trope of the Thaw and one that Khrushchev would emphasize in his 'secret speech' at the Twentieth Party Congress in February 1956. Nevertheless, Zorin's critique of high-level ministerial corruption was far too incendiary for the Ministry of Culture, which swiftly banned the play after its first performance. Zorin was heavily rebuked and fell ill; Lobanov too suffered a heart attack and was forced to quit his role at the theatre.[20]

In his speech at the Second All-Union Soviet Writers' Congress held in December 1954, the new general secretary of the Writers' Union Aleksei Surkov denounced the maligned 'theory of conflictlessness' in a Stalinist fashion but offered little promise of any further easing of restrictions. However, speeches by Konstantin Simonov, Mikhail Sholokhov and Valentin Ovechkin offered some resistance and called for widening the parameters of socialist realism. Ovechkin's speech was the boldest, criticizing the 'scandalous' way bonuses and prizes had been awarded under Stalin.[21] That same month, Aleksandr Sukhovo-Kobylin's grotesque nineteenth-century satire *The Case* opened at the Lensovet Theatre (see Chapter 2). Over the next two years, a series of revivals of classic plays from the 1920s and 1930s brought avant-garde methods back to the stage. Many of these productions took place in the aftermath of Khrushchev's 'secret speech' in 1956 – a year that also witnessed the emergence of a new theatre-studio, the Sovremennik (Contemporary), in Moscow for the first time in eighteen years. In the late 1950s, new plays emerged that questioned the dominant socialist realist template. In 1959 Aleksandr Volodin's *Five Evenings* caused a sensation at the Sovremennik Theatre-Studio in Moscow and the Bolshoi Dramatic Theatre in Leningrad (see Chapter 5). That same year Aleksei Arbuzov's *An Irkutsk Story* became the most popular play of the decade, staged in hundreds of theatres across the country, including at Moscow's Mayakovsky Theatre in a production directed by Nikolai Okhlopkov which opened in February 1960. Arbuzov's play was notable for the way it used stylized devices such as pantomime and a chorus, the first new Soviet play in the post-war era to do so.

A series of theatre appointments beginning in the mid-1950s marked a change in atmosphere that saw artistic merit prioritized over fealty to the party. In 1956 Nikolai Akimov was reappointed artistic director of the Leningrad Comedy Theatre, after a four-year hiatus at the Lensovet Theatre, and Georgii Tovstonogov was appointed artistic director at the Leningrad Bolshoi Dramatic Theatre. In 1957, Valentin Pluchek was rewarded for the success of his productions of Mayakovsky and made artistic director at the Moscow Satire Theatre. In 1963 Iurii Liubimov was made artistic director of the Moscow Taganka Theatre and Anatolii Efros was appointed to the same position at the Lenin Komsomol Theatre. These directors had a significant influence on the way the theatre landscape changed in Moscow and Leningrad during the Thaw, both in the merger of stylized and realist forms and in their boldness to use the stage as a platform for political critique.

The Thaw ushered in a number of administrative changes to the organization of theatres in the Soviet Union. In 1953 Glavrepertkom (the Central Repertoire Board) was abolished and its functions distributed to Glavlit (the main literary censor) and the newly established Main Administration for Theatres and Musical Institutions. Government oversight of theatres was instituted primarily in-house, by a theatre's literary manager (*zavlit*) and artistic council, which were supervised by the Ministry of Culture. In Moscow, theatres were overseen by the central directorate of culture of the Moscow City Council (Glavk), which was a sub-branch of the Ministry of Culture. The aim of these changes was to decentralize theatre management in order to boost productivity, but it also added layers of extra bureaucracy. Writers were now permitted to send their plays directly to theatres and publishers (as long as they were members of the Writers' Union) and any alterations or edits required by the censor were made in the theatre, rather than by a committee. However, the playwright was powerless to reject alterations to their work and could not withdraw a play once it had been submitted. The Ministry of Culture only reviewed plays after they had been accepted by a theatre's literary manager or published, but plays could still be banned prior to performance if the censor disapproved after watching a dress-rehearsal. Theatres continued to receive state subsidies, with the major academic theatres patronized the most generously. Training for the stage was also subsidized with all students receiving free tuition and bursaries for living costs, except those whose parents earned very high salaries. In December 1956, the Ministry of Culture abolished the tiered system of grading, which fixed budgets and personnel numbers according to a theatre's rank and therefore restricted upward promotion for younger actors. This opened the door for a new crop of actors and gave directors greater choice when allocating parts.

## The avant-garde: Aesthetics and politics

The Thaw was experienced in the Soviet theatre through both a nostalgic return to pre-Stalinist styles and genres and as a forward-looking impulse that sought to invent forms that would speak to a new generation. Both of these tendencies could be defined as 'avant-garde'. The innovators of the 1920s that survived the Stalinist purges rekindled their art under Khrushchev, while simultaneously a new vanguard took the theatre in novel and unforeseen directions. The first use of the term 'avant-garde' to denote artists as progressive leaders in society was by the French utopian socialist Henri de Saint-Simon.[22] In the 1820s, towards the end of his life, Saint-Simon devised a radical religious doctrine called 'The New Christianity' which envisaged artists as the high priests of a new society built on love and universal harmony. Saint-Simon was certainly not the first to argue that art should be devoted to social aims, but he was the first to mobilize the militaristic concept of a 'vanguard' (*avant-garde* in French) to define the leaders of the forthcoming society, of which he believed artists would be the most important. Throughout the course of the nineteenth century, the term 'avant-garde' became commonly used as a means to characterize radical and progressive artistic movements. In the twentieth century, the term would take on new significance as it became identified with modernism and expressionism, was rejected by the Communist Party of the Soviet Union in the late 1920s and was consequently embraced in the West after the Second World War as a symbol of liberal democracy.[23] The commodification of avant-garde culture in the West and its instrumentalization as a weapon in the Cold War helped to cement a binary opposition between avant-garde and popular mass culture. This binary was characteristic of both Soviet aesthetic discourse, which contrasted avant-garde formalism with socialist realism, and Western Marxist theories of culture such as those articulated by the Frankfurt School philosophers Max Horkheimer and Theodore Adorno in their *Dialectic of Enlightenment* (1947) and before them by the US art critic Clement Greenberg. In his seminal essay on the avant-garde, first published in 1939, Greenberg famously opposed avant-garde art and literature to what he called *kitsch* – popular and commercial art produced for and consumed by a mass audience.²⁴ Greenberg argued that the artists and writers of the avant-garde, in searching for new forms of expression, had ceased to depict common experience and had turned in on themselves, making the medium of their craft the subject of their work (similar arguments were also used by Soviet critics in the 1930s to harangue 'formalists'). Such is the case, Greenberg argued, with abstract and 'non-objective' painting, which becomes an expression of an absolute into which content and signifiers are dissolved. By contrast, *kitsch* draws on the simulacra of genuine culture to create a commodity for mass consumption that distracts and entertains. Greenberg's definition of the avant-garde, one that fully separates the sphere of art from that of life, would dominate in Western culture during the twentieth century.

More recently, however, Jacques Rancière has brought about a paradigm shift in the way the term is understood, arguing that Greenberg's narrow definition of the avant-garde was misconceived. Not only, Rancière contends, does Greenberg's approach betray an elitist scorn for the idea that ordinary working people should engage with art and culture, but it also obscures the real revolution that was taking place in aesthetics: the development of a new idea of art capable of 'giving infinite resonance to the most ordinary minutes of everyday life'.²⁵ Rancière's partition of eras of art making and thinking into 'regimes' provides a useful re-evaluation of the notions of modernity, modernism and postmodernism. His ideas on the relationship between aesthetics and politics will be used in this book as a framework to understand the changing practices and discourses of theatre in the Soviet Union.

In his work, Rancière outlines the development of a new, transformative idea of art, from the mid-eighteenth century to the mid-twentieth century. It is the idea of an art which seeks to express the profound complexity, infinite variety and contingency of life – a life which is ultimately unrepresentable in its totality. Modernism is for Rancière an expression of separation. It is the exposure of the gap between the world as it is and the world as we would wish it to be, between the world as it is experienced by people and the forms of representation used to capture that experience. It is in this sense that Rancière describes historical modernism – both artistic and political – as a 'counter-affirmation about modernity'.²⁶ This counter-affirmation denied Hegel's verdict that the 'golden age' had been reached and claimed instead that

> The contemporary world is structured by a separation that must be abolished. Here the subjective richness of assembled humanity remains foreign to humans,

frozen in dogmas of revealed religion, the mechanics of state administration or the product of work appropriated by capital; the signs of the future are still ciphered there in the fossils of past revolutions or barbarous hieroglyphics of industrial and colonizing innovation. The revolution to come is the conscious re-appropriation of this subjective richness fixed in the objective world and the deciphering of these enigmatic signs.[27]

The task the avant-garde set itself was to re-appropriate the 'subjective richness' of the world and decipher it for new audiences. For Rancière this is fundamentally a democratic process, a process of equality that insists that art can be experienced by anyone and take anything as its subject because everyone and everything are a part of the world. This is the new idea of art that was born at the end of the eighteenth century, an art that exists when it takes the collective life of the people as its subject.

Rancière traces the genealogy of art as a singular concept back to the publication of Johann Winckelmann's *History of the Art of Antiquity* (1764), Immanuel Kant's theorization of beauty and Friedrich Schiller's concept of the 'aesthetic education of man'. Of course, prior to this there existed many different arts and artistic practices, but the notion of 'Art' in the singular only emerged in our modern understanding, he argues, when it became tied to a notion of 'History' as the story of a people. For there to be a history of *art*, rather than a history of artists or a history of the arts, art has to exist as a singular concept. By using his knowledge of ancient artefacts to tell the history of the Greek people and by drawing a link between Greek sculpture and the freedom of Athenian democracy, Winckelmann established a correlation between art and political emancipation that would reverberate throughout the romantic era in the works of the German Idealists. This is the beginning of what Rancière calls 'the aesthetic regime of art': a period when art as a singular concept becomes the manifestation of the collective life of a people in the form of style.[28] In the aesthetic regime, the old representative system breaks down. This system was part of what Rancière calls 'the representative regime of the arts' in which individual arts are organized according to the principle of *mimesis*, which differentiates artistic practices that create imitations of things from other social practices, such as those producing goods and wares.[29] This act of classification also subjected the arts to a set of intrinsic norms: a hierarchy of genres, the suitability of certain forms for certain subjects, the privileging of speech and narrative over description and representation and criteria for assessing the quality of an artwork. In the theatre, for example, tragedy depicted royalty and the nobility while those without rank or title were the subjects of comedy. In painting, historical and biblical canvases were privileged over genre painting and still life.[30] Rancière notes that 'in this sense the logic of representation enters into a relationship of global analogy with an overall hierarchy of political and social occupations'.[31] In other words, a layperson could not be the hero of an Elizabethan tragedy because their destiny was not considered important in the way that a king's was and so the privileged relationship between the artistic form (tragedy) and the subject (king) reflects the actual hierarchy of the society in which the drama is written and staged. Rancière's argument is borne out further when we look at the architecture of the Elizabethan stage, which, in its assemblage of medieval symbols, reflected the social and divine order of the time.[32]

In the 'aesthetic regime of the arts', however, the former system of representation vacillates and there is no longer a strict correlation between subject matter and mode of representation. Rancière identifies examples of this vacillation across the different artistic genres. In literature it was epitomized by Gustave Flaubert's democratic depiction of all subject matter with the same microscopic attention to detail and Walt Whitman's 'unanimist poetics' whereby the meticulously curated details of prosaic life possess the value of equality 'from all being microcosms of the whole'.[33] In sculpture it was defined by Auguste Rodin's metonymic models of body parts, which symbolize the infinite potentiality of life rather than the closed unity of the organic body. In such fragments we witness not the relation between the specific to the general, but 'the symbolic relation of the part to the unrepresentable whole that expresses its actuality'.[34] In the aesthetic regime, the old distinctions between 'high-brow' and 'low-brow' genres collapse in the face of art's aesthetic indifference towards its subject. Thus, the movement to define art as something singular and to open it up to life in all its heterogeneity are part of the same process, but herein a problematic logic is revealed. As Rancière points out, 'art exists as a separate world since anything can belong to it'.[35] The process of defining art in the singular simultaneously leads to the blurring of the boundaries that separate arts from other activities, as seen for example with the Arts and Crafts, Art Nouveau and Bauhaus movements. The social codes that differentiated between 'fine arts' practised by people of leisure and 'mechanical arts' produced by workers deprived of the right to leisure time were dissolving with the growth of the industrial proletariat. But by dispensing with the categorizing principle of *mimesis* (an artwork is something that imitates something else) and by blurring the boundaries between traditional artistic practices and other activities, the aesthetic regime both defines art in the singular and calls this singularity into question. This is what Rancière describes as 'a form of thought that has become foreign to itself'.[36] Art becomes a singular concept at the same time that the criteria for identifying this singularity are being eroded.

Art in Rancière's 'aesthetic regime' is not a fixed category but a constant blurring of the difference between art and non-art.[37] Art exists at the point where the gap between the world and the inadequacy of its modes of representation and thought are exposed. In this respect it is tied irrevocably to politics as a force for demanding equality and representation to those who are excluded from the social order. Rancière argues that artistic and political activities both effect a redistribution of the 'sensible' (i.e. the system determining what can be sensed and perceived).[38] Both art and politics are contingent notions, forms of *dissensus* (disruption) which reconfigure common experience: politics does so by suspending the hierarchical relations that partition the social order through processes of subjectivation; art does so through 'practices and modes of visibility that reconfigure the fabric of the sensible'.[39]

## Avant-garde theatre in the aesthetic regime

Rancière contends that theatre in the aesthetic regime bore witness to the fracturing of the old neoclassical system of conventions that linked subjects to genres and specific modes of expression, privileging the ideal proportions of the body.[40] And this idea makes sense if we look at the ways in which theatre was performed on two of the major European stages in the late Renaissance period. The neoclassical system was perhaps best exemplified by the seventeenth-century French theatre, which regulated dramatic speech through use of the *alexandrine* and in doing so restricted the expression of emotions to the actor's voice and a series of set gestures. These gestures had been catalogued by Descartes in his *Traite des passions* in 1649 and were conveyed on the stage via a taxonomy similar to Charles Le Brun's model for painters. In Elizabethan England, actors were also trained in classical rhetoric and oratory, especially those with a grammar school education, and they used the guides of Quintilian and Cicero who outlined which gestures were appropriate for which emotions.[41] Celebrated actors like Richard Burbage, who were famous for the versatility of their role playing and ability to express a nuanced range of emotions, were the exception rather than the norm. Even then, the way an actor experienced emotion on stage was conceived differently to our contemporary understanding. Emotions were known as 'passions': independent entities that needed to be activated and experienced passively. In neoclassical acting theory, the actor represents these 'essences' of nature in a general manner, depicting universal passions rather than individual emotions.[42]

As Rancière suggests, the overthrow of this system began in the mid-eighteenth century with the embrace of the principle of *mimesis* by Denis Diderot and others, as the means to express thoughts and emotions truthfully, in place of the stock conventions and clichés of the neoclassical system. Diderot sought to elevate the truthful expression of thoughts and passions above formal principles of harmony and proportion, an idea of total expression in which every movement conveys a thought that is personal to the character.[43] If we look at what was happening in England, we see this same shift exemplified by Aaron Hill's theories of acting and the realistic methods of Charles Macklin and David Garrick at Drury Lane, who abandoned the bombastic declamatory style of the late seventeenth century for greater naturalism in their speech, movement and costumes. A significant part of Garrick's 'naturalness' came from the dexterity and agility of his movement which was often compared at the time to that of pantomime or burlesque.[44] For Diderot also, the expressive potential and flexibility of pantomime was a corrective to the rigid and regulated neoclassical system and influenced a new performance style that accentuated the body over the voice. Nevertheless, 'natural' actors still relied on stock gestures to a far greater degree than on the twentieth-century stage. Naturalism in the eighteenth century meant personalizing the link between emotion and gesture, rather than doing away with stylized gestures altogether.

The break with the representative regime was taken even further in the nineteenth century by symbolists such as Maurice Maeterlinck who called for an 'immobile theatre', a drama of inaction and indifference to replace the Aristotelian focus on the dramatic plot.[45] Rancière reminds us of the central importance of the well-constructed plot in Aristotle's definition of tragedy, with its chain of actions linking wills and destinies through cause and effect. He notes that its intelligently drawn characters, who act according to rational motives directed towards a particular end, were opposed by Maeterlinck to a new idea of theatre in which meetings with the unknown are given form and space on stage. This was not a retreat to interiorized psychology but the abandonment of the whole system of linkages that related inner feelings to exterior speech and gestures. In its place, 'the silent sensations through which any individual whatsoever experiences the silent action of the world' are staged.[46] Rancière sketches how the rejection of text and plot drew on the traditions of the mimes and circus clowns who react to stimuli with unmotivated indifference, their tricks and tumbles leading to unexpected consequences and foiled expectations, which become the source of comedy.[47] And he notes how the influence of these folk theatre traditions was particularly strong on the Russian symbolists, most memorably with Meyerhold's staging of Aleksandr Blok's play *The Little Fairground Booth* (1906) which combined the clowns of the Commedia dell'arte with the grotesque marionette forms of the puppet show. The grotesque principle was for Meyerhold the urge to jolt the spectator out of their comfort zone, not allowing them to settle for an instant through the use of 'shocks' that combine dissimilar elements.[48] The use of clowning tricks, acrobat stunts and tumbling became a feature of Soviet theatre after the revolution, not only a symptom of the freedom of bodily movement from the shackles of the plot but also the merger of 'high-brow' and 'low-brow' genres characteristic of the 'aesthetic regime'.

The tendency to pit symbolism antagonistically against naturalism during the 1910s and 1920s masked the fact that both of these movements were part of the same break with the old representative system. Konstantin Stanislavsky's rejection of *remeslo* ('stock-in-trade'), that is the use of stock clichés and gestures on the stage, is part of this rupture. But while naturalism preserved the integral role of the dramatic text in the performance, symbolism took the schism with the old system further. It did so by distancing the theatrical spectacle from its reliance on plot and speech in favour of the free movement of bodies in space, as part of the new art of mise en scène. The elevation of the mise en scène (staging) to the level of an art form that rivalled the importance of the play text also saw the status of the director rise equal to or above that of the dramatist. For a director like Meyerhold, the conflict between form and content (between mise en scène and text) was the very art of the grotesque which aimed to 'subordinate psychologism to the ornamental objective'.[49] Mise en scène becomes the site where all the different art forms are unified (architecture, music, dance, etc.) and focused onto the actor's body. Drama is transformed into spectacle, able finally to convey what words cannot. Freed from the confines of the plot with its logic of causality, the stage space becomes an opening onto the unknown and the infinite. But while Maeterlinck believed in turning action into immobility, Russian symbolists like Viacheslav Ivanov sought to erase the division between actor and audience, transforming Maeterlinck's passive resignation into a theatre of mass action. In this radical vision, theatre no longer narrates actions but directly expresses the potential of life contained within the energy of bodies moving freely in space. In the art of mise en scène, music is used throughout the performance to structure the dynamics of movement and emotion, rather than incidentally, whenever a character is required by the text to break into song. Lighting is no longer limited to the role of illuminating action on stage (via footlights) but becomes 'active', contributing in its own way to the play of shadows and moods, intervening to show what is not expressed in speech. Naturalistically painted backdrops are replaced by architectural structures – flats, platforms, staircases – which organize the stage according to the movements of the actors, while the border between stage space and auditorium is blurred.

These were some of the practical innovations introduced by avant-garde stage designers such as Adolphe Appia and Edward Gordon Craig, who left an indelible mark on the visual language of the theatre. Appia and Craig both shared a vision of uniting the different stage arts within the art of mise en scène, but with different consequences for the role of the actor. As Rancière notes, Craig's solution was to turn the actors' bodies into marionettes, overwhelmed by the architectural space of the stage, as seen in his designs for *Hamlet* at the Moscow Art Theatre (1911). Whereas Appia, in his staging of Wagner at Hellerau (1912), freed the actors' bodies from representing characters in order to affirm the life potential contained within their energy and collective movements.[50] Both Appia and Craig eventually realized that taking theatre to such extremes would simultaneously sound its death knell. But, as Rancière notes, the modern art of mise en scène would find its principles and its strategies at the juncture of these impossible realizations.[51] Their ideas lived on in the stylized use of platforms and flats, in rhythmic choreography and mime as Meyerhold and other avant-garde directors played with the tensions between the actor's body and the plastic space, without ever completely abandoning the text and its plot.

## Disrupting the regime

The primary focus of this book is the change that took place in the Soviet theatre during the Thaw. In the chapters that follow I illustrate the ways in which actors, directors, stage designers and writers revived the proscribed methods and practices of the avant-garde and in the process began to dismantle the rigid Stalinist aesthetic hierarchy which mandated psychological realism in the Moscow Art Theatre style and vilified avant-garde formalism as a treacherous aberration. In doing so these figures contributed to a call for greater tolerance of diversity that reverberated throughout the period: at first in timorous *pianissimo*, later in bold eruptions of *sforzando*. The calls for greater variety of artistic means and methods were often phrased in terms of redefining the parameters of socialist realism, the official method of all Soviet arts, including theatre. The supremacy of socialist realism was not questioned (at least overtly), but the argument that socialist realism should be a broad church incorporating a wide variety of approaches deconstructed the logic of the hierarchical system that privileged it, eating away at its structure from the inside. Singularity of artistic method was tied implicitly to singularity of political doctrine in Soviet epistemology, and to do away with the former risked challenging the latter. The revival of avant-garde theatre during the Thaw was therefore often tempered by pragmatism and hesitancy. Directors and actors remained wary of punitive repercussions despite the changes in political climate. Smuggling avant-garde devices past the censor dressed in socialist realist clothing became a popular tactic. Techniques such as breaking the fourth wall, clowning and acrobatics, shadow puppetry and musical orchestration of the action returned to (at least semi) prominence, where they competed on stage with realist methods of character acting and stage design. These hybrid productions reintroduced audiences to performance styles that had not been seen on the major Soviet stages for many years, opening up new and potentially edifying ways for spectators to interpret their lived experience and their place in society. The democratic merger of different theatre styles, from the past and from abroad, suggested the underlying equality of all modes of expression to depict all kinds of experience. By operating in the interface between mediums and genres, this hybrid theatre disrupted established norms and created new frames of visibility. It prompted audiences to think by 'making strange' the world they saw on stage and reminded them of their agency as performers in their own personal story.[52]

Another important theme of this book is the way the revival of avant-garde theatre and its concomitant nostalgia for 1920s cultural values was interlinked with the de-Stalinization process under Khrushchev. What we see repeatedly is that de-Stalinization of society both informs and derives from the deconstruction of the Stalinist aesthetic system: they are connected in a relationship of interdependence. One example of this is the rehabilitation of victims of Stalinist repression. As we will see in Chapters 2 and 3, the first attempts at reviving Meyerhold's artistic legacy happen on stage prior to his political rehabilitation in 1955. At the same time, the posthumous quashing of his sentence opened the door for greater understanding and circulation of his ideas in the contemporary theatre. Critiques of Stalinist bureaucracy and the 'cult of personality' were also dramatized on the stage, both via subtle allusions in the mise en scène and through satirical characterization. We see this most explicitly in the productions of Evgenii Shvarts's fairy-tale satires in the early 1960s, plays which had been banned under Stalin but which finally reached the stage during the Thaw (see Chapter 6).

A third theme is the new openings and beginnings which rejuvenated the Soviet theatre during the Thaw. In June 1954 the Moscow Estrada Theatre opened in the building of the former Al'kazar Variety Theatre on Triumfal'naia Square, providing a permanent home to Moscow's variety performers for the first time since the closure of the Music Hall in 1936. The Estrada Theatre would remain on the square until 1961 when it moved into new premises in the famous House on the Embankment on Zamoskvoreche Island, opposite the Kremlin, where much of the Soviet elite lived since the early 1930s. Taking its place on Triumfal'naia Square in 1961 was the Sovremennik Theatre-Studio led by the young director Oleg Efremov. Devoted to the Stanislavsky system, the Sovremennik breathed new life into realist theatre, but antagonized the Ministry of Culture by staging works that broke with orthodox socialist realist narratives (see Chapter 5). Following somewhat in Efremov's footsteps, although ten years his senior, the director Iurii Liubimov used a student production of Brecht's *The Good Person of Szechwan* as the springboard to the creation of a new theatre company, the Taganka, which became a centre for avant-garde innovation and dissidence in the 1960s and 1970s. In this way the roots of the dissident movement of the later Brezhnev period, which helped create the conditions for *glasnost'* and the eventual collapse of the Soviet Union, can be traced back to the disruptive and iconoclastic theatre makers of the Thaw.

Before we look in detail at some of the most important theatre productions of the Thaw, we will first embark on a whistle-stop tour of the changing landscape of Soviet theatre from the post-revolutionary experiments of the avant-garde in the early 1920s to Stalin's death in 1953. Chapter 1 tells the story of the dizzying ascent of the Moscow Art Theatre from a reviled bourgeois institution to *the* premier drama theatre in the Soviet Union, its elders canonized and its model enshrined as a blueprint for others to follow. At the same time, it shows the troubled fall of avant-garde directors such as Meyerhold and Tairov, the purging of writers and the closure of theatres that fell outside the increasingly narrow parameters used to define acceptable theatre practice. We will follow closely the development of the official method of socialist realism and ask what it meant for the theatre specifically: in terms of playwriting, acting and the mise en scène. The post-war period saw the atrophy of creative innovation as theatre productions became homogenized and 'cosmopolitan' theatre critics and Jewish cultural figures were purged. We will survey all of these developments in order to understand better the significance of what followed afterwards.

Chapter 2 starts our journey through the turbulent years of the Thaw and explores the brief but influential tenure of Nikolai Akimov as artistic director of the Lensovet Theatre in Leningrad from 1952 to 1955. Akimov had lost his position at the Comedy Theatre in 1949 during the anti-cosmopolitanism campaign but managed to revive his fortunes at the Lensovet Theatre by staging the nineteenth-century satires *Shadows* by Mikhail Saltykov-Shchedrin and *The Case* by Aleksandr Sukhovo-Kobylin. We will examine the compromises Akimov made by diluting his usual eccentric theatricalism with realism to suit the new actors at his disposal and consider the way he used creative solutions in the mise en scène to critique the Soviet bureaucratic system and lawless police state. The ghosts of Stalinism haunted these productions, both in their stylized form and in their dramatization of the persecution of the 'Other'.

In Chapter 3 we relocate from Leningrad to Moscow, where between 1953 and 1957 the Satire Theatre restaged all three of Mayakovsky's major plays for the first time since Meyerhold's original productions. By restaging Mayakovsky and remembering Meyerhold, the Satire Theatre helped canonize the former and rehabilitate the latter – overseeing an important shift in the way avant-garde theatre was perceived and practised. The rehabilitation of victims of the Stalinist purges was a crucial step in allowing society to learn and move on from the past. But in the cultural sphere, rehabilitation of repressed individuals did not necessarily translate into widespread restoration of their artistic legacies. The Satire Theatre productions were thus a stepping stone to greater public acceptance of tendencies that had earlier been denounced as 'formalist'. In the process, directors such as Valentin Pluchek and Sergei Iutkevich contributed to a growing discourse that sought to redefine the parameters of socialist realism to become more inclusive of a diverse range of styles.

This theme continues in Chapter 4, which explores in detail the debates surrounding theatre style which emerged following Khrushchev's 'secret speech' in 1956. The chapter focuses on two particular stage revivals between 1955 and 1956 which contributed to these debates: Vsevolod Vishnevskii's *An Optimistic Tragedy* at the Aleksandrinskii Theatre in Leningrad and Nikolai Pogodin's *Aristocrats* at the Mayakovsky Theatre in Moscow. Both productions interpreted archetypal socialist realist plays in an innovative manner that used a wide range of stylized devices and techniques to deliver a political message. By doing so they helped to redefine the narrow understanding of socialist realism that had become entrenched in the previous era and ensured that the dismantling of the Stalinist aesthetic hierarchy took place in concert with Khrushchev's de-Stalinization programme.

In Chapter 5 we turn away from the revival of avant-garde theatre and take a close look at the first new theatre collective to emerge during the Thaw – the Sovremennik Theatre-Studio in Moscow. The Sovremennik was formed in 1956 by a group of young graduates of the Moscow Art Theatre School, who were determined to restore the values of integrity and authenticity cultivated by Stanislavsky and Nemirovich-Danchenko. Staging new plays by a fresh generation of writers such as Viktor Rozov, Anatolii Kuznetsov and Aleksandr Volodin, the Sovremennik developed a cult following among students and the intelligentsia, while treading a fine line between official approval and opprobrium for its sometimes-controversial choice of repertoire. With its avowedly Stanislavskian approach to acting but relaxed attitude to non-realistic stage design, the Sovremennik indicated a future direction of travel for theatre in the post-Thaw era: one that replaced socialist realism with a Soviet 'neorealism'.

Chapter 6 returns to the theme of rehabilitation, but in this case the rehabilitation of a playwright. Evgenii Shvarts's fairy-tale satires were often banned in the Stalinist era on account of their ambiguous critiques of autocracy and corruption, which could just as easily be applied to the Soviet Union as to their stated target – Nazi Germany. We will focus our attention on two specific productions of Shvarts's work: *The Naked King* at the Sovremennik Theatre-Studio (1960) and *The Dragon* at the Leningrad Comedy Theatre (1962). Both of these plays caused a sensation with audiences, which flocked to get tickets, but incurred the wrath of the Ministry of Culture on account of their mockery of Soviet relations of power. Performing a grotesque inversion of established hierarchies, these productions provided audiences with a cathartic release through 'carnival laughter' and questioned the viability of the Soviet fairy-tale utopia which Khrushchev had promised would soon be in reach.

Taken together these chapters reveal a society undergoing great change; a society in a process of negotiation between the legacies of the past, an impatient desire for reform in the present and long-term aspirations for the future. In the new productions and plays of the Thaw this transition between eras, values and identities was performed on stage. Audiences greeted these changes with confusion and dismay but also with joy and humour, looking forward with hope into the wide-open space of the unknown.

# 1

# Soviet theatre under Stalin

Implicit in the idea of the Thaw is the assumption of a long Stalinist freeze preceding it. However, the Stalinist era was not monolithic but was shaped by its own climactic shifts between periods of cultural restriction and relaxation. The Cultural Revolution of 1928–31, which accompanied the aggressive Stalinist overhaul of industry and agriculture, was followed by a period of easing off in which radical literary groups were disbanded and militant reformers in the education system were sacked. Persecution of cultural figures continued intermittently but became more targeted in 1936 as the anti-formalism campaign picked up steam and the Great Purges began. However, the onset of war in 1941 brought with it another easing in censorship and cultural restrictions as the party sought to mobilize popular support for the war effort. This short thaw was then followed by another clampdown in the post-war period under Stalin's new chief of culture Andrei Zhdanov. Even during periods of restriction and persecution there were opportunities for unexpected theatre productions or performances to slip through the net.

Yet the Stalinist era was also markedly different to the Thaw in a number of ways. The centralization of the cultural sphere increased until the late 1930s, at which point it plateaued and remained highly centripetal until Stalin's death. In the late 1940s, Soviet theatre became heavily bureaucratized as the dual-management system was axed and the role of the artistic director became subordinated to that of the administrator. Artistic directors no longer had overall control of repertoire, which was assigned to a literary manager, appointed by the party. In 1949, state subsidies were cut, forcing administrators to run a profit. The quality of theatre productions diminished and audience numbers fell sharply. In 1940 there were 83.7 million visits to the theatre in the Soviet Union, but by 1950 this had dropped to 68 million.[1] Another characteristic feature of Soviet theatre under Stalin was the formation of a rigid hierarchy of styles and methods: avant-garde theatre fell into a downward spiral and psychological realism of the Moscow Art Theatre (MAT) variety was firmly in the ascendency. In what follows, we will take a close look at the emergence of this hierarchical system – at the establishment of socialist realism, the purging of avant-garde 'formalists', and the homogenization of theatre practice according to the MAT model – using the framework provided by Rancière: the interplay between 'representative' and 'aesthetic' regimes. The Stalinist period was a time of radical change in cultural habits, norms and values. But as the machinery of party and government became increasingly centralized and sclerotic, so too did the Procrustean cultural apparatus, leading to creative paralysis and stagnation in the final years of Stalin's rule.

## Early Soviet theatre and the avant-garde

After the 1917 Revolution, there was an explosion of cultural activity across the country, nowhere more so than in the theatre. Theatre at this time was diverse, experimental, participatory and dynamic. New independent cultural groups such as the Proletkult (Proletarian Cultural Organization) formed with the aim of providing the proletariat and peasantry with the means and agency to create art themselves. Under the auspices of the Proletkult, hundreds of amateur theatre collectives were set up around Russia, often attached to factories, social clubs or military brigades, which performed short one-act propaganda plays known as *agitki*. The Proletkult also organized 'mass spectacles', open-air performances with thousands of participants, such as Nikolai Evreinov's iconic recreation of the storming of the Winter Palace on location in 1920, using many of the original revolutionaries as extras in their own history. The Proletkult theorist Platon Kerzhentsev argued that the purpose of revolutionary theatre was to turn spectators into actors, achieving a synthesis between public and performers.[2] And such attempts to restore agency to spectators were mirrored in Germany by Brecht's anti-naturalist theatre, which required audiences to disassociate themselves from the drama in order to think critically about the problems it raised.

The mass participatory zeal of early Soviet theatre was perhaps best exemplified by the TRAM movement (Theatre of Young Workers) set up by Mikhail Sokolovsky in Leningrad in 1925. TRAM was an amateur theatre run for and by young workers, intended not only to reflect the reality of young people's lives but to correct and improve them. Avowedly anti-professional, with a repertoire based solely on plays written by young workers, the Leningrad

TRAM inspired numerous replicas which sprang up around the country. Another theatre movement that spread across the Soviet Union in the early years of the Revolution was Terevsat (Theatre of Revolutionary Satire) set up by Mikhail Pustynin in Vitebsk. Pustynin was director of his local branch of the Russian telegraph agency (ROSTA), and he used the theatre as a means of delivering news and propaganda to those who were unable to read newspapers. Structured in the form of a revue-show, Terevsat's 'living newspapers' contained songs, dancing, puppet shows, comic sketches and other miniatures. Terevsat toured the country and the Civil War front before affiliates were established in other cities.

Although many of these collectives disappeared in the early 1920s, the form of the 'living newspaper' survived in the work of the Blue Blouse groups which began in 1923 and brought propagandistic variety revues to workers' clubs, factories and village halls around the country. Like many other amateur or independent groups, the Blue Blouses disbanded in the early 1930s as the government began to exert greater control over the content and style of performances. But in the 1920s, the variety revue-show and 'living newspaper' were emblematic of a particular avant-garde dynamic which saw the substitution of plot with mise en scène, the juxtaposition of different styles and genres, and the democratic merger of high-brow forms such as drama, opera and ballet with the popular entertainments of circus, puppet show and music hall. These disruptive innovations were characteristic of what Rancière calls the 'aesthetic regime of the arts', wherein the old representative system, which bound certain art forms to certain subjects and privileged the word over other forms of representation, was fracturing and giving way to a new idea of art capable of expressing the heterogeneity of life as experienced by everyone. In the ballet, for example, the choreographer Fedor Lopukhov experimented with new productions based on movement rather than plot, inspired by dancers such as Isadora Duncan and Mikhail Fokin. At the same time, the trends of 'circusization' (*tsirkizatsiia*) and 'music-hallization' (*miuzik-khollizatsiia*) swept Petrograd and Moscow leading to new collectives such as Sergei Radlov's Theatre of Popular Comedy and the Factory of the Eccentric Actor (FEKS) which used professional circus performers and music-hall singers in their shows. One pioneer of the 'music-hallization' of theatre was Nikolai Foregger, who set up the Mastfor workshop in Moscow in 1921. Mastfor staged parodies of contemporary theatrical hits alongside its own musical 'parades' – cabaret-style shows that combined songs and dancing. Foregger used his workshop to showcase Western dance trends such as the tango and foxtrot, alongside original pieces of choreography like the 'dance of the machine'. In this routine, dancers in black-and-white leotards created different machine-like structures with their bodies – the most famous being the 'human conveyer belt' – which replicated the mechanical movements and patterns of industrial machinery.[3]

The hum of industry was a ubiquitous background to the Soviet theatre in this period. Meyerhold used American engineer Frederick Winslow Taylor's experiments in the scientific management of labour as the theoretical justification for his biomechanical system of acting, which developed the actor's ability to control their bodily movements and emotional apparatus optimally within the stage space. In Meyerhold's biomechanical actor the distance between idea and form, author and work, is collapsed – she is both 'organizer and organized'.[4] In this way, Rancière notes, the biomechanical actor as 'engineer of his own mechanics' goes someway to achieving the Wagnerian dream of the 'total work of art', the pure synthesis of forms embodying their own potential.[5] The actor as master of their own material was also a fundamental principle of Aleksandr Tairov's 'synthetic theatre', which he developed at the Kamernyi Theatre in the 1920s. Tairov's 'master-actor' was able to combine multiple talents – speaking, dancing, gymnastics, singing, fencing, boxing, acrobatics and so on – enabling a flexibility and dynamism of performance on stage. Tairov believed, like Meyerhold, that the actor's art should be conscious: the actor should resist full identification with the role and convey to the audience the emotional essence of the character instead. To this end, Meyerhold developed the technique of 'pre-acting' as a way of transmitting the underlying meaning of a scene to the audience through the use of mimetic expressions and gestures before the actor begins to speak their lines. In this way the actor steps out of the role momentarily to reveal the context in which his or her words should be understood.

This distancing effect, which Meyerhold borrowed from the Japanese and Chinese theatres, was also employed productively by Evgenii Vakhtangov at the Moscow Art Theatre's Third Studio in the early 1920s. Vakhtangov's iconic production of Carlo Gozzi's *Princess Turandot* in 1922 saw actors repeatedly switch in and out of character, improvise freely and communicate directly with the audience. The ability to look at their character ironically from the side was a skill that Meyerhold, Tairov and Vakhtangov all demanded of their actors, a technique that anticipated Brecht's later 'Verfremdungseffekt'. The overall purpose of this kind of non-naturalistic acting is to make the audience think, to prompt it to use its critical faculties and its imagination to complete the production themselves. Meyerhold believed that a theatre production must be left unfinished to ensure that the spectator becomes involved in the process of consummation. This not only points towards a fundamental egalitarianism at the root of stylized acting methods, which were intended to engage the audience rather than alienate it but also represents a key intersection with the 'constructivist' impulse within avant-garde culture more broadly. Constructivism, after all, did not set out to reflect the world but to remake it. As Rancière observes:

> Revolutionary artists do not make revolutionary art. They do not make art at all. This does not mean that there is no art in what they do. They use their art – that is to say, their consciousness of the new goals of life and their practical savoir-faire – to develop materials to make things, material elements of the new life.[6]

Occupying the boundary between art and non-art, between artistic practices and mechanical labour, the constructivists – with their designs for buildings, textiles and pottery – set about producing the building blocks of the new utopia. And this was also the role envisaged for the Soviet theatre. In a lecture given in 1929, Meyerhold declared: 'The theatre is becoming a bridgehead for the formation of a new human being, the theatre is helping to launch a new training programme for the people.'[7] The task of the Soviet theatre was envisaged as nothing less than to create a new kind of active, emancipated human being. But to do so it had to treat spectators as equal co-creators in the making of the artwork. Although much of this grand, demiurgic sentiment continued into the era of high Stalinism, with writers exhorted to become 'engineers of the soul'; the underlying sense of equality, in all its radical diversity and hopeful fragility, would be lost.

## Stalin consolidates power

Throughout the year 1926, a 'united opposition' formed against Stalin within the highest echelons of the Communist Party. Its key members were Trotsky, Lenin's wife Nadezhda Krupskaia and former Stalin supporters Lev Kamenev and Grigorii Zinoviev. Alarmed at the way Stalin had used his position as general secretary to consolidate power, the 'united opposition' released a signed declaration in July denouncing the suppression of free debate in the party. At a meeting of the Politburo in late October, Trotsky angrily called Stalin 'the grave-digger of the Revolution'.[8] As one leading Bolshevik noted solemnly: 'we understood that the breach was irreparable.'[9] At the Fifteenth Communist Party Conference held shortly afterwards, delegates unanimously condemned the 'united opposition', following vitriolic speeches by Stalin and Nikolai Bukharin. Trotsky and Kamenev were sacked from the Politburo, while Zinoviev was replaced as chairman of the Communist International (Commintern) by Bukharin. Over the next two years, Stalin set about crushing all opposition to his rule, honing the instruments of control – the state bureaucracy, press and secret police – that would become characteristic of his dictatorship.[10]

Just over a month after the Fifteenth Party Conference, Vsevolod Meyerhold's production of Nikolai Gogol's *The Government Inspector* (1836) premiered on 9 December 1926 at the Meyerhold State Theatre in Moscow. The production represented Meyerhold at the height of his creative talent, crystalizing his theories of symphonic choreography and biomechanics, but it also came to be seen as a turning point in his career. Acclaimed by kindred spirits such as Andrei Belyi, but decried by party critics and *komsomol* youths, Meyerhold's iconoclastic interpretation of Gogol's famous comedy became the most hotly debated production of the season. The fallout would have a lasting effect on Meyerhold's artistic reputation and his relationship with the party apparatus. As Walter Benjamin noted ominously, after attending a public debate on the production in January 1927: 'from now on, there is a front against Meyerhold.'[11]

At the same time that critics were turning on Meyerhold, the 'academic' theatres were also under attack, accused of catering to bourgeois audiences and of failing to stage plays about Soviet life. On 5 October 1926, the Moscow Art Theatre premiered a dramatization of Mikhail Bulgakov's banned Civil War novel *The White Guard* (1924), re-titled *Days of the Turbins* to pacify the censor. Bulgakov was forced to make substantial alterations to the text in order to show the defeat of the whites and victory of the Bolsheviks as inevitable. All references to Trotsky were removed from the script, ensuring his airbrushing out of history on both the theatrical and political stages that autumn. But despite these revisions, the reaction from critics was almost unanimously hostile. The production hung on for three seasons before being banned in June 1929 along with the rest of Bulgakov's oeuvre. In the wake of the controversy over *Days of the Turbins*, the MAT came under increasing pressure to stage pro-Soviet works. In 1927 it found success with Vsevolod Ivanov's *Armoured Train 14-69*, a play about Bolshevik partisans during the Civil War, staged in celebration of the tenth anniversary of the Revolution. The young actor Nikolai Khmelev played the role of Bolshevik intellectual Peklevanov in the production to great acclaim. In *Days of the Turbins*, Khmelev had courted controversy as the lead protagonist Aleksei Turbin by playing the white colonel as a man of great inner strength and faith, embodying these values with a dignity of movement and a resolute manner of speaking that placed sharp emphasis on the first half of each phrase.[12] Now Khmelev brought a similar degree of psychological nuance to the role of Peklevanov in *Armoured Train*, delivering his lines in a low voice full of concentrated conviction, rather than relying on heroic declamation.[13] His performance demonstrated that MAT acting techniques could be used fruitfully to interpret the new heroes of Soviet drama and the production as a whole became a turning point in the fortunes of the MAT. Anatolii Lunacharskii, the head of the Commissariat for Education (Narkompros), had strongly criticized *Days of the Turbins*, but he hailed *Armoured Train* as a 'triumphant production' and reserved special praise for the gifted young actors in the cast who had conveyed a 'new spirit' and appeared 'much closer to the regime of our epoch' than one might have expected.[14] The production marked the first step in the canonization of the MAT as the premier drama theatre in the Soviet Union. Consequently, as the 'front against Meyerhold' and other 'formalists' developed, the MAT, with its tradition of psychological realism, began to rise in favour.

The consolidation of Stalin's political control between 1926 and 1927 also saw a tightening of censorship within the arts that continued into the 1930s. Of course, censorship had also been a feature of cultural life under the Tsars, with the imperial monopoly on theatre productions only lifted in 1882.[15] Under the Tsarist regime, the five imperial theatres were subsidized by the state and had their repertoires strictly controlled by the ministry of the imperial court. After the Revolution, the imperial theatres, plus the MAT, were awarded 'academic' status by the Bolsheviks and received large state subsidies. All Soviet theatres and their repertoires were controlled by the central repertory committee, Glavrepertkom, formed on 9 February 1923 and attached to the main literary censorship department, Glavlit. Glavrepertkom authorized repertoires, censored new plays, compiled and circulated lists of banned plays and monitored rehearsals of plays in production. After watching a rehearsal, a representative of Glavrepertkom could approve, ban or demand changes to a production, working with the theatre's 'artistic council' to ensure that necessary alterations were made. Artistic councils were advisory boards established by the party to increase political oversight of theatres. They included representatives from the party, as well as from trade unions, *komsomol* and local factories to ensure a correct political approach. In the first half of the 1920s, the roles of Glavrepertkom and Glavlit were largely preventative rather than prescriptive. However, from 1926 onwards Glavlit's remit was extended to include preliminary censorship of all literature published in the Soviet Union, with editors given greater prescriptive oversight. In 1928 the government brought all the various censor agencies under the newly created umbrella organization Glaviskusstvo (Main Administration of Matters Pertaining to Belles Lettres and Art). Glaviskusstvo exercised general control over literature, theatre, music, fine arts, cinema, the circus and amateur performances, although Glavlit and Glavrepertkom continued to operate as offices within it. A year later, Stalin removed the more liberal-minded Lunacharskii as head of the Narkompros, and replaced him with Bolshevik military leader Andrei Bubnov, the man who would go on to lead the aggressive anti-formalist campaign in the mid-1930s.[16]

## The first Five-Year Plan and Cultural Revolution

In 1927 the Soviet leadership began a radical overhaul of the country. The first Five-Year Plan oversaw a rapid transition from the New Economic Policy (NEP) to a fully planned state-run economy in order to stimulate the growth of heavy industry and catch up with the West militarily. It also resulted in the forced collectivization of the peasantry into state-controlled collective farms (*kolkhozy*) to ensure a steady supply of grain to the cities and for export abroad. The centralized state apparatus played a key role in forcing through these changes and would go on to become a defining feature of Stalinist society. Alongside the transformation of the economy and agriculture, a 'cultural revolution' began in May 1928, which was both party-sanctioned and the culmination of a decade of simmering tensions at grassroots level.[17] The Cultural Revolution saw widespread attacks on the intelligentsia and other 'specialists' in society. Prominent show trials such as the Shakhty trial in 1928 and the Industrial Party Trial in 1930 were used to whip up public fear and hostility towards alleged 'wreckers' and 'saboteurs' within industry, academia, state departments and cultural institutions. Militant groups such as RAPP (Russian Association of Proletarian Writers) were emboldened and encouraged by the leading party organs to attack 'fellow travellers' and other cultural non-conformists with the slogan 'tear off the masks!' (*sryvaite maski*); encoding within society a suspicion of surface appearances in favour of an 'inner truth' that was said to be deliberately concealed from view.[18] In the theatre, those seen as an impediment to the sovietization of repertoires were accused of 'Golovanovism': named after the lead conductor of the Bolshoi orchestra who, alongside a group of Bolshoi actors, had tried to resist change. In a letter to the RAPP-affiliated playwright Vladimir Bill-Belotserkovsky on 2 February 1929, Stalin declared Golovanovism an 'anti-Soviet phenomenon' before criticizing Bulgakov's plays *Flight* and *The Crimson Island* and labelling the Kamernyi Theatre, which had staged the latter, as 'really bourgeois'.[19] Four months later, Bulgakov's plays were banned from the stage, and he begged the government to let him emigrate. Alongside Bulgakov, playwrights Nikolai Erdman, Sergei Tretiakov and Vladimir Mayakovsky were attacked by RAPP critics for writing subversive content or for their 'formalist' style. Mayakovsky killed himself in April 1930 – his suicide note alluding to the barbs he had suffered at the hands of RAPP critics.

RAPP and its acolytes presented themselves as harbingers of the new: the only true representatives of proletarian culture in a binary world that lumped all opponents together in one protean mass. But they operated within a system of power relations that was highly unstable and prone to sudden shifts and reversals. For a while, RAPP had harboured ambitions of taking over the MAT, removing Stanislavsky and Nemirovich-Danchenko, and transforming it into its own house theatre.[20] In January 1931, RAPP held a theatre conference in Moscow and passed an acerbic resolution which attacked theatre directors including Stanislavsky, Meyerhold, Tairov, Vakhtangov and even vilified the 'disease' of amateur theatre and the TRAM movement.[21] These attacks were then repeated at a plenary session of the RAPP leadership held in December at the end of the year. In his concluding report, the playwright Aleksandr Afinogenov attacked both the Stanislavsky system (for its 'idealistic and metaphysical roots') and the Meyerhold system of biomechanics.[22] Afinogenov's attack on Stanislavsky was particularly ironic given that his own (suitably titled) play *Fear* (1931) was due to open at the MAT two weeks later. *Fear* is one of the best-known Soviet plays of the Cultural Revolution and depicts the persecution of bourgeois specialists in academic institutions. Its main protagonist, Professor Borodin, is eventually ousted from his position at the Institute of Physiological Stimuli for his reactionary views that the Bolsheviks govern through fear alone. The ideological conflict in the play centres around a speech that Borodin gives in Act Three lamenting the all-pervasiveness of fear in Soviet society, which is then rebutted by an old Bolshevik. In the speech, Borodin, played at the MAT by Leonid Leonidov, declares that 'fear compels talented intellectuals to renounce their mothers, to fake their social origin, to wangle their way into high positions ... fear stalks everyone'.[23] The line would turn out to be prescient for Leonidov as suspicion of hidden identities intensified during the Great Purges. In 1936, the actor was passed over for one of the inaugural People's Artist of the Soviet Union awards because of his Jewish background. In official documents, the words 'real name Wolfenson' appeared in brackets after his stage name Leonidov – ensuring that the actor's 'mask' was torn off and the 'inner truth' of his family origins revealed.[24]

In response to the attacks by RAPP on the MAT and his system, Stanislavsky appealed to the Soviet government for help. In his lifetime, Lenin had been a strong supporter of the MAT and had been instrumental in the decision to award it protected 'academic' status in 1919, privately ranking it first among all the theatres in the country.[25] Stalin, who made much of following in Lenin's footsteps, was also known to have a fondness for the MAT and was rumoured to have seen its production of *Days of the Turbins* between ten and fifteen times. Consequently, in the days following the December plenary session of RAPP's leadership, the Soviet government moved quickly to affirm its support for the MAT. On 15 December 1931, the Presidium of the Central Executive Committee of the USSR published a resolution that brought the MAT under its direct control. Nine months later, on 17 September 1932, the MAT was renamed the Maksim Gorky Moscow Art Theatre of the USSR to mark the fortieth anniversary of the start of his literary career.[26] Gorky (Peshkov) had returned to Russia in 1931 to become a state-sponsored figurehead for Soviet literature and over the next few years the MAT staged a cycle of four of Gorky's plays, including, in 1934, *Egor Bulychev and Others* (1932), his first play written in the Soviet era. The MAT was now the most privileged drama theatre in the Soviet Union, overseen directly by the central executive committee and given special latitude and favours that no other theatre received. It was the start of a process that would reconfigure the landscape of Soviet theatre and turn the MAT, and a simplified version of the Stanislavsky system, into the standard models for theatre productions and actor training across the country.

On 23 April 1932 the Politburo of the Central Committee issued a resolution which brought a sudden end to all independent cultural groups, replacing them with official state-run unions for the various artistic professions: writers, musicians, painters, architects and so on. Theatre workers in Soviet Russia were served by the All-Russian Theatre Organization (VTO), which had separate branches for the other Soviet republics. The entire cultural sphere was now centralized under state control – all officially approved creative labour was subordinated to and controlled via membership of these unions. Militant groups like RAPP, which had flown too close to the sun with their harassment of the MAT, were abolished, although many of its leaders received prominent roles in the new Writers' Union, such as Aleksandr Fadeev who later became its general secretary.

## Stalinist culture and socialist realist theatre

The period of 1932–3 was one of crisis in the Soviet Union. The rapid pace of industrialization had seen massive expansion of industrial output but also resulted in soaring inflation, goods shortages and widespread absenteeism. Forced collectivization had led to the deportation of over a million *kulaks* (rich peasants), the execution of tens of thousands more and widespread famine in the countryside during which an estimated five million people starved to death. In response, the party applied the brakes and enforced a retreat that saw production targets slashed, the legalization of peasant markets in the countryside and the reintroduction of wage differentiation and greater material incentives for managers and bosses. This new emphasis on hierarchy within the workplace was combined with a return to greater social conservatism. Male homosexuality was re-criminalized in 1934, and in 1936 divorce laws were tightened and restrictions placed on abortion. The 1936 'Stalin' Constitution decreed that class distinctions had now been abolished, promoting the idea of the *narod* (people) rather than the proletariat, and precipitating a return to national and patriotic forms in art.[27] Writing from exile, Trotsky referred to this retreat as a 'Soviet Thermidor' and noted that under Stalin the Soviet state had acquired a 'totalitarian-bureaucratic character'.[28] The legacy of the Cultural Revolution continued, however, in the increased role of the *vydvyzhensty* (the upwardly mobile proletariat) in the state bureaucracy, which formed the middle-class base of popular support for Stalinism in the 1930s and 1940s.[29]

In the cultural sphere, the policies of centralization and greater prescriptive oversight continued. On 1 November 1935 a decree from the Narkompros ordered all theatrical performances and films to be reviewed by the censors at least ten days prior to their official opening. Then on 16 December the All-Union Committee for Artistic Affairs was established which took control over all aspects of cultural life. From the end of the first Five-Year Plan all 560 professional theatres in the Soviet Union were state controlled and financially accountable to the Narkompros, either directly or via municipal departments. Every theatre had an artistic director, who was in charge of repertoire and artistic matters, and an administrator who was responsible for financial affairs and liaised with the state. By law, one of the administrator's two assistants had to be a member of the Communist Party. The theatre's literary advisor proposed suitable plays for performance which were read by a literary committee, including one party member acting as a political advisor. Repertoire lists and budgets were sent to Narkompros for approval prior to the start of the year. In this way, state oversight was built into almost all aspects of a theatre's working life.

In the 1930s, the increased centralization of cultural matters took place alongside a shift in the way discourse and knowledge was produced. As Katerina Clark has argued, Stalinist epistemology was a variety of Neo-Platonism, which posited a higher knowledge of reality beyond surface appearances.[30] This knowledge was accessible only to the Bolshevik 'fathers' who occupied the top echelons of the great Soviet pyramid. The 1930s Neo-Platonic system replaced a 1920s cult of positivism with a cult of higher-order knowledge that fetishized daring heroic feats and Nietzschean over-reaching. Standing at the apex of this pyramid were Lenin and Stalin, who functioned as guardians of a singular 'messianic truth', from which all divergence or disagreement, however small, was treated as a form of heresy.[31] As a manifestation of this doctrinal truth, the strict party line was a necessary function of the one-party state, regarded as an immutable law even if its practical implementation in everyday life could be ambiguous and inconsistent. Every society, as Foucault points out, has its 'regime of truth': 'the ensemble of rules according to which the true and false are separated and specific effects of power attached to the true.'[32] In the Stalinist 'regime of truth', the types of discourse which functioned as truths were often (although not always) determined within the Kremlin and radiated out across society via the centralized organs of the press and party structures. Of course, the decision-makers within the Kremlin often took their cue from the wider society of which they were a component part; however, control over the shaping of authoritative discourses became particularly centralized under Stalin, and moreover, the production of knowledge was *imagined* this way in Stalinist epistemology.[33] Moscow was envisaged as a 'higher order' place, with the Kremlin at its centre and inside the Kremlin – Stalin's study, functioning, according to Clark, as the 'sacral space where he had access to higher forms'.[34] The spatial hierarchy that centred Stalin in his Kremlin study was an illustrative component of what became known as the 'cult of personality'. As Stalin's control over the party and government increased, a leader cult grew up around him both in the everyday practice of power and in the myths that were engendered about him in the press and the arts. It was claimed that Stalin's intellectual genius and mastery of the Russian language were unmatched. Many of his speeches were canonized and presented as sources to inspire writers, while at the same time significant quotes and theories were frequently attributed to him. Such was the case with the term 'socialist realism' which the party claimed Stalin had coined in a conversation with Gorky at his flat in October 1932, despite the fact that Ivan Gronskii, the head of the organizing committee of the Soviet Writers' Union, had first used it in a speech five months earlier.[35]

Socialist realism was officially unveiled at the First Soviet Writers' Congress in August 1934 and was presented as the basic method of all Soviet literature, which demanded from writers the 'truthful' and 'historically concrete' depiction of 'reality in its revolutionary development'.[36] Of course, the word 'truthful' in this definition referred to the messianic truth of Marxism-Leninism, dedicated to 'the task of ideologically remoulding and educating the working people in the spirit of socialism'.[37] The writer, like the composer, sculptor and painter, must depict reality according to the singular and hegemonic Stalinist worldview which sees history in dialectical terms as the victory of the new Soviet arcadia over the old, moribund world. In literary prose this resulted in the famous 'modal schizophrenia' of a form that combined romantic epic with nineteenth-century realism.[38] In his keynote report on socialist realist drama at the First Soviet Writers' Congress, Valerii Kirpotin (secretary of the organizing committee of the Union of Soviet Writers) outlined its main aspects as optimistic in character, socialist in content and simple in expression.[39] He criticized the 'abstract' and 'stylized' forms of Vladimir Mayakovsky and Vsevolod Meyerhold, arguing that they carried a 'fatal danger' for the Soviet theatre. However, he insisted that the techniques of psychological realism were also insufficient for socialist realism, which required a broader scope and greater emphasis on the most heroic and significant elements of life. This final point would be ignored, however, as a simplified version of the Stanislavsky system became dominant across the Soviet theatre in the late 1930s.

Socialist realist dramaturgy of the Stalinist period followed the same overarching template as the Soviet novel, which can be defined according to Katerina Clark's well-known concept of the 'master plot'.[40] The 'master plot' of socialist realism was structured along the 'spontaneity-consciousness dialectic', which dramatized the journey of Soviet heroes and heroines from the 'spontaneity' of class ignorance to the 'consciousness' of ideological enlightenment. In this manner it fictionalized the foundational Bolshevik doctrine of the 'vanguard' as bringer of consciousness to the masses.[41] The hero's attainment of a new consciousness was typically aided by a mentor figure from the party and impeded by reactionary forces, which varied according to the work. The acquisition of Bolshevik consciousness (its messianic truth) was depicted as the integral factor in the building of the socialist utopia.

Although the historical context, geographical setting, combination of character types and internal plot devices differed markedly across the wide spectrum of socialist realist dramaturgy, this basic 'master plot' remained consistent throughout. And although each dramatist had their own stylistic idiosyncrasies, there were certain common features across the canon, including realistic settings, schematic character types and clichéd rhetoric that imitated the slogans and phrasing of political speeches and newspaper leaders. Popular socialist realist dramas of the mid-1930s were Vsevolod Vishnevskii's *An Optimistic Tragedy* (1933), Boris Romashov's *Fighters* (1934), Nikolai Pogodin's *Aristocrats* (1934) and Aleksandr Korneichuk's *Platon Krechet* (1934) and *Truth* (1937). As the canon developed, playwrights began to incorporate obligatory references and appeals to Stalin as a *deus ex machina*, sometimes even including Stalin and Lenin as characters in the play. Examples of such works include Pogodin's *Man with a Gun* (1937), Konstantin Trenev's *On the Bank of the Neva* (1937), Arkadii Perventsev's *Southern Liaison* (1949) and Vishnevskii's *The Unforgettable 1919* (1949).

In terms of set design, socialist realism came to mean adherence to the naturalistic style of the MAT and the Malyi Theatre, with their use of the three-walled box set, real properties and authentic period costumes. Stage backdrops were painted according to correct proportions and rules of perspective, while lighting and sound effects were strictly naturalistic.[42] The use of music was limited to live performances by the characters onstage if required by the plot, while mass scenes were choreographed to achieve maximum verisimilitude. All elements of dance, tumbling, gymnastics and acrobatics were excised from the performance. These were the principles that Stanislavsky had learned from the theatre company of the Duke of Saxe-Meiningen, directed by Ludwig Chronegk, when it toured Moscow for the second time in 1890 and which subsequently became staples of socialist realist theatre. Stanislavsky's influence was also integral to the way acting methods became standardized under Stalinism, as a reductive interpretation of his acting system became canonized and eventually mandated to theatres and schools across the Soviet Union.[43]

Stanislavsky's system was not a fixed method but a constantly evolving search for the key to an actor's truthful performance on stage. It was a search that he was often forced to conduct outside the walls of the main MAT as his personal feud with Nemirovich-Danchenko led him to be frozen out of its day-to-day operations. In fact, after 1908 Stanislavsky only returned to a position of creative prominence at the MAT in the three years between 1925 and 1927 when Nemirovich-Danchenko was away on tour with his Music Theatre. The receptivity of the MAT actors to the system was also inconsistent, particularly as it kept changing over time; however, we know from Stanislavsky's letters that by 1909 most of the troupe had adopted it.[44] At that stage, the key element of the system was the idea of 'affective memory' (later called 'emotional memory'), influenced by French psychologist Théodule-Armand Ribot's work on the use of memory as a stimulus for a patient's emotional state. Stanislavsky encouraged his actors to draw on their memories of past experiences to find that spark of inspiration which would lead to truthful acting on stage. The goal was 'to experience analogous feelings to the role every time it is repeated', a process that by the late 1920s he was calling 'emotional experiencing' (*perezhivanie*).[45] Stanislavsky contrasted 'emotional experiencing' to the technique of 'representation' (*predstavlenie*) in which the identification with the emotional state of the character happens only in rehearsal and not at final performance. With the method of *predstavlenie*, he argued, emotions become mechanized and risk turning into clichés, as the actor merely 'represents' them onstage. This was the tradition of Denis Diderot and Constant Coquelin, which Stanislavsky believed was inferior to the art of *perezhivanie*. Below both of these methods came *remeslo* or 'stock-in-trade', in which the actor utilizes all the clichés and tricks of the profession to convey different emotions to the audience. Stanislavsky acknowledged that all three of these tendencies can usually be detected in any one performance but believed it was the actor's task to return to the correct path of genuine experiencing whenever they felt themselves lapsing into representation or declamation.

In the late 1930s, the hierarchical scale which ranked the school of *perezhivanie* above that of *predstavlenie* and *remeslo* became entrenched in cultural discourse. The actor Boris Babochkin observed at the first All-Union Conference of Theatre Directors in June 1939: 'There is but one method in the Soviet Union. It is Stanislavsky's method, the method of the realistic theatre in which is summed up a century's experience in the Russian theatre. We have no other method.'[46] In this manner the Stanislavsky system was canonized as the only acceptable means of interpreting the heroes of socialist realism on stage and imposed on theatres around the country. However, it was a simplified version of the system which focused on the use of 'emotional memory', the analysis of tasks and playing the inner subtext of the role. The iteration of the system as Stanislavsky was refining it in the 1930s, namely the 'Method of Physical Actions', was not widely known outside of his Opera Theatre, remained unpublished until after his death in 1938 and, therefore, was not part of the canonized system. Although the 'through-action' had been included in Stanislavsky's pedagogy since around 1913, the Method of Physical Actions placed a much greater emphasis on action as the basis of the actor's work on a role. Improvising a series of actions in order to discover a set of corresponding feelings, prior to the introduction of the script, became a crucial element of the system, which also ironically brought it much closer to Meyerhold's practice as he was developing it in the 1930s.[47] Stanislavsky's students at the Opera Theatre, Mikhail Kedrov and Vasilii Toporkov, who worked on his production of Molière's *Tartuffe* and staged it after his death, guarded the Method of Physical Actions closely and turned the system into a blueprint to be applied universally to all types of dramaturgy.[48] Although there was considerable scepticism towards the Method of Physical Actions from the MAT's established stars, it found greater traction with the students at the MAT School, which finally opened in 1943 and became a model for theatre schools up and down the country.[49]

## A tale of two art theatres

In the late 1930s, Stanislavsky was celebrated for his 'deeply national talent' and described as part of the great national tradition of Russian realism.[50] It was a tradition that traced its roots back via Aleksandr Fedotov, Stanislavsky's teacher, to Mikhail Shchepkin, who introduced the principle of full incarnation of the role to the Malyi Theatre in the early nineteenth century.[51] In this sense, the canonization of Stanislavsky and the MAT formed part of the Stalinist return to national and patriotic themes in the cultural sphere. While Stanislavsky and the MAT were seen as Russian, native and *narodnyi* (of the people), the 'formalists' were characterized as foreign-influenced, cosmopolitan and bourgeois. There was thus a chauvinistic impulse behind both the anti-formalism campaign of 1936 and the symbolic placement of the MAT at the top of the theatrical pyramid, mirroring Moscow's position at the centre of the Stalinist spatial hierarchy. As chief artistic director of the MAT, Vladimir Nemirovich-Danchenko's influence on the shaping of socialist realist theatre was also considerable. An effective manager but averse to innovation, he resented the prestige attached to Stanislavsky's system and was virulent in his opposition towards formalism and Meyerhold (his former pupil at the Moscow Philharmonic Society). The main tenets of his directorial approach were a professional work ethic, detailed analysis of character and fidelity to the author's text, the latter in particular becoming integral to socialist realist theatre. Nemirovich-Danchenko's most celebrated production of the 1930s was an adaptation of Tolstoy's *Anna Karenina* (1937), starring Alla Tarasova as the eponymous heroine. Stalin was so impressed with her performance that she was made a deputy to the Supreme Soviet, one of many who took advantage of the revolving door between the MAT and the government in that era.[52] Close ties were also fostered between the MAT and the Soviet Writers' Union: the MAT actress and Partorg Angelina Stepanova was the wife of Aleksandr Fadeev, general secretary of the Writers' Union from 1946 to 1953. On 27 April 1937 the MAT was awarded the Order of Lenin, and on 26 October 1938 it received the Order of the Red Banner of Labour to mark its fortieth anniversary, cementing its hallowed status in the constellation of Soviet theatres.

The privileged standing of the MAT as *the* model Soviet drama theatre left its sister the Second MAT in a precarious position. The Second MAT was established as the first MAT studio in 1912 by Stanislavsky and his assistant Leopol'd Sulerzhitskii with a group of young actors, including Richard Boleslavskii and Evgenii Vakhtangov. It was renamed the Second MAT in the autumn of 1924 and led by Mikhail Chekhov. Following in the studio tradition, the Second MAT distanced itself from the MAT in its choice of repertoire and its openness to innovation and stylized forms of stage production. After an internal struggle, Mikhail Chekhov was forced out of the theatre and he emigrated in 1928. The Second MAT was then reorganized under the leadership of Ivan Bersenev with the aim of including more Soviet plays in the repertoire. Examples of this new repertoire, such as Sergo Amaglobeli's *The Good Life* (1934) – a forerunner of post-war 'conflictless' dramaturgy – proved popular with audiences. However, on 28 February 1936 the liquidation of the Second MAT was announced via a resolution of the People's Commissars and the Central Committee. Its premises were handed over to the Central Children's Theatre and its troupe disbanded and incorporated into the Moscow Regional Professional Union Theatre. The Second MAT was taken completely unawares by the decision, but on closer inspection of the resolution's wording the logic behind the government's reasoning became apparent. It stated that the 'so-called Second MAT is not living up to the MAT name and is a mediocre theatre'.[53] During the Stalinist purges, concealing your 'true' identity behind a false name was a common accusation; and in the theatre hierarchy the MAT name was now sacrosanct. As Anatolii Smelianskii noted, in those days the phrase 'so-called' could be a death sentence.[54]

## The anti-formalism campaign and the Great Purges

The liquidation of the Second MAT was announced a month after the start of the anti-formalism campaign, which began with an infamous editorial in *Pravda*, published on 28 January 1936, attacking Shostakovich's opera *Lady Macbeth of the Mtsensk District*. The editorial, titled 'A Muddle instead of Music', described the opera as a 'discordant, chaotic flood of sounds' and criticized the composer for 'replacing singing with shrieks' and creating music only for the tastes of 'aesthete-formalists'.[55] Shostakovich was accused of borrowing his 'convulsive, epileptic' rhythms from jazz, a mixing of high and low cultures that was bound to antagonize a cultural establishment implicitly minded to preserve the purity of artistic genres and their rightful place in the hierarchy of forms. But the newspaper's harshest criticism was reserved for the opera's 'crude naturalism'; the way it depicted the act of love-making through musical expression. The reviewer undoubtedly had in mind the opera's controversial third scene, in which the orchestra communicates the climax of the love-making between Katerina and Sergei with twelve quick upward trombone glissandi, followed shortly afterwards by downward glissandi to indicate 'flaccidity'.[56] Stalin and Molotov had watched a performance of the opera at the Bolshoi Theatre two days earlier on 26 January and had evidently been unimpressed. Shostakovich was expelled from the Moscow Conservatory and *Lady Macbeth* was removed from the repertoire. More significantly, the attacks on Shostakovich launched a widespread campaign against 'formalism' (Western-influenced modernist art) and 'naturalism' (vulgar, sexually explicit art).[57]

Emerging in the mid-1920s, the pejorative label 'formalism' was used to condemn any art that appeared more interested in mode of presentation than in subject matter. It was employed widely during the Cultural Revolution as a means to attack the avant-garde and also invoked frequently at the First Soviet Writers' Congress in 1934 as the antithesis of socialist realism. In the theatre, the main target of the anti-formalism campaign was Meyerhold; the *Pravda* editorial had accused Shostakovich's opera of transferring into music 'the most negative features of Meyerholdism'. In an attempt to rebut the accusations, Meyerhold gave a speech in Leningrad on 14 March entitled 'Meyerhold against Meyerholdism' in which he admitted to making 'major errors' in past productions but also blamed critics for failing to understand his work.[58] He defended Shostakovich and absolved himself of all responsibility for 'Meyerholdism', which he laid at the door of his 'epigones', such as Sergei Radlov and Nikolai Okhlopkov. But Meyerhold's refusal to be cowed went down badly with the Committee for Artistic Affairs. He was rebuked in the press for not going far enough in his 'self-criticism' and turned into a scapegoat in the anti-formalism campaign, singled out for the lack of Soviet plays in his theatre's repertoire and for his long-standing opposition to the MAT.[59]

Over the next year, the pressure continued to build on Meyerhold and others who had been given the label 'formalist', as Soviet society was gripped with the first Moscow show trial of Kamenev and Zinoviev. After being secretly promised their freedom in return for public confessions of guilt, the two men were then sentenced to death and executed in August 1936. Two more show trials followed in January 1937 and March 1938 leading to the execution of thirty prominent

Bolsheviks, including Iurii Piatakov, Karl Radek and Nikolai Bukharin. The years 1937 and 1938 were the height of the Great Purges, known in Russian as the *Ezhovshchina* after Nikolai Ezhov, the head of the People's Commissariat for Internal Affairs (NKVD) at that time. During this period over a million people were arrested on spurious charges and sent to the Gulag and nearly 700,000 people were executed in prison. The purge of prominent Bolsheviks and Communist Party officials extended throughout every branch of government, party, industry, military and, finally, the police, with innocents denounced by their co-workers, subordinates or neighbours and arrested as 'enemies of the people'.[60]

In the theatre, the period was marked by a series of mergers, liquidations and arrests. On 15 November 1936, *Pravda* published an article by Platon Kerzhentsev, the chair of the Committee for Artistic Affairs, denouncing the Kamernyi Theatre, describing it as 'alien to Soviet art'.[61] In response to the criticism, Aleksandr Tairov fell ill and retired to his bed. 'Tairov is finished', Kerzhentsev's deputy Boiarskii told the troupe, 'consider him gone already. You need to think about yourselves.'[62] In August 1937, the Kamernyi Theatre was merged with Nikolai Okhlopkov's Realistic Theatre as punishment to both directors for their 'formalist' mistakes. In September that year, the Leningrad TRAM was merged with the Red Theatre (another theatre born out of the amateur tradition) and renamed the Lenin Komsomol Theatre. In January 1938 the Central TRAM in Moscow was merged with Ruben Simonov's theatre studio and renamed the Moscow Lenin Komsomol Theatre. Later that year, in October, the Perm TRAM was reorganized as the Perm Regional Drama Theatre.[63] The directors of merged theatres (as opposed to liquidated ones) often managed to survive the purges. Both Tairov and Okhlopkov avoided arrest: however, many others caught up in the whirlwind either disappeared into the Gulag or perished in prison. In 1937, the avant-garde directors Igor Terent'ev and Les' Kurbas were executed, along with playwrights Vladimir Kirshon, Sergei Tretiakov and Isaak Babel'. The directors Natalia Sats and Aleksei Dikii were sentenced to five years in the Gulag. On 17 December 1937, Meyerhold also came under attack when *Pravda* published an article by Kerzhentsev which accused the director of 'turning himself into an alien body in the organism of the Soviet theatre'.[64] In his letter to Bill-Belotserkovskii in 1929, Stalin had defended Meyerhold as a director who 'despite some disgusting traits . . . is undoubtedly bound to our Soviet community, of course, and cannot be numbered among the category of "aliens"'.[65] Now, eight years later, Meyerhold had been moved into this vague, amorphous group, accused by the top-ranking cultural authority of isolating himself from Soviet reality and becoming a virus within the Soviet body politic.

In Stalinist society the use of labels such as 'formalist' constructed a notion of otherness that was used to ostracize cultural figures and turn them into public scapegoats. As the most prominent formalist (and historic opponent of the MAT) Meyerhold became the Soviet theatre's symbolic 'Other': an enigma, in Levinas's sense, that while undefinable in phenomenological terms, serves as the basis on which the subject is constituted as an ethical being.[66] The practice of identifying this enigmatic 'Other' in the Soviet press was a particular discursive strategy within a broader mode of discourse, in Foucault's sense of a discourse – as an accumulation of 'statements' (i.e. attitudes, beliefs, practices, customs) that reveal the relations of power which determine who is allowed to speak and what they can say.[67] The designation of Meyerhold as 'Other' turned him and his theatre into the antipode against which those toeing the party line could constitute themselves. It gave them a voice and took away his, first artistically and then conclusively. On 8 January 1938 the liquidation of the State Meyerhold Theatre 'as alien to Soviet art' was announced in *Pravda*.[68] However, Meyerhold was given a lifeline by Stanislavsky, who invited him to join his Opera Theatre. After Stanislavsky's death, on 7 August 1938, Meyerhold succeeded him as artistic director and oversaw the rehearsals of his final production *Rigoletto*, which premiered on 10 March 1939. That same month, at the Eighteenth Party Congress, key figures in the Politburo repudiated the 'mass purging of communists' and 'excesses' of vigilance. This signalled the winding down of the Great Purges. The random arrests and use of torture were reined in and Ezhov himself was arrested in April, tried and then shot a year later. It appeared as though Meyerhold had survived.

In April 1939 there were tentative signs of a change in approach towards the theatre from the top. In an article in *Pravda* on 16 April, secretary of the Soviet Writers' Union and Central Committee member Aleksandr Fadeev criticized the process of 'homogenization' encouraged by the Committee for Artistic Affairs and argued that while the MAT is 'of course our best theatre . . . that does not mean that all theatres should resemble the MAT'.[69] Later that month, at the end of a week-long meeting of the Presidium of the Writers' Union, Fadeev again called for greater tolerance of diversity in the theatre and described Meyerhold as 'an outstanding artist' whose 'work must not be covered up'.[70] However, a month later Fadeev was summoned to the Kremlin by Stalin and shown confessions that had been recently extracted by the NKVD which incriminated Meyerhold as a foreign spy and member of a Trotskyite cell. 'Now I hope you can see who you were supporting in your speech', said Stalin. 'So, with your permission, we intend to arrest Meyerhold.'[71] Possibly aware of his impending fate, Meyerhold gave a dejected speech on 15 June at the first All-Union Conference of Theatre Directors which was full of uncharacteristic self-criticism and platitudes towards Stalin. Nevertheless, in his closing remarks, the new chairman of the Committee for Artistic Affairs, Mikhail Khrapchenko, criticized Meyerhold for admitting to mistakes in a superficial manner and failing to acknowledge how his theatre had become 'hostile to the Soviet people'.[72] A week later, on the morning of 20 June Meyerhold was arrested in Leningrad before being transferred to the Lubianka prison in Moscow where he was tortured until he confessed to being part of a right-wing Trotskyite organization, a confession he later sought to retract. On 14 July, his wife, the actress Zinaida Raikh, was stabbed to death in their Moscow apartment by two intruders. The apartment was then appropriated by Lavrentii Beria, head of the NKVD, who gave it to his staff. Meyerhold was tried *in camera* on 1 February 1940 and shot the following day in the basement of the Military Collegium.

Meyerhold's death was emblematic of the Stalinist cultural regime's rupture with the avant-garde and its glacial push towards homogenization of the theatre. As a 'formalist' director who was also a devoted communist and party member, Meyerhold was a particularly troublesome thorn in the side of Stalinism's hegemonic system: an implicit challenge to its anointment of MAT realism as the exclusive means of depicting the 'messianic truth' of Soviet reality on stage. Over the course of the 1930s, Meyerhold's stubborn refusal to undertake 'self-criticism', his failure to stage contemporary Soviet plays and his past links with Trotsky (through his friendship with Olga Kamenova, Trotsky's sister and Kamenev's wife) were all contributing factors in his transformation into the symbolic 'Other' of Soviet theatre. This meant that during times of arbitrary justice such as the Great Purges, when the principles of 'socialist legality' were followed, Meyerhold was always a potential, if not likely, target of false confessions extracted by torture.[73]

## Stalinism as a return to the representative regime

As we have seen, in Soviet avant-garde theatre of the 1920s, the art of the prop maker became as important as the art of the dramaturg; the mise en scène – equal or superior to the dramatic text. This was evident, for example, in Meyerhold's production of *The Magnanimous Cuckold* (1922), in which Liubov

Popova's constructivist machine-set usurped Fernand Crommelynck's dialogue as the main driver of the action. The rising status of the art of mise en scène was, like the merger of 'high-brow' and 'low-brow' forms, a process of equality, a levelling of the hierarchical ordering of creative activities and professions, and an expression of the suitability of all forms to depict all subjects. Stalinism may have shared something of the avant-garde's desire to transform life rather than represent it,[74] but it also differed from it fundamentally in its rejection of this basic democratic impulse (the re-appropriation of the 'subjective richness' of the world on behalf of everyone) and in its sectarian devotion to the preservation of hierarchy. Although Stalinism paid lip-service to the importance of a mass culture, its preference was for a mass of atomized and subordinated consumers, rather than a mass of emancipated individuals. Its modes of cultural organization were proselytizing and stratifying rather than democratic.

If the innovations and experiments of Soviet avant-garde theatre were evidence of what Rancière calls art in the 'aesthetic regime', then theatre under Stalin, we can argue, effected a return to the norms of the 'representative regime'. In this regime, speech and the word took precedence over other stage forms (dance, architecture, music, etc.) and the relationship between modes of artistic expression and the subjects they depicted was strictly codified and regulated. The 'positive hero' of socialist realism had to be embodied on stage with psychological authenticity and realistic movement against a background of period detail and real properties. Stylized methods of stage choreography, speech delivery and set design were devalued in the hierarchy of forms and ostracized from practice. In the culture of high Stalinism, the pollution of the drama stage (and the opera and ballet) with the 'small forms' of music hall, circus, puppet show and pantomime was labelled 'formalist' and became anathema. The term 'conventionality' (*uslovnost'*) was also widely used to demarcate unacceptable methods and styles in the theatre that produced a non-realistic effect.[75] One symptom of this devaluing of the 'small forms' in the Stalinist period was the closure of both the Moscow and Leningrad music halls in 1936.

The Stalinist aesthetic system was supported by a framework of ancillary norms, values and institutional structures – prizes, awards, positions on the Supreme Soviet, censorship boards, editorships in journals and so on – which helped regulate the visibility of specific forms of theatre on the stage. Appointments and promotions to positions of authority in the cultural apparatus depended on a willingness to follow orders from above and to manifest the party line. Awards such as the 'People's Artist of the Soviet Union', which began in 1936, were used to bestow official praise and indicate the correct artistic tendency. In the inaugural set of awards, presented in September 1936, the Moscow Art Theatre heads Konstantin Stanislavsky and Vladimir Nemirovich-Danchenko were honoured, alongside MAT actors Vasilii Kachalov and Ivan Moskvin. Meyerhold and Tairov were excluded, which according to Nemirovich-Danchenko 'indicated the line'.[76] From 1941 the Stalin Prizes were awarded annually to honour achievements in the arts, literature, science and scholarship. In the theatre, Stalin Prizes were given to dramatists, actors, directors and stage designers. The prestige, material perks and large financial sums bestowed on winners meant that theatre became homogenized according to the standards set by the Committee for Artistic Affairs and Politburo which oversaw the work of the Stalin Prize Committee.[77] In this manner it resembled the centralized French state of Louis XIV which used the Prix de Rome to encourage political allegiance from its painters and established the Comédie-Française in order to standardize French neoclassical theatre according to strict cultural codes.[78] Of course, the performance methods of the French neoclassical actor, who conveyed the universal passions through stock gestures and declamatory verse, were very different to that of the Stanislavskian actor, who personalized their hero's emotions through the strategic use of memory. Nevertheless, the overall hierarchy of conventions which privileged one particular method as the only correct means of depicting the dramatic subject was highly similar. Just as the tightly regulated French neoclassical theatre was a symptom of the Sun King's autocratic control, so the aesthetic hierarchy in the Soviet theatre was a manifestation of Stalin's one-party state.

It must be noted, however, that the shift from the 'aesthetic regime' back to the 'representative regime' in Stalinist culture of the 1930s did not happen in the form of a clean, eschatological break. Elements of both regimes co-existed in time and even together within individual theatre productions.[79] We see this merger of regimes particularly in the productions of Aleksandr Tairov and Nikolai Okhlopkov, who despite operating at the intersections of dance, spoken word and architecture typically retained a text and a plot in their productions. Early socialist realist theatre productions such as *An Optimistic Tragedy* at Tairov's Kamernyi Theatre and *Aristocrats* at Okhlopkov's Realistic Theatre fashioned a novel link between design and text: the mise en scène became a focus for the conveyance of emotions and ideas, but these were harnessed in service of the key ideological aims of the play text. In a similar vein, in 1933 the Theatre of the Red Army Baltic Fleet in Kronstadt staged a production titled *Red Verdun* about Stalin's role in the defence of Tsaritsyn (later renamed Stalingrad) during the Civil War. It combined ensemble dancing, music, chorus singing and duelling matches, which completely overshadowed the dialogue.[80] The mise en scène, rather than the word, became the primary medium in which the panegyric to Stalin was constructed. These early examples of socialist realist theatre demonstrated its potential for variety and innovation while serving a didactic end. But as the 1930s progressed, socialist realist theatre became defined and practised within increasingly narrow parameters and a simplified version of the Stanislavsky system and MAT stage naturalism was adopted in theatres across the country.

Before he died, Stanislavsky had advocated for all Soviet theatres to be reorganized into permanent repertory companies in the MAT model, an initiative that was implemented by a Sovnarkom decree in 1939. This decree had a number of positive benefits: actors received security of employment and theatres could plan their repertoires on a long-term basis. It also introduced a uniform tariff of salaries for actors across the country based on a tiered system of grades. Theatres were awarded a grade from one to four and had their budgets and personnel allocations approved on the basis of that grade. Salary tariffs were fixed for each position in the grade, which ensured stability of income for actors but also led to stagnation as older cast members clung on to the fixed number of highly remunerated positions.[81] This meant that younger actors could not be promoted up the salary scale and so many left the profession in the 1940s.

## The homogenization of Soviet theatre in the post-war period

After pursuing a more relaxed approach to cultural matters during the Second World War, the party reimposed stricter measures in 1946. Stalin placed Andrei Zhdanov in charge of the cultural sphere which began the reactionary period known as 'Zhdanovism' (*Zhdanovshchina*). Zhdanovism entailed rigorous censorship, bureaucratic management of the arts and the cultivation of 'Soviet patriotism'. As a result, the Soviet theatre stagnated. Innovative production methods were weeded out as theatre companies were cajoled into reproducing a vapid interpretation of the MAT style and rewarded with Stalin Prizes when they acquiesced. Directors who failed to conform, such as Aleksandr Tairov and Nikolai Akimov, were sacked; while theatre critics who spoke out were purged in the 'anti-cosmopolitanism' campaign. A new phalanx of playwrights churned out anti-Western potboilers or happy 'conflictless' dramas in response to the second of three Central Committee resolutions released between August and September 1946.[82] The second resolution, issued on 26 August, concerned the direction of Soviet theatre and expressed dismay that out of 119 productions staged at 9 of the leading theatres across the country, only 25 were devoted to contemporary themes.⁸³ To remedy this, the resolution imposed on all theatres a production quota of at least two new plays on Soviet themes each year.

In order to help theatres meet these demands, the Soviet Writers' Union promoted three up-and-coming playwrights: Anatolii Sofronov, Nikolai Virta (Karel'skii) and Anatolii Surov. Alongside plays attacking the West, these dramatists also turned to social themes of rebuilding Soviet industry and agriculture after the war. Sofronov's *In One Town* (1947) and *Moscow Character* (1948) depicted party officials and factory managers who become better at their jobs by learning to follow the party line. Sofronov won Stalin Prizes for both plays, while Aleksei Dikii's production of *Moscow Character* at the Malyi Theatre in 1948 also won a Stalin Prize (first class). Virta's *Our Daily Bread* (1947) dramatized the struggle to meet grain production targets in the *kolkhoz* and the fight against black market speculators. *Our Daily Bread* won a Stalin Prize (second class) in 1948 and was staged at the MAT that year by Maria Knebel'. In her production Knebel' followed the Stanislavsky system closely, ensuring the actors focused on the psychological nuances of their characters. The mise en scène was organized with an exhaustive level of naturalistic detail, from the muddy Kirzov boots worn by the cast to the noise of the rain which had to be kept at just the right volume to ensure that the actors' voices could be heard by the audience.⁸⁴ Anatolii Surov's *Dawn over Moscow* (1950) portrayed the director of a Moscow textile factory who unwittingly holds back production by failing to embrace new ideas. In the end, the director is made to see the light by a group of progressive-minded workers, including her own daughter, and the factory is reset onto the correct path. In 1951 Surov won a Stalin Prize (second class) for the play, as did Iurii Zavadskii for his production at the Mossovet Theatre. *Dawn over Moscow* was paradigmatic of the 'theory of conflictlessness' (*teoriia beskonfliktnosti*) which gained traction in the post-war years as genuine optimism for a conflictless future coincided with a paralysing fear of contradicting the party's rose-tinted vision. The 'theory of conflictlessness' claimed that since Soviet society was now free of class antagonism, drama should no longer portray serious conflicts. As a truthful reflection of everyday Soviet reality, drama should depict instead the struggle of 'good versus better': the friendly competition between good and better citizens who share the same communist worldview.⁸⁵ In post-war 'conflictless' drama the epic social clashes between reactionaries and progressives are gone, replaced by accidents, misunderstandings, love triangles and comic mishaps. Friends and colleagues encourage each other to achieve their goals in an optimistic spirit of fraternal solidarity and good-natured rivalry.

Criticism of the theory appeared sporadically in journals and newspapers in the post-war period. But a backlash against it properly emerged in early 1952, following the publication of a piece by Nikolai Virta in which he rehashed the key tenets of the theory. Reviewing the film *The Village Doctor* (1951, dir. Sergei Gerasimov), Virta compared it favourably to his own play *Our Daily Bread*, claiming that the film's lack of any 'antagonistic conflicts' was a more authentic representation of reality.[86] During a Politburo meeting in February 1952, Stalin noted that he had heard of a theory in which there are no conflicts. 'But how you can write plays without conflict?' he asked. 'We do have conflicts. There is conflict in life. These conflicts must be depicted in dramaturgy.'[87] Following Stalin's pronouncement, a vitriolic press campaign was launched in *Pravda* attacking the 'theory of conflictlessness' as a malign distortion of Soviet reality.[88] At the Nineteenth Communist Party Congress held in October that year, Stalin's chief ideologue Mikhail Suslov dismissed the idea of 'conflictlessness' as unreflective of the difficult struggle the country faced to reach communism.[89] Despite never having written a conflictless play himself, Virta was made a scapegoat for the theory and eventually expelled from the Soviet Writers' Union in April 1954. Anatolii Surov, who *had* written a conflictless play, was expelled at the same time (allegedly for drunken behaviour).

The attacks on 'conflictlessness' in 1952 bore many similarities with the campaign against 'cosmopolitanism' that began on 28 January 1949 with an article in *Pravda* titled 'On One Antipatriotic Group of Theatre Critics'. The date was not selected by chance – it was exactly thirteen years to the day since the start of the anti-formalism campaign. The *Pravda* article denounced a group of Western-leaning theatre critics writing in the journals *Teatr* and *Sovetskoe iskusstvo*, for impeding the development of Soviet literature with their 'harmful rootless cosmopolitanism'.[90] Among those accused were Aleksandr Borshchagovskii, Iosif Iuzovskii, Abram Gurvich, Grigorii Boiadzhiev and Leonid Maliugin. These critics and many others were expelled from the Writers' Union and sacked from their positions on editorial boards and the literary committees of theatres. The pretext for the campaign was a conference on contemporary Soviet drama in Moscow theatres, which took place at the Central House of Writers on 29 and 30 November 1948. At this conference, Borshchagovskii and Maliugin gave scathing assessments of Stalin-prize-winning plays by the three party-sponsored dramatists: Sofronov, Virta and Surov. The critics also rebuked the heads of the MAT and the Malyi for staging drama of such poor quality. They were joined by the playwright Nikolai Pogodin (Stukalov) who criticized the way Soviet theatres were becoming replicas of the MAT and bemoaned their lack of identity.[91] The party's draconian response to this criticism then snowballed into a widespread cultural purge. A year earlier, in January 1948, Zhdanov had denounced Vano Muradeli's opera *The Great Friendship* (1947) in a meeting of the Central Committee. Zhdanov accused the composer of 'formalist tricks' and drew a link between the opera and Shostakovich's *Lady Macbeth of the Mtsensk District*.[92] Subsequently, many of the newspaper articles in the anti-cosmopolitanism campaign associated the 'bourgeois cosmopolitans' with formalism, linking the two campaigns and using the labels interchangeably as a means to ostracize cultural figures.[93]

A conference of dramatists and critics was held in Moscow from 16 to 18 February 1949 in order to discuss the issue of 'cosmopolitanism'. Led by Sofronov and Surov, speaker after speaker denounced the theatre critics, with most using the conference as an opportunity to gain revenge for bad reviews of their work. In one speech, the dramatist Boris Romashov claimed that the 'decadent' cosmopolitans had their own 'genealogy' that was rooted in the 'bourgeois era of Meyerhold'.[94] In press reports of the conference, Meyerhold was depicted as the 'forefather' of the cosmopolitans, 'idolized' by them as an anti-Soviet figure.[95] It was the first time that Meyerhold's name had been mentioned in either of the main central newspapers, *Pravda* and *Izvestiia*, since his execution.[96] Although his surviving family had still received no confirmation of his death, Meyerhold's name was now invoked in order to tarnish the theatre critics with the same symbolic otherness. The nature of this otherness was twofold. Meyerhold's name carried both a cultural symbolism that linked it to the avant-garde and the patrilineal mark of his Jewish ancestry – he was born Karl Teodor Kazimir Meyergol'd to a German émigré who converted from Judaism to Lutheranism. Meyerhold changed his name aged twenty-one when he became a Russian national and converted to the Russian Orthodox faith.[97]

This is significant because, from its very beginnings, the anti-cosmopolitanism campaign had an anti-Semitic subtext. The vast majority of the critics targeted were of Jewish origin and the term 'cosmopolitan' (*kosmopolit*) in Russian has a history of anti-Semitic usage.[98] Those denounced in the campaign often had their Jewish surnames revealed, for example the critic Efim Kholodov had his real name 'Meyerovich' unmasked in an article published three days after the anti-cosmopolitanism campaign was launched.[99] Such practices were also common during the Great Purges a decade earlier. During the first Moscow show trial of Kamenev and Zinoviev in August 1936, the press referred to the two former Politburo members by their Jewish surnames, Radomyslsky and Rosenfeld, rather than their Bolshevik *noms de guerre*. Stripped of their political status, their Jewishness was performatively unveiled and used to link them to Trotsky (also Jewish, surname Bronstein) and to stir up anti-Semitic hostility from the public. Stalin's personal anti-Semitism combined with latent prejudice historically embedded within Russian society provided an important context to both the Great Purges and the anti-cosmopolitanism campaign.

In the late 1940s, the targeting of Jewish cultural figures took place alongside the dismantling of Jewish organizations, such as the Jewish Anti-Fascist Committee (JAC) which was abolished in November 1948 and its members arrested. One of the JAC's most prominent members was People's Artist of the USSR Solomon Mikhoels, who had chaired the committee during the war and travelled the world raising money for the Soviet war effort. Mikhoels was one of the Soviet Union's most famous actors and had been the artistic director of the State Jewish Theatre since 1928. On 13 January 1948, Mikhoels was assassinated on Stalin's orders while in Minsk. State security agents dumped his body at a crossroads in town and staged a car crash to make it appear as if he had died in a road accident. A year later, in 1949, the Jewish State theatre was shut down and Mikhoels's replacement as artistic director, Benjamin Zuskin, was arrested. On 12 August 1952, a group of thirteen former JAC members were executed in the basement of Moscow's Lubianka prison, including Zuskin and the writers Itsik Fefer, David Bergel'son, Lev Kvitko and David Gofshtein. They were charged with being part of a Zionist conspiracy that aimed to overthrow the Soviet Union.

The Stalinist anti-Jewish repressions culminated in January 1953 with the 'Doctors' Plot' (*Delo vrachei*), another fabricated conspiracy which saw a group of predominantly Jewish Kremlin doctors, including Mikhoels's brother Miron Vovsi, arrested on charges of conspiring to murder leading Soviet politicians. A month prior, on 1 December 1952, Stalin informed the Presidium of the Central Committee that 'Jewish nationalists' had infiltrated the medical profession and were working as agents of American intelligence. The plot was then revealed on 13 January 1953 in a communiqué published in the Soviet press accusing US tycoons and their British partners of planting spies in the Kremlin disguised as doctors. Although the Jewish identity of the doctors was not referred to explicitly, the arrests set off a wave of anti-Semitic hysteria which led to the incarceration of many more doctors and other Jewish public figures, including one of the original 'cosmopolitan' theatre critics, Iogan Al'tman. Readers of *Pravda* wrote in to report that Jews were being harassed and assaulted in the street. Official plans were drafted to deport all Soviet Jews to Siberia, with the construction of new concentration camps to house them already underway. The violence continued until Stalin's unexpected death on 5 March 1953 which brought everything to a halt. On 3 April, thirty-seven doctors and their families were released from prison (two had died during their incarceration).[100]

One of the most prominent Jewish victims of both the anti-cosmopolitanism campaign and the homogenization of Soviet theatre in the late 1940s was Aleksandr Tairov. On its return from evacuation in 1943, Tairov's Kamernyi Theatre had begun work on a new production of Chekhov's *The Seagull*. Styled as a 'concert production', Tairov stripped the play of all naturalism and set it to the music of Tchaikovsky. The open stage was circled by grey drapes which changed colour with the music. Spotlights picked out vague silhouettes in the background and illuminated the actors, who sat around tables in full evening dress. Tairov distilled the play's theme into the conflict between different theatre styles, with Treplev's new forms competing against traditional realism, as represented by Trigorin and Arkadina. Particular emphasis was placed on the scene in Act Three in which Treplev tells the latter: 'You are rigid. You have taken first place in art and you consider only what you yourselves do to be legitimate and genuine. You chase away and stifle everything else.'[101] It was Tairov's way of asserting his own creative independence and rejecting the standardization of theatre styles in the MAT model. To do this with *The Seagull*, the MAT's foundation stone, was a bold provocation.

On 28 January 1945 Tairov was awarded the Order of Lenin in recognition of his achievements in the Soviet theatre. However, the onset of Zhdanovism a year later brought about a change in atmosphere. In September 1947 the Central Committee's official journal *Kul'tura i zhizn'* published an article on the Kamernyi Theatre entitled 'Bourgeois Theatre in a Blind Alley', echoing Stalin's description of the theatre back in 1929. To Tairov's critics, his decision to begin work on a new production of Oscar Wilde's *Lady Windermere's Fan* a year later was merely confirmation of his shameless indulgence of Western bourgeois plays at the expense of Soviet ones. The production was banned by the Committee for Artistic Affairs, and on 19 May 1949, at the height of the anti-cosmopolitanism campaign, Tairov was fired as artistic director of the Kamernyi Theatre, which he had led since 1914. Tairov and his wife, lead actress Alisa Koonen, were initially transferred to the Vakhtangov Theatre, but their attempts to work on new productions were obstructed by the theatre's management. The pair were eventually dismissed in January 1950 after being awarded state pensions. Tairov wrote a desperate letter to Mikhail Suslov in March begging for work in any of Moscow's theatres, but it was to no avail. After undergoing renovations, the Kamernyi Theatre reopened in August 1950 as the Pushkin Drama Theatre. Tairov fell ill and died a month later, on 25 September.

The Kamernyi Theatre's final performance was *Adrienne Lecouvreur* by Ernest Legouvé and Eugène Scribe, one of its most popular productions, which had premiered in 1919. On the night of 30 May 1949, the theatre was packed. Koonen played the lead role with her usual aplomb, and there was thunderous applause at the end. Tairov refused to join the cast onstage for the curtain calls but Koonen was given her own standing ovation. At that moment, a young student from the MAT School jumped up onto the stage and pinned a badge of the MAT seagull onto Koonen.[102] The stunt was most likely meant as a compliment, a gesture of acceptance.[103] But it also conveyed a more pointed symbolism: as a statement of ownership, possession and hegemonic domination. It was an unwitting act of revenge for Tairov's brazen appropriation of *The Seagull* six years earlier and a tell-tale symptom of the homogenization of the Soviet theatre under Stalin.

2

# Leningrad in the shadow of the Other
## Akimov at the Lensovet Theatre, 1952–5

In October 1952 the Nineteenth Congress of the Communist Party of the Soviet Union was held in the Kremlin Palace in Moscow. It was the first party congress since 1939 and would be the last during Stalin's lifetime. Stalin used the congress to restructure the party leadership, promote new faces to the top of the Central Committee and establish a political legacy that would perpetuate his 'cult of personality' after he was gone. The honour of delivering the 'general report' was given to Georgii Malenkov, second in the party hierarchy and widely seen as Stalin's most likely successor. In the report, which had been edited and approved by Stalin, Malenkov spoke of the Soviet Union's economic development, the threat of a new 'Cold War' with the West and issues pertaining to Soviet cultural life. Regarding the latter, Malenkov criticized the lack of satire in Soviet fiction and dramaturgy and proclaimed: 'we need Soviet Gogols and Shchedrins' in order to eradicate from society those elements that hinder our forward progress.[1] Malenkov's call for new Soviet satires was the culmination of a concerted campaign to replace 'conflictless' literature with a genre more befitting the challenges the Soviet Union faced in the Cold War era.[2] At a meeting of the Politburo on 26 February that year, Stalin had criticized the standard of contemporary Soviet drama, dismissing the idea that you can write plays without conflict. 'We need Gogols, we need Shchedrins', he insisted, in order to 'cure the evil' in our society.[3] The phrase 'we need Gogols and Shchedrins' was then planted in the press during commemorations for the centenary of Nikolai Gogol's birth on 4 March and turned into a mantra, employed repeatedly to encourage writers to be bolder in targeting anti-Soviet elements in their works.[4] In fact, calls for new Soviet Gogols and Shchedrins could be traced back to the 1920s, when a heated debate on the nature and relevance of satire in Soviet society was carried out intermittently in the press.[5] While some argued that satire was redundant in a post-revolutionary society, wherein the state was on the side of the people, others maintained that satire was needed as a means to eradicate the last vestiges of bourgeois capitalist society that continued to hold the Soviet Union back.[6] Now, twenty-five years later, satire was once again being promoted officially as a means to consolidate the power of the state and to purge society of those hindering its progress by targeting the social 'Other'.[7]

The marginalization of those considered to be anti-Soviet or unpatriotic had been ongoing for much of the Stalinist period. It was particularly evident in the anti-cosmopolitanism campaign, which began in 1949 and saw prominent theatre critics and other cultural figures, many of whom were Jewish, arrested and purged. As we saw in the previous chapter, there was a clear anti-Semitic subtext to these attacks on 'rootless cosmopolitans' which took place alongside increased repressions against Jews across Soviet society in the final years of Stalin's rule. Together with the arrest and murder of prominent Jews, anti-Semitism was also manifest in the restriction of discussion of the Holocaust and the downplaying of the suffering of Russian Jews at the hands of the Nazis. Ilia Ehrenburg and Vasilii Grossman's *Black Book*, a documentary account of the massacre of Jews in the USSR, which they compiled for the Jewish Anti-Fascist Committee between 1943 and 1946, was denied publication by Stalin. Grossman would later depict Stalinist anti-Semitism in his novel *Life and Fate* (1960) which was confiscated by the KGB and not published in the Soviet Union until 1988. In the theatre during the late 1940s, the conflation of cosmopolitanism and formalism was commonplace, with Vsevolod Meyerhold singled out as the 'forefather' of the 'decadent cosmopolitans'.[8] A genealogy linking formalists of the 1930s with cosmopolitans in the 1940s was frequently invoked, transforming these terms into generalizing labels used to identify and persecute the 'Other'. But if Meyerhold was the symbolic 'Other' of the Soviet theatre stage, then Leningrad was the symbolic 'Other' of Soviet geopolitical space.

Ever since its creation by Peter I at the start of the eighteenth century, St Petersburg had been locked in rivalry with Moscow. Peter's decision to move the Russian court and capital to this new city, built as a 'window onto Europe' was a direct challenge to Moscow's mythic status as the 'third Rome', the last holy city of orthodox Christianity.[9] If Moscow was a holy city, then, according to the myth, St Petersburg was cursed – a necropolis built on top of the bones of dead serfs who had given their lives for Peter's vanity project and were buried in the boggy marshland of the Neva delta. For two centuries, old Moscow was in the shadow of grand, European-styled St Petersburg until Lenin moved the capital city back to Moscow in 1918, fearing a German invasion. The locus of power shifted once again. Renamed Leningrad in 1924 after the Bolshevik leader's death, the city became stifled politically and culturally. As Stalin increased his grip on the central party apparatus in Moscow during the mid-1920s he sought to isolate his key rival Grigorii Zinoviev, who was the head of the Leningrad party organization: the power struggle between Stalin and Zinoviev was conceived toponymically as part of the historic rivalry between Moscow and St Petersburg. As we saw previously, Zinoviev and fellow old Bolshevik Lev Kamenev were purged in 1935, accused of being at the centre of a Trotskyite-Zinovievite bloc based in Leningrad that was conspiring to undermine Stalin. Both were tortured and then sentenced to death in a show trial in August 1936. In this way the image of Leningrad as a centre for political heresy and social otherness became fixed in public discourse during the Stalinist period. Despite the city's heroic resistance to the Nazis during the war, for which it received the Order of Lenin, Stalin remained deeply suspicious of Leningrad gaining too much influence. In August 1946 he ordered Andrei Zhdanov, in charge of cultural affairs, to issue a warning strike against the city's cultural apparatus in that infamous first Central Committee resolution.[10] Two years later, in the wake of Zhdanov's sudden death, Politburo members Lavrentii Beria and Georgii Malenkov began a purge of the Leningrad political elite, arresting hundreds of party members who were charged with state crimes and either sent to the Gulag or executed. What became known as the 'Leningrad Affair' saw a re-assertion of Moscow's dominance over Leningrad. The museum commemorating the Leningrad Blockade was liquidated in February 1953 and its story labelled a myth intended by Stalin's enemies to diminish his personal role in the victory over the Nazis.

It is therefore both surprising and unsurprising that some of the first signs of change in the Soviet theatre appeared in Leningrad. Surprising because the city and its political authorities, subjected to periodic attacks from the Kremlin, had become quite risk-averse when it came to cultural matters; unsurprising because of Leningrad's long history of alterity in relation to Moscow and its vibrant tradition of alternative forms of theatre. One example of this tradition was the Jewish comedian Arkadii Raikin, who made his name on the Leningrad variety circuit in the 1930s and 1940s, offering satirical skits that ridiculed everyday Soviet life. Although his shows were constantly policed by the Leningrad censor, he became one of the most popular performers in the Soviet Union, favoured by political leaders from Stalin to Brezhnev, and thus able to get away with lampooning Soviet bureaucracy and corruption in ways that others could not.[11] Raikin was an example of the outsider working on the fringes who becomes adopted (co-opted) by the mainstream. Yet it was not Raikin's vein of satire that Malenkov was advocating in his speech at the Nineteenth Party Congress in 1952. The call for new 'Soviet Gogols and Shchedrins' was a demand for works that would aid the Soviet state in marginalizing anti-Soviet others. In response to Malenkov's appeal, a number of writers dashed off new Soviet satires, the most memorable of which was Sergei Mikhalkov's *Crayfish* (1952), a social comedy which owed an obvious debt to Gogol's *The Government Inspector*.[12] *Crayfish* even included a parody of Gogol's famous ending in which the townspeople are struck dumb on hearing the news that the real government inspector has arrived from St Petersburg. In Mikhalkov's version, a party of wedding guests freeze as a crocodile enters, raising a pitchfork in order to select its victim – a reference to the popular satirical magazine *Krokodil* (The Crocodile). One corollary of Malenkov's speech was that it legitimized the restaging of Gogol's and Mikhail Saltykov-Shchedrin's own works at a time when theatres were struggling to find contemporary plays of sufficient quality. One director who took advantage of this was Nikolai Akimov in Leningrad, who staged Shchedrin's play *Shadows* and Gogol's *The Government Inspector* as part of a trilogy of productions, which also included Aleksandr Sukhovo-Kobylin's *The Case* (1861), that explored the nature of the state bureaucratic machine in Russia and offered veiled critiques of the Soviet system.

Akimov was himself a victim of the anti-cosmopolitanism campaign, having been sacked as artistic director of the Leningrad Comedy Theatre in August 1949 on charges of 'cosmopolitanism, formalism, constructivism, expressionism and naturalism'.[13] Given a second chance at the Lensovet Theatre in Leningrad, Akimov began rehearsing Shchedrin's play *Shadows* in the autumn of 1952. This obscure and little-known work from the mid-nineteenth century is a satire of Russian civil society in the Juvenalian mode – railing against corruption and vice with a bitter sense of irony. Akimov's decision to revive the play proved to be a fortuitous one. The production was a great success and proved to be a harbinger of the Thaw, both in terms of its Aesopic subtext and its innovative staging that blended realism and grotesque stylization. It was a template that Akimov would repeat to great acclaim a couple of years later with his production of *The Case*. In their political themes, these productions challenged audiences to ask difficult questions of the overbearing, sclerotic Russian (Soviet) state. In their form, they broke with the norms of Soviet theatre established during Stalinism, by combining a psychologically realist approach to characterization with a stylized mise en scène and rhythmic musicality. In this way, they set a new course which would be followed by other directors and theatres during and after the Thaw. Performance practices which had previously been denounced as 'formalist' became a part of audiences' viewing experiences and cultural vocabulary once again.

## From the Comedy Theatre to the Lensovet

Nikolai Akimov began his career as a set designer working in variety theatres and music halls in Leningrad in the early 1920s. He made his name at places such as the Crooked Mirror Theatre and Free Comedy Theatre before transitioning to work on stage plays at the Leningrad Bolshoi Drama Theatre and the Aleksandrinskii Theatre. Eventually he became known as a 'director-artist' who directed productions as well as designing them. Akimov's work was therefore steeped in the avant-garde tradition of theatrical design: often expressionistic and using grotesque manipulations of space and proportion. As a director, he placed great emphasis on visual forms – costumes, set design, properties and lighting – in the construction of the mise en scène, an approach that the artist Moisei Levin described as 'pictorial direction'.[14] His proclivity for the physical stunts and tricks of the circus was influenced by studios such as the Factory of the Eccentric Actor (FEKS), established by Grigori Kozintsev, Leonid Trauberg and Sergei Iutkevich in Petrograd in 1921. FEKS enshrined 'eccentrism' [*ekstsentrism*] as the theatrical means to capture the tempo of modern life via the merger of circus, music hall, street performance and cinema. Another important influence on Akimov's work was the music hall, which he saw as the blueprint for the creation of a 'synthetic theatre' that combined different genres and art forms together. From 1933 to 1934 he set up an experimental theatre studio attached to the Leningrad Music Hall to explore these ideas further. Akimov's work at the studio was undoubtedly influenced by Aleksandr Tairov's concept of a 'synthetic theatre' in which different theatrical forms combine harmonically in one unified production. Akimov also borrowed ideas from Evgenii Vakhtangov and Meyerhold to create his own particular aesthetic. Meyerhold's emphasis on rhythm as the foundation of all dramatic expression resonated with Akimov's interpretation of the mise en scène, as did Vakhtangov's vision of theatre as a festival: the idea that theatre should be celebratory, joyful and expressive. Like Vakhtangov (and Tairov), Akimov saw the art of performance as residing in the combination of expressive devices that nevertheless centre the actor as an intelligent co-creator in the making of a production. In Akimov's method, theatre is the art of 'collective play' and the collective must take responsibility for bringing a play to life and engaging the audience.[15] This focus on expressive theatrical devices and visual forms led to Akimov's work being labelled 'formalist', a judgement that was cemented by the furore surrounding his production of *Hamlet* at the Vakhtangov Theatre in Moscow.

Akimov's *Hamlet* has gone down in Russian theatre folklore as a scandalous aberration. It premiered in April 1932 to a near universal barrage of invective from critics which would haunt the director for the rest of his life. Akimov's crime was to reinterpret Shakespeare's play as a tragi-farce, casting the comic actor Anatolii Goriunov to play Hamlet as a brash joker who appeared in one memorable scene in a night gown, feigning madness while holding a carrot. Orphelia, played by Valentina Vagrina, was a drunkard who drowns after stumbling into a river on the way back from a party.[16] *Hamlet* ran for a year before it was axed from the repertoire, but Akimov's heresy would not be forgotten, as became apparent during a conference for theatre workers held in Moscow on 9 April 1936. The conference was used by the Committee for Artistic Affairs as an instrument of coercion in the anti-formalism campaign and Akimov's *Hamlet* was repeatedly referenced in speeches as an exemplar of formalist deviance. When his turn came, Akimov defended himself by pointing out that *Hamlet* was just one of many theatre productions he had worked on over the years and was not reflective of his approach today. He distanced himself from formalism as a particular tendency but nevertheless called on his fellow directors to be brave in their creative practices, insisting that 'great works are not made with trembling hands'.[17] This was a risky move by Akimov, but there were no immediate consequences. Back in Leningrad, he managed to survive the Stalinist purges thanks to a combination of luck and the popularity of his Comedy Theatre with audiences.

However, Akimov's luck ran out during a fateful tour of Moscow with the Comedy Theatre in the summer of 1949. Productions that had been in the repertoire for years in Leningrad were suddenly thrust into the spotlight on the Moscow Art Theatre's subsidiary stage and scrutinized by the capital's critics. The anti-cosmopolitanism campaign was in full swing and the press was on the lookout for scapegoats. Unfortunately for Akimov, a mix up by one of the Kremlin chauffeurs saw members of the Politburo brought to his production of Eugène Labiche's farce *The Journey of Mr. Perrichon* (1860) at the MAT subsidiary stage on Moskvin Street, instead of *Boris Godunov* at the MAT main stage on Kamergerskii Lane. Expecting Pushkin's tragedy, the high-ranking officials soon realized their mistake and promptly left after only eight minutes. But to the watching press, members of the Politburo had walked out of a performance and this was taken as a sign.[18] A review of the Comedy Theatre's tour in *Pravda*, titled 'Recurrences of Formalism', rounded on Akimov for employing 'formalist effects' in his productions and called for the eradication of 'recurrences of aestheticism and formalism' from the theatre.[19] Targeting his ire particularly at 'western comedies' in the Comedy Theatre's repertoire such as *The Journey of Mr. Perrichon* and Lope de Vega's *The Dog in the Manger* (1618), the critic griped about the director's use of 'outdated comic devices' and complained: 'The spectator is distracted by meaningless stunts, tumbles, slaps, the throwing of bouquets, ridiculous gestures, the wearing of clothes inside out, breaking crockery and similar rubbish. It is often simply impossible to catch the text of the play.'

The distraction of the audience through ambivalent and reactive physical gestures (à la Charlie Chaplin) at the expense of the consistent logic of a text is for Jacques Rancière a defining feature of performance in the aesthetic regime of the arts.[20] In the first two decades of the twentieth century, such stunts and devices – borrowed from the popular forms of music hall, cabaret and circus – were elevated to the level of 'high-brow' art, where they jostled for attention with the once sovereign plot. The democratizing merger of high and low art was part of the breakdown of the old representative system, which had distinguished artistic practices from other social occupations via the principle of *mimesis* (imitation rather than utility) and reflected the real social hierarchies of power in its ranking of artistic genres and its privileging of speech, action and narrative over form, stasis and description.[21] As we saw in Chapter 1, the Stalinist theatre underwent a return to this representative system, which linked norms, practices and the criteria to evaluate them within a hierarchical model that privileged the school of *perezhivanie* and with it the centrality of the 'through-action' (*skvoznoe deistvie*). The notion of the 'through-action' was a twentieth-century revision of Aristotle's 'unity of action', which transferred responsibility for dramatic coherence from the shoulders of the dramatist onto the actors themselves.[22] It was this acting method that was deemed most suitable for the depiction of the new Soviet person, the 'positive hero' of socialist realism. Aligned with the 'Meiningen' approach to stage verisimilitude, it placed the actor/character and their actions and speech at the centre of the performance. Conversely, Akimov's use of stylized tricks and routines, which crowded out the dialogue of the plays being performed, were a rejection of this representative system. His productions at the Comedy Theatre were evidence of the way in which avant-garde elements could survive in the Soviet repertoire through directorial sleight of hand even in the late 1940s. Yet although they were tolerated by the cultural authorities on their 'home' stage at the Comedy

Theatre in Leningrad, the intrusion of these forms onto one of the stages of the prestigious Moscow Art Theatre, centre of the Soviet theatrical universe, was an unforgiveable breach of the representative norms that linked forms, genres and institutions in Stalinist culture.

Following publication of the review in *Pravda*, Akimov was summoned to a meeting of the Committee for Artistic Affairs on 9 August while the rest of the company travelled on to Sochi to continue the tour. At the meeting, Akimov was accused of harbouring 'cosmopolitan' and 'formalist' tendencies and as evidence the chair brought out an article Akimov had written back in 1922 in which he praised Vincent van Gogh. The meeting quickly descended into farce, however, when it turned out that none of the other committee members knew who van Gogh was. The chair had to explain to those in attendance that this was a 'dreadful artist whose paintings were full of broken arms and legs'.[23] For the chair, van Gogh's (alleged) expressionistic fragmentation of the body was a transgression of the strict codes of classical bodily proportion enshrined in socialist realist art. Likewise, Akimov was guilty of a similar charge in the theatre – disrupting Aristotle's classical unity of action with 'meaningless' stunts, tricks and routines that switched the audience's focus away from the dramatic text and towards a visual language of playful festivity. The committee demanded that Akimov issue a *mea culpa* but, just as in 1936, the director showed no contrition in his speech, insisting that he was not guilty of any wrongdoing. Unsurprisingly, his stubbornness went down badly with the committee, and on 13 August Akimov was fired as the artistic director of the Comedy Theatre. A resolution by the Committee for Artistic Affairs published that day in *Sovetskoe iskusstvo* criticized the director for failing to acknowledge his formalist mistakes and accused him of copying the worst elements of Meyerhold's art.[24] The Comedy Theatre was allowed to continue performing but a large number of plays were cut from its repertoire and audience numbers gradually decreased. On 29 September a Central Committee resolution was published in *Pravda* noting that the task of purging the theatre of the 'recurrences of formalism and bourgeois aestheticism' had recently been carried out at the Kamernyi Theatre, with the removal of its artistic director Aleksandr Tairov, and at the Leningrad Comedy Theatre with the firing of Nikolai Akimov.[25] This necessary work would allow socialist realism to become stronger, the resolution argued, as 'formalists', 'decadents' and 'cosmopolitans' were swept from its path. For Tairov this marked the end of his career. Akimov, however, continued to find work as a freelance director and designer at various theatres around the country. In 1952 he was invited to return to Leningrad to become the artistic director of the Lensovet

Theatre thanks to sympathetic officials working within the Leningrad Party Obkom (regional committee).²⁶

The Lensovet Theatre (originally the New Theatre, renamed in August 1953) has straddled the artistic divide between realism and theatricalism since its formation in the autumn of 1933. It was founded by Isaak Kroll', former director of the Leningrad Satire Theatre, who brought together a company of actors picked from across the variety theatre scene, including Aleksandr Zhukov, Elizaveta Mosolova and Roman Rubinshtein. Kroll''s leadership came in for criticism during the anti-formalism campaign, and he was eventually removed as artistic director by the Leningrad city council executive in March 1937. His final production, an adaptation of Aleksandr Pushkin's *The Tales of Belkin* (1831), was cancelled before its opening night on account of its overuse of pantomime in place of dialogue.²⁷ Kroll' was replaced by Boris Sushkevich, a former pupil of Stanislavsky's at the Moscow Art Theatre and a director at the Second MAT. Although Sushkevich had experimented with different production styles at the Second MAT, he was well versed in the Stanislavsky system and his brief at the Lensovet was to push the theatre away from the tradition of the 'small forms' and towards the methods of psychological realism that were being canonized in theatres across the country. Sushkevich and his wife, the former MAT actress Nadezhda Bromlei, changed the culture within the company, encouraging the actors to focus on the psychological delineation of their characters rather than outward stylization. After Sushkevich's death in 1946, the Lensovet Theatre entered a period of stagnation. Audience numbers fell, the theatre began to accrue debt, and twice a week the building was used for cinema screenings. Into this void, in 1952, stepped Nikolai Akimov who implemented changes straight away, overhauling the repertoire and introducing his own rehearsal methods. Most of the company had been trained in the Stanislavsky system and were unaccustomed to stylized theatre techniques. Nevertheless, Akimov managed to win over the majority of the younger actors to his project while simultaneously adapting his own approach to the existing culture in the theatre. Perhaps wisely, Akimov decided to begin his stint at the Lensovet Theatre with Viktor Gusev's harmless musical comedy *Springtime in Moscow* (1941). The show premiered on 29 June 1952 to great fanfare and popular acclaim. But although the authorities in Moscow could not find fault with his choice of play – an upbeat socialist realist comedy – the Committee for Artistic Affairs took umbrage at the poster Akimov had designed for the production, warning him that depicting 'sunny Moscow' at night time was a political error.²⁸ Nevertheless, by March 1953 the show had played over one hundred times and an adaptation for the cinema starring Galina Korotkevich as lead protagonist Nadezhda Kovrova was released that spring.

## *Shadows*, 1952

There was a strong degree of prescience in a number of Akimov's early productions at the Lensovet Theatre that picked up a mood of change not only in the aftermath of Stalin's death but prior to it, suggesting that the Soviet leader's passing on 5 March 1953 should not be interpreted as an absolute watershed when marking the onset of the Thaw. One such production was *Shadows* by Saltykov-Shchedrin. A satirical drama set in the late 1850s, on the eve of the liberal reforms introduced by Tsar Aleksandr II, *Shadows* was virtually unknown in Russia before its premiere at the Lensovet on 31 December 1952. The play is an excoriating attack on the Russian state bureaucracy but, unusually for its time, targets both conservatives and liberals. It is thought to have been written sometime in the 1860s but was neither staged nor published in Shchedrin's lifetime. The text lay forgotten in the writer's archive until it was discovered in 1914 and staged on 26 April that year in a one-off production at the Marinskii Theatre in St Petersburg, directed by Aleksandr Zagarov. Attacked in the press for 'insulting the dead', the play was mothballed until Akimov decided to revive it in 1952.[29]

*Shadows* begins with the arrival of Nikolai Bobyrev (played by Vladimir Petrov) and his wife Sofia (Galina Korotkevich) in St Petersburg. Bobyrev is a liberal dreamer hoping to find a meaningful career in the capital. He shows up at the office of an old school friend and like-minded liberal, Petr Klaverov (Valentin Lebedev), who in a short space of time has risen up the ranks of the civil service and runs a department in the state administration. Klaverov agrees to give Bobyrev a job because he has designs on Bobyrev's wife Sofia, with whom he was romantically involved many years ago. With Sofia's mother as a willing accomplice, Klaverov and his entourage introduce the young ingénue to Petersburg high society and dazzle her with trips to the theatre and late-night cafes. Sofia believes his advances are genuine but in fact Klaverov has other motives. He has managed to rise swiftly up the ranks of the civil service due to his willingness to provide his superior, the old Prince Tarakanov ('Cockroach'), with lovers. Klaverov sold his former girlfriend Klara on to Tarakanov in exchange for a promotion, and he now hopes to do the same with Sofia. Eventually Bobyrev learns of Klaverov's betrayal and drunkenly confronts him at a party creating a scene. The next morning Sofia runs away to Klaverov's place and asks him to take her in, but his reluctance makes her realize that he has been insincere all along. A courier arrives with a letter from Bobyrev, but instead of challenging Klaverov to a duel he timidly apologizes for making a scene the night before. Sofia is mortified that her husband is not prepared to defend her honour and she leaves with her reputation in tatters. Youthful idealism and romantic hopes are dashed as cynicism, selfishness and subservience prosper in a city where people are slowly losing their humanity.

Set in the mid-nineteenth century, the play is a critique of the Russian imperial system and so was deemed palatable by the Soviet censor. Nevertheless, audiences were able to draw parallels between the corrupt and self-serving officials of the Tsarist bureaucracy and their twentieth-century Soviet counterparts. These were parallels that Akimov's innovative use of stylized devices did nothing to discourage – in fact, the uncanny atmosphere they created gave space for imaginative interpretations. Most notable in this respect was the use of shadow theatre in between scenes. These interludes, created using silhouettes in front of a spotlight to cast shadows on a screen, established a contrast between the flesh and blood characters on stage and the spectral world lurking behind them. Akimov used this device to express the overall concept of the production – exposing the system that turns living people into phantoms. In the dance of shadows that breaks up the action, real life becomes transformed into a grotesque abstraction. Following each act, the same characters in silhouette form would spring to life, performing new para-textual episodes in pantomime. At the end of Act Two, for example, which closes with Sofia accepting an invitation from Klaverov to go to the ballet that evening, a shadow interlude depicted Sofia and a group of revellers dancing the can-can (a common Soviet trope for bourgeois debauchery). This episode recounts what is only suggested in the text: Sofia's introduction to high society by Klaverov and his friends will lead to her debasement. Likewise, prior to the start of Act Four, a shadow scene depicted Sofia rushing to Klaverov's apartment in a sled to naively ask for his protection. The sled was drawn by a toy horse with spindly legs galloping on the spot and through this comic yet fragile image a sense of Sofia's childish naivety was conveyed.[30] The most memorable of these shadow projections was an image of the equestrian statue of Tsar Nikolai I, which stands in St Isaac's Square in St Petersburg. The outline of the Tsar on horseback was projected onto a curtain during the prologue – yet critics and audiences were at first confused. After all, the play is set during the more liberal reign of his successor Aleksandr II, so why open with an image of the feared and heavy-handed Nikolai? The underlying idea of Shchedrin's play is that a new era may have arrived, but the corrupt bureaucratic system has remained the same.

Akimov sought to represent this idea symbolically through the shadow of the deceased Tsar looming over the action, but this device took on new meaning when Stalin died only a few months after the premiere. During performances, the curtain would rustle periodically, sending a ripple through the shadow as though bringing him back to life. It struck one critic as though the ghost of the recently departed was still demanding fresh sacrifices from beyond the grave.[31]

In the production, Akimov used music innovatively to illustrate the idea of a bureaucratic system that transforms people into shadows. In Act One, Klaverov's colleague Naboikin eagerly tells Bobyrev about the new era that is upon them: 'Previously', he says, 'we carried out orders mechanically . . . but nowadays we carry them out according to our own personal convictions.'[32] But as the conversation continued, the sounds of a marching band could be heard drifting up from the street below. Gradually, unconsciously the two men began to pace back and forth on stage in time with the drumbeat, oblivious to the fact that they were marching in step with the soldiers down below. With this sequence, Naboikin's empty rhetoric about a new liberal dawn is figuratively undermined – the bureaucrats are still marching to the oppressive tune of the previous era like clockwork soldiers. The director then brought this music back in the final scene, set in the same office as the first act, with the same mahogany furniture and the same vista of St Petersburg outside the window. In this way, the marching music became a leitmotif for the immutable status quo, two more lives may have been ruined, but the regimented social order remains unmoved.

At the time in which the play is set, Petersburg society was gripped by an 'operetta-mania' (in Shchedrin's words) with the works of Jacques Offenbach some of the most popular with the Russian public.[33] Akimov consequently used music from Offenbach's operettas in the production, partly in the interest of period authenticity and partly to satirize the faux-cultured airs of Klaverov and his circle. This came to the fore in Act Three, when Sofia and her entourage return from a late-night party and continue their revelry at the Bobyrevs' apartment. Before their return, Bobyrev has drunkenly played a few couplets at the piano from the Bolero in Act Three of Offenbach's operetta *La Périchole* in which the hero is praised for daring to protest against the authorities. The pathos of this sentimental moment, in which Bobyrev resolves to stand up to Klaverov, is then parodied minutes later when Sofia and her circle arrive home noisily and proceed to sing another Offenbach number, this time from the operetta *La Belle Helene*, at the same piano. In this scene, Akimov devised a number of skits with the actors in order to accentuate the vaudeville tones of the action. First Sofia's mother Ol'ga Dmitrievna (played by Vera Budreiko) disappears into the bedroom (offstage) with Naboikin before the two reappear moments later having swapped accessories – Ol'ga now in a top hat and Naboikin wearing a white feather boa – and proceed to drunkenly dance the can-can across the stage.[34] Next, Sofia sings an adaptation of the chanson from *La Belle Helene* that the party had listened to that night at the opera, accompanied on the piano by Naboikin. However, unbeknownst to the others, Ol'ga's friend Obtiazhnov has brought back some musicians from the restaurant and hidden them in the hallway (offstage). At a pre-arranged signal, just as Sofia is finishing the aria, the musicians strike up a raucous accompaniment to the delight of the guests. Sofia begins to dance the can-can herself, cavorting around the apartment, leaping onto the furniture and finally the grand piano when suddenly the music stops and she falls exhausted onto the piano top. As the guests gather around her, she looks at them in bewilderment and asks: 'Tell me, messieurs, why is it so wearisome to live on the earth?'[35] Behind the joyful façade a spiritual emptiness temporarily reveals itself, which is hastily covered up by the other (male) guests who subtly remind Sofia of her place and the social codes which govern her behaviour. The abrupt switch from gaiety to despair is meant to disorient the audience, and within moments another shock arrives in the form of a drunken Bobyrev lumbering out of his study to confront Klaverov over his deception. The guests watch in horror as Bobyrev breaks rank and calls his boss a 'scoundrel', but at this point the director switches tone once again. Removing his handkerchief to anxiously wipe his brow, Obtiazhnov inadvertently gives the musicians the signal, and once again they start up the can-can melody at the worst possible moment, before quickly falling silent in confusion. Melodrama gives way to comedy, pathos turns into farce.[36]

Both the sudden switches of tone and the orchestration of the actors' movements to music were reminiscent of Meyerhold, who had used these principles memorably in his 1926 production of Gogol's *The Government Inspector*, structuring the movements and utterances of the actors according to the tempo and cadence of the musical score. It was a technique also used frequently by Tairov who envisaged the stage space as a 'keyboard' on which the actor plays via their rhythmic movements.[37] Akimov clearly borrowed from these traditions when he structured the action in Act Three, but his approach was not to everyone's taste. One critic, reviewing the production for the newspaper *Vechernii Leningrad*, criticized the director's use of music insisting that 'the operatic musical numbers by Offenbach were unnecessary and . . . purely superfluous'.[38] However, overall the response from critics was positive. The reviewer for *Pravda* praised the Lensovet collective for their 'creative bravery' in using biting satire and irony while never losing sight of the human characteristics of the play.[39] He commended the production for enriching Soviet theatre art and predicted that it would have a long and successful run. Writing in *Literaturnaia gazeta*, Ruben Simonov (the artistic director of the Vakhtangov Theatre) praised the production as a 'creative success' for the director, noting that Akimov's use of expressive devices to accentuate situations and characters was justified because he had 'penetrated the ideological substance of the play' to reveal its 'great living truth and psychological depth'.[40] In other words, the realistic treatment of characters and settings redeemed the more stylized elements of the production. Simonov noted that in the interpretation of some of the smaller comic roles, 'one could clearly feel the hand of the director leading them to the level of the grotesque' but insisted that Akimov was never guilty of 'overstepping the boundaries of truth'.[41] The production's use of shadow theatre was overlooked by both critics, perhaps because it would have been harder to justify stylistically and might have therefore undermined the argument, implicit in both reviews, that Akimov's move to the Lensovet had led to a kind of creative *perekovka* (reforging).

There is no doubt that Akimov adapted his usual directorial approach when he began work at the Lensovet Theatre and the production of *Shadows* was emblematic of this change. Alongside his eccentric theatricalism was a new focus on truthfulness in the actor's performance and a close attention to verisimilitude in set design, properties and costumes. Many of the items in Klaverov's office and the Bobyrevs' apartment, from writing desks to porcelain figurines, were sourced by Akimov from second-hand shops in Leningrad. Likewise, the top hats, shawls and coats worn by the characters were authentic period pieces. Sets were constructed in the three-walled box design, carefully decorated to represent the tastes of the mid-nineteenth century down to the most minute detail. This 'Meiningen' approach to design was matched by a method of character development that generally avoided stock clichés and encouraged the actors to build up a complex and nuanced picture of their character and the motivations driving them. Akimov prompted the actors to research the 'given circumstances' of the play, to familiarize themselves with Shchedrin's oeuvre and to take the initiative during rehearsals to add colour and depth to their character's psychological profile.[42] This combination of a Stanislavskian approach to characterization and a realist set design with stylized episodes and devices (a variation on what is sometimes known as the Vakhtangov method)[43] was not only a pragmatic move by Akimov as he adapted to working with a cast trained in the MAT tradition, but it also laid out a blueprint for other directors to follow during the Thaw. It was a blueprint that married certain taboo stylistic innovations of the avant-garde with the system of acting and scene arrangement that had become canonized during the Stalinist period.

One example of this approach could be found in the character Svistikov, Klaverov's elderly lackey. The director was adamant that Svistikov should be played not by an experienced actor of villains but by a serious dramatic actor, casting the thirty-seven-year-old Anatolii Abramov in the role. The aim was to avoid the character turning into a stock type and to ensure that even this servile sycophant had depth to him. Nevertheless, Act One opened with a pantomime skit in which Svistikov was booted through the door of Klaverov's office out into the corridor where petitioners were waiting, flying acrobatically through the air before sprawling on the floor with a beaming smile.[44] This kind of stunt obviously required a younger actor, justifying the decision to cast Abramov in make-up rather than one of the older members of the company. Throughout the play, Svistikov followed his superiors around bent double in an obsequious pose, his curved back a physiological cipher of the strict hierarchy encoded into Russian society. Thus, Svistikov epitomized the director's approach to characterization in the play: complex psychological incarnation of the role combined with moments of slapstick comedy and stylized movement.

Another example was the scene in which Prince Tarakanov the younger (played by Aleksandr Giul'tsen) recounts an argument between his uncle, Prince Tarakanov senior, and a young liberal, Serkin, that took place at the club. In response to Serkin's teasing over the new liberal reforms being introduced, the old Prince Tarakanov stuck out his tongue at him. To illustrate this part of the story his nephew twisted his red pocket handkerchief into a ribbon and when the moment came – out of his mouth flew the ribbon: the anti-liberal Prince senior reduced to a synecdochic red tongue. This playful trick was also demonstrably grotesque, and yet in a piece published in 1954 Akimov insisted that when creating the production 'the grotesque was not allowed into this sphere'.[45] The director stated that they had deliberately avoided the standard 'Shchedrin style' – gloomy grotesque, caricatured make-up and stylized characterization – in favour of a 'truer form': a mix of psychological verisimilitude and satirical exaggeration that is suggested by the text itself.[46] Denying any use of the grotesque was undoubtedly a strategic ploy on Akimov's part. Like many directors and critics of the time, he was accustomed to using irony, ambiguity and denial for reasons of self-preservation.

At a public discussion of the production held on 12 January 1953, Akimov defended his staging methods and responded to questions from spectators and

**Figure 1** Valentin Lebedev and Galina Korotkevich in *Shadows* at the Lensovet Theatre in Leningrad, 1952. Courtesy of the Museum of the St Petersburg Academic Lensovet Theatre.

critics. One of the most controversial topics for debate was the role of Sofia. Akimov had encouraged Korotkevich to play Sofia as a sympathetic figure: naïve and foolish at the start, but world weary and defiant by the end of the play, a reading which diverged from Shchedrin's description of the character. Key to this was the final scene when on hearing from her husband's letter that he would not be defending her honour, Korotkevich simply laughed rather than breaking down with emotion. Both actor and director felt that such a stoic response perfectly encapsulated her position – all there was left to do was to laugh at the world and at those who had mistreated her.[47] She left the stage with her head held high, escorted by Prince Tarakanov the younger and her mother. Akimov's reasoning was that unless the audience felt some positive sentiment towards Sofia, they would not be sufficiently repulsed by Klaverov's deception. But some participants at the public discussion were left unsatisfied, complaining that Sofia was 'unfit for society', 'of low morality' and was 'not deserving of our sympathy'.[48] These opinions were also echoed by critics, with one reviewer unhappy at the decision to downplay Sofia's 'vampish traits' since this reduced the 'social power' of the character.[49] Refusing to depict Sofia as merely a 'fallen woman', Akimov and Korotkevich emphasized instead her journey from credulous naivety to mature insight. This was another example of Akimov embracing Stanislavskian methods of building a role – encouraging the audience to empathize with the character by making nuanced adjustments to her behaviour. In this respect, *Shadows* was a different type of theatre production to those Akimov had staged at the Comedy Theatre. It was a compromise of different methods and traditions, a heteroglot approach that would go on to become paradigmatic of the Thaw.

The shrewdness of Akimov's approach was revealed a few months later when, in May 1953, another production of *Shadows* opened at the Moscow Pushkin Theatre (formerly Tairov's Kamernyi Theatre). The play's director Aleksei Dikii was harshly criticized in the press for his boldly theatrical interpretation, which saw the actors break the fourth wall by addressing the audience directly. The actor Boris Babochkin was also reprimanded for playing Klaverov as a foppish buffoon whose ad-libbed monologues and 'vaudevillian gestures', delivered with a wink to the audience, made him too sympathetic and 'weakened the satirical sting' of Shchedrin's play.[50] Aided by Iurii Pimenov's exaggeratedly grand and parodic set, Dikii focused the entire production on a single supertask: unmasking the state apparatus, which is rotten to the core.[51] The director had been arrested and sent to the Gulag in 1937 on charges of formalism but returned to play the role of Stalin himself numerous times on stage and screen after the war: a Faustian bargain which ensured his survival. Now with Stalin gone, Dikii drew on his full repertoire of theatrical tricks to rail against the system that had wronged him. It was to be his swansong. He died two years later on 1 October 1955.

## *The Case*, 1954

In December 1954, Akimov followed up the success of *Shadows* by staging *The Case*, the second play in a trilogy by Aleksandr Sukhovo-Kobylin written between 1852 and 1869.[52] Thematically the most sombre and fatalistic of the trilogy, *The Case* is based partly on Sukhovo-Kobylin's personal experience of the Russian criminal justice system after he was imprisoned and then controversially acquitted of the murder of his lover Louise Simon-Dimanche. *The Case* picks up the story six years from the end of the first play in the trilogy, *Krechinsky's Wedding*, which sees Lidochka Muromskaia unjustly implicated in a scam cooked up by her fiancée Krechinskii. In the intervening years this scandal has turned into a long-running police investigation against Lidochka and her father Petr Muromskii. The case against the Muromskii family, although based on flimsy evidence, has been dragged from one government department to another for years. The slow unyielding machine of the Russian state bureaucracy has sucked them in and chewed them up. The play begins with Muromskii and his daughter arriving in St Petersburg to try and finally resolve the case. Muromskii visits Maksim Varravin, the head of the government department where his case has been sitting for the past five months, willing to pay a bribe to bring everything to a conclusion. But Varravin and his assistant Tarelkin demand a sum so large that it would leave him almost penniless. Muromskii takes the case higher up the chain to Varravin's superior, the so-called 'Important Person' (*Vazhnoe litso*), but the outcome is even worse – he orders the entire case to be re-investigated. Broken and humbled, Muromskii gathers together all the money he can find and visits Varravin once again to pay him the bribe. But Varravin tricks Muromskii by pocketing the money on the sly before calling him back into the office to retrieve his package. Realizing that he has been duped, Muromskii rages at the theft before collapsing. After he is carried out, the 'Important Person' and his superior the 'Very Important Person' enter and order an investigation into the matter. Tarelkin then reports that Muromskii has died in his carriage on the way home. Varravin departs, leaving Tarelkin to curse his boss for taking the money for himself.

Like *Shadows*, *The Case* is set in St Petersburg and critiques the corrupt Russian bureaucracy and oppressive police state. But if Akimov had been restrained and elliptical when staging *Shadows*, he was much bolder with *The Case*, allowing the play's denunciatory force to resonate loud and clear through the mise en scène. Once again, Akimov used an ingenious prologue to articulate the meta-concept of the play. It began with a clap of thunder, then a blackout, followed by a spotlight which picked out a smartly dressed young man who nervously read the author's foreword to the play, the first time this foreword had been used in a performance. The young man (resembling the Prologue of the Elizabethan stage) was at pains to convince the public that nothing depicted in the play was beyond the realms of possibility. Then the curtains opened to reveal a large, ramped staircase which curved in an arc from stage right to stage left. Frozen on each level of the staircase, bathed in green light, were all the characters of the play, ordered in their social rank to create a tableau vivant of the imperial hierarchy. At the top were the 'authorities' standing upright and proud, dressed in their smart uniforms with gold trim. Below them stood the 'powers', influential bureaucrats like Varravin who execute the will of the authorities, and below them came the 'subordinates', the clerks and minor officials who do the bidding of the 'powers': filing, copying, running errands, their poses becoming increasingly hunched and deferential towards those above them. The young man walked among these frozen figures and introduced each one to the audience in turn, like a tour guide in a waxworks museum. At the very bottom on the stage floor, he reached the 'nonentities or private individuals' among whom sat the weak and frail Muromskii (played by Ivan Nazarov) in a decrepit armchair. Finally, Muromskii rose out of the chair and approached the edge of the stage, slowly raising his hands towards the audience as though pleading for mercy. When Meyerhold had staged *The Government Inspector* in 1926, he solved the problem of Gogol's famous mute scene by raising a screen to reveal life-size effigies of the horror-struck townspeople in grotesque poses, frozen in time. Spencer Golub has noted that these terrified waxworks not only prefigured the real Stalinist terror to come but also 'destroyed the logical reality of historical chronology', paralysing time just like Lenin's embalmed body in the mausoleum on Red Square.[53] Akimov used this same idea at the start of *The Case*, petrifying the characters into their fixed rank to show not only the rigidity of the bureaucratic system but also to germinate the idea of the nineteenth-century *chinovnik* reincarnated as the Soviet *apparatchik*, continually frozen and unfrozen in perpetuity, history condemned to repeat itself as tragedy and then farce.

The stage device of a staircase was one that Edward Gordon Craig had conceptualized in his experimental drama *The Steps* in which the staircase

**Figure 2** The prologue in *The Case* at the Lensovet Theatre in Leningrad, 1954. Courtesy of the Museum of the St Petersburg Academic Lensovet Theatre.

functions as a character in its own right, expressing different moods.⁵⁴ In *The Case*, the staircase became the architectural embodiment of a structure of power relations that produced and regulated the Tsarist subject. Although the Table of Ranks had disappeared with the revolution, a new hierarchy of power had emerged in the Soviet Union based around membership of the Communist Party – an irony that was not lost on audiences in 1954.⁵⁵ There was also something of Craig's concept of the 'Übermarionette' in Akimov's wax-work bureaucrats who moved about the stage like automata directed by a higher power. In Act Two, set in the reception room of a government department, these bureaucrats were everywhere: rushing around, carrying papers, opening doors, bowing to their superiors, 'gliding past in their never-ending useless activity'.⁵⁶ In one scene, light music played in the background and the clerks seated at their desks began swaying in time to the rhythm, their goose quills bobbing up and down, scratching along with the melody in perfect unison. But this playful episode encompassed a more sinister conceit – the unthinking conformism and detached indifference of the Russian (read Soviet) bureaucratic machine. Nowhere was this idea more sharply realized than in the figure of Varravin, the director of the government department who calmly and impassively entraps Muromskii and drives him to his death. Pavel Pankov played Varravin not as an evil sadist but as an ordinary bureaucrat dutifully carrying out his role in a corrupt and callous system. Varravin has worked his way up through the Table of Ranks, from the bottom rung to near the top, abasing himself before those above him and showing no mercy to those below him – both product and gatekeeper of the state apparatus. To help illustrate this, Akimov added an extra detail to the scene in which Varravin first receives Muromskii in his office. Getting ready to leave after having toyed with his victim, Varravin put on his coat and picked up a jar of jam and a toy horse, taking these gifts back home to his wife and son at the end of a hard day's work. The symbol of Sofia's naïve innocence in *Shadows* reappears in *The Case* as a mark of Varravin's paternalistic normality. Nine years later, the political theorist Hannah Arendt would coin the phrase 'the banality of evil' to describe Adolf Eichmann, one of the main organizers of the Nazi 'final solution'.⁵⁷ Reporting on his trial in Jerusalem, Arendt characterized Eichmann not as a 'monster' or psychopath but as an ordinary person who committed evil acts because he had bought into the system and followed orders unquestioningly. In the final scene of *The Case*, when Varravin heard that Muromskii had died, he automatically made the sign of the cross over his chest, as though oblivious to the role he had played in the old man's death. The incongruous humanity of this gesture echoed the ironic banality of the gifts intended for his family, both signifiers of the cog in the wheel that just does its (murderous) job.

As the critic Vera Shitova noted: 'Varravinism [*Varravinshchina*] insinuates itself into people's lives.'[58] Her use of the neologism *Varravinshchina*, with its suffix '-shchina' (-щина) commonly used in Russian to denote a pejorative ideology, also brought to mind the Russian term for the Stalinist purges: the *Ezhovshchina*. The ghosts of that era undoubtedly haunted the production of *The Case* as they did wider Soviet society that year. Audiences could not have failed to note the doorman positioned on duty outside the office of the 'Important Person' who wore a grey uniform resembling that of a Soviet prison guard.[59] The amnesty of 27 March 1953 had seen over 1.2 million prisoners released from the Gulag, and on 1 September the Ministry of Internal Affairs (MVD) special board responsible for most of the false convictions of the Stalin era was abolished.[60] In the spring of 1954, a commission was set up to re-examine the cases of those serving time for counter-revolutionary crimes, as 'lawfulness' (*zakonnost'*) became the new slogan of the Soviet leadership. Although next to no information about the rehabilitation process or returnees appeared in the press, those who were released described their experiences to friends and relatives, allowing for information about the camps to spread informally and widely.[61] *The Case* premiered at the Lensovet Theatre as these first tentative steps of de-Stalinization were taking place. It would be another two years until Khrushchev condemned Stalin and his 'cult of personality' directly in the infamous 'secret speech' on 25 February 1956. Nevertheless, with its denunciation of the corrupt and unlawful police state that preys on ordinary citizens, the Lensovet production became a small piece in the vast jigsaw puzzle of unofficial public reconciliation with the Stalinist past, performing on the theatre stage what was at that time still being excluded from the political podium.

In this respect, Akimov's decision to foreground the victimization of Muromskii by making his death visible on stage, rather than happening 'invisibly' off stage, was key. On realizing that he had been entrapped by Varravin and cheated out of both his money and a successful resolution of the case, Muromskii raged, demanded to be taken to see the Tsar – a futile appeal to the highest earthly authority – before uttering a final cry, grasping at his throat and falling to the floor. His body was carried offstage in silence. The critic Konstantin Rudnitskii described what happened next:

Moments after Muromskii's death the stage remained empty. Then from its depths, calm, business-like, a bureaucrat walked across the stage carrying a file in his hands. Another came to meet him, just as calm, and also with a file in his hands. Then a third, a fourth – silent, indifferent, hurrying, occupied with their own urgent business. It was as if nothing had happened.[62]

The ritualistic pantomime of bureaucrats, coming and going with their files and papers, embodied the ruthless functionality of the system. The wheels continued to turn, oblivious to the death of the old man, who became just another depersonalized victim. In Vasilii Grossman's novel *Life and Fate* there is an episode in which Evgenia Shaposhnikova visits the Lubianka prison in Moscow to inquire about her former husband who has been arrested on counter-revolutionary charges. Waiting in line, Evgenia is struck by the expressivity of the human backs, necks and shoulders in front of her 'which seemed to be crying, to be sobbing and screaming'.[63] Emmanuel Levinas highlighted this passage in his discussion of the 'face' of the Other which determines our ethical responsibilities. His point was that 'the face is not exclusively a human face', rather the term 'face' can describe the backs, the necks, the shoulders of the people standing in the queue which scream, cry and sob and stand for 'the extreme precariousness of the other'.[64] Judith Butler has argued that in this sense the face becomes a 'figure for what cannot be named, an utterance that is not strictly speaking linguistic'.[65] For Butler, 'the face of the Other is that vocalization of agony that is not yet language or no longer language, the one by which we are awakened to the precariousness of the Other's life'.[66] As Muromskii uttered his final dying cry, that non-verbal vocalization of his suffering, the precariousness of his life and of all life was revealed in that moment. Muromskii's cry became the face of the Other, persecuted by the authoritarian police state that asserts its authority by denying its ethical responsibilities to those it is obligated to protect.

## Return to the Comedy Theatre

Six years after that fateful tour to Moscow, which led to his sacking, Akimov returned with the Lensovet Theatre in the summer of 1955. Much had changed in the intervening years, including the first tour of a Western theatre company to the Soviet Union since the start of the Cold War.[67] This time around, however, there was no hostility towards Akimov and his theatre. *The Case* was singled out for particular praise by critics, with one boldly insisting that it was only by supporting artists and collectives in their struggle for creative independence that such productions were possible.[68] But while Akimov had managed to improve considerably the fortunes of the Lensovet Theatre during his tenure, his former Comedy Theatre had undergone a period of stagnation. That summer an article was published in the *Leningrad Pravda* comparing the Comedy Theatre to a ship without a captain and demanded the return of Akimov to his spiritual home.[69] The article was almost certainly planted by Akimov's ally and guardian Vera Ivanovna, who was at that point in charge of the theatre department of the Leningrad Obkom, but it would also have been unthinkable without the new political climate of the Thaw.[70] The actors of the Comedy Theatre sent a delegation to the Ministry of Culture requesting the return of their director, and Akimov was officially invited back at the start of 1956. But on his return, Akimov confounded those who had expected him to continue working in the same vein as he had done at the Lensovet Theatre. The 'Vakhtangov compromise' of psychological realist acting with stylized effects was quietly shelved, and Akimov reverted to the open embrace of festive theatricalism and comic vaudeville.

In 1958 he staged Gogol's *The Government Inspector* (premiered on 29 November), which formed the final part of his trilogy of productions that critically examined the corrupt Russian bureaucratic state. Like Meyerhold before him, Akimov approached the play in an irreverent manner, breaking with tradition to interpret the play anew. Believing that audiences tended to be bored when watching the play and that the source of this boredom was rooted in 'the constant violation of the work's genre' he was determined to stage *The Government Inspector* as a light comedy.[71] This was clear in his rendering of the final mute scene which was performed like a music-hall number with the characters cheerfully adopting strange poses: some squatting, some standing on their heads, others holding up chairs; terror was replaced with an eccentric circus routine. But this was not just an empty spectacle: the vaudeville ending was integral to Akimov's vision of the play. As Marina Zhezhelenko has observed, in the end the townspeople have no fear of the real government inspector because they are convinced that, like the imposter, he too can be bribed.[72] Corruption has reached such grotesque proportions that it erodes even fear of authority. Whereas Meyerhold transposed the play from Gogol's provincial backwater to imperial St Petersburg in order to strengthen its satirical power, Akimov created a picturesque fairy-tale kingdom to illustrate the way in which a beautiful façade can be used to mask something more sinister. Khlestakov was played by Nikolai Trofimov not as a chancer or a dandy but as a kind-hearted young man with a beaming smile who sings the 'Marseilles'. The allusion to the positive hero of socialist realism was unmistakable. The satirical fairy tale was a genre that Akimov returned to repeatedly throughout his career in his collaborations with

Evgenii Shvarts. Four years after staging *The Government Inspector*, Akimov would realize his long-held ambition of staging Shvarts's *The Dragon* at the Comedy Theatre in 1962, as we shall examine more closely in Chapter 6.

The three productions which made up Akimov's trilogy on the Russian state system – *Shadows*, *The Case* and *The Government Inspector* – marked the changing landscape of Soviet theatre during the early stages of the Thaw. These productions tacitly critiqued the Stalinist regime, with its lawless police state and corrupt bureaucracy, while at the same time deconstructing the Stalinist aesthetic system, by reviving avant-garde theatre forms that had been ostracized from the stage. The breakdown of this hierarchical model, which matched specific genres and practices to a deserving subject, and the introduction of a plurality of styles of performance, often in hybrid form, provided spectators with fresh and unexpected ways of interpreting their social reality. It is no surprise that some of the first opportunities in the theatre to see and think from anOther perspective were initiated by 'cosmopolitan' Akimov in the city of Leningrad, a locus of alterity to the Stalinist hegemony centred in Moscow. In what the Soviet critic David Zolotnitskii referred to as 'the ghostly season of the Thaw', the shadows of Vakhtangov, Tairov and Meyerhold loomed large over these productions, in particular that of Meyerhold, who was not officially rehabilitated until November 1955.[73] In Akimov's productions at the Lensovet Theatre, 'Meyerholdism' survived as an aesthetic trace, while the question of Meyerhold's corporeal absence remained unaddressed in wider society. Over in Moscow, the revival of Meyerhold's theatrical style and the rehabilitation of his person were thrust into the spotlight at the Satire Theatre, where Valentin Pluchek staged Vladimir Mayakovsky's plays for the first time since his death in 1930. Pluchek was forced to perform a similar balancing act to the one practised by Akimov, offsetting the agit-prop theatricalism of Meyerhold's original productions with the modes and conventions of realism, as we shall see in the next chapter.

3

# Restaging Mayakovsky and remembering Meyerhold

## The Moscow Satire Theatre productions, 1953–7

On the 29 July 1958, a statue of Vladimir Mayakovsky, the futurist poet and dramatist, was unveiled in Moscow's Triumfal'naia Square. The event was attended by writers, party officials and other dignitaries, including the poet's sister. During the unveiling, a speech was given by the poet Nikolai Tikhonov, former general secretary of the Soviet Writers' Union and arch Stalinist, in which he paid tribute to 'the great poet of the proletarian revolution'.[1] The event marked the culmination of a long process of canonization which had begun in the mid-1930s. After his suicide in 1930 at the age of thirty-six, Mayakovsky's legacy had been tarnished by his links with Futurism, LEF (Left Front) and the 'formalist' schools of the Moscow Linguistic Circle and the Society for the Study of Poetic Language (OPOYAZ). In the early 1930s, Mayakovsky's work was frequently denounced as formalist, and his reputation as a dramatist suffered particularly due to his association with Vsevolod Meyerhold. Valerii Kirpotin's report on socialist realist drama at the First Soviet Writers' Congress in 1934 had even singled out Mayakovsky and Meyerhold for specific criticism.[2] It took a direct intervention from Lilia Brik (Mayakovsky's one-time lover and muse), in a letter written to Stalin, for Mayakovsky's legacy to be secured. Stalin, who had long admired the poet, forwarded the letter on to Nikolai Ezhov, head of the NKVD, with an infamous note that read, 'Mayakovsky was and remains the best, most talented poet of our Soviet epoch. Indifference to his memory and his work is a crime.'[3] Stalin's personal approval initiated the canonization process. In December 1935 Moscow's Triumfal'naia Square was renamed Mayakovsky Square and in 1938 the Mayakovsky Metro station opened on the square's north-east side. Mayakovsky's poetry began to be read at public meetings around the country, praised in journals that had previously criticized him and included in the national curriculum. In May 1947 the Secretariat of the Writers' Union authorized Goslit to issue a mass one-volume edition of Mayakovsky's poetic works, proposed the commissioning of an academic biography and ordered a film to be made about the poet's life.[4] However, despite all these commemorative acts, there was no official interest in restaging his plays. While Mayakovsky's legacy as the poet of the revolution was being assured, his contribution to Soviet theatre was being ignored.

Meyerhold's ostracization and eventual execution during the Great Purges impacted heavily on the reputation of Mayakovsky's drama. Meyerhold had directed all three of Mayakovsky's major plays, and the two artists had great respect for one another, working as co-directors on these productions, an arrangement that Meyerhold did not countenance with any other dramatist.[5] This close artistic relationship meant that, in many ways, Mayakovsky's plays could be seen as collaborative projects. Mayakovsky wrote the texts specifically for Meyerhold's theatre and drew inspiration from his previous productions while writing them.[6] Their shared roots in the Russian avant-garde led to a symbiotic relationship of reciprocal influence. Mayakovsky had spent time at Meyerhold's experimental studio on Borodinskaia Street in the years before the Revolution, while Meyerhold's productions of Mayakovsky's *Mystery Bouffe* in 1918 and 1921 signalled an important stage in the development of his directorial vision. It was in these productions that Meyerhold first realized the idea of actors' uniforms (*prozodezhda*), and where the concept of the 'poster-style' (*plakatnost'*) in the theatre was consummated.[7] Because of the nature of their artistic relationship, any attempt to revive Mayakovsky's plays would inevitably entail a re-engagement with Meyerhold.

Efforts to bring Mayakovsky's plays back to the stage were largely unsuccessful prior to the Thaw. Valentin Pluchek, director at the Moscow Satire Theatre, noted that there was a 'conspiracy of silence' surrounding Mayakovsky's plays in this period.[8] Meyerhold had attempted to stage a theatrical homage to Mayakovsky in 1936, which was rejected by the Committee for Artistic Affairs. In 1940, Aleksandr Tairov's Kamernyi Theatre staged *The Bedbug* while on tour in East Asia but was denied permission by the committee to include the play in its repertoire back in Moscow. That same year, Valerii Sysoev, who had played the 'Person of the Future' in *Mystery Bouffe* (1921 version), performed fragments of *The Bedbug* in a solo show at small variety theatres in Moscow, and did the same with *The Bathhouse* in 1941.[9] This was symptomatic of the status of Mayakovsky's drama in the Stalinist aesthetic hierarchy. His 'formalist' plays were considered apt for the variety show revue but not fit for the major national stages. Stalinist culture often tolerated the 'small forms' when staged in their 'rightful' place; but the elevation of these forms to the status of high-brow art – one of the defining features of the avant-garde – was a transgression of the representative conventions linking specific forms with specific genres and had to be resisted. Thus, as we saw previously, Nikolai Akimov was allowed to stage his Western farces at the Comedy Theatre in Leningrad but presenting them on tour at the venerable Moscow Art Theatre became an infraction serious enough to warrant his sacking.

However, the change in atmosphere following Stalin's death encouraged directors to return to Mayakovsky's drama once again in the hope that they would now be accepted for performance. In the autumn of 1953, the Moscow Satire Theatre, then located on the southwest side of Triumfal'naia Square in the building of the former Al'kazar Variety Theatre, embarked on an ambitious project to bring Mayakovsky's three major plays back to the Moscow stage after an absence of over twenty years. These productions were significant not only because they removed the final obstacle in Mayakovsky's path to full canonization (the reputation of his dramas) but also because they enabled a re-engagement with the avant-garde theatre of Meyerhold. But just as Akimov was obliged to do at the Lensovet Theatre, the Satire Theatre directors Valentin Pluchek and Sergei Iutkevich trod a fine line in their directorial approach between expressive theatricality and realism: between a faithful restoration of Meyerhold's radical mise en scène and interpreting the plays in a fashion that would be more palatable to officials and audiences. Pluchek and Iutkevich were in a precarious position. Follow Meyerhold's original production style too closely and they would risk accusations of formalism in the press, the cancellation of the production and be held responsible for further damaging Mayakovsky's reputation as a dramatist. Pluchek recalled that in the run up to the premiere of *The Bathhouse*, the cast and directors were acutely aware that failure would entail 'the burying of Mayakovsky-the-dramatist for many more years to come and the fixing of the line that his plays had no value'.[10] Yet Mayakovsky's plays had been written in the language of Futurism and demanded a certain degree of stylization in order to realize them as dramatic pieces. Consequently, the directors ended up striking a balance: diluting the most theatrical elements of the original productions with realist methods while emphasizing the dramas' value for political agitation. This enabled them to argue that Mayakovsky's plays could be defined as socialist realist because of their revolutionary content, regardless of their style and form. The Satire Theatre productions emerged at a time when the rigid parameters of socialist realism were being questioned across the arts and redefining Mayakovsky's plays as classics of socialist realism undoubtedly contributed to this discourse.

By restaging Mayakovsky and remembering Meyerhold these productions disrupted many of the established norms of the Soviet theatre that had become cemented under Stalinism: norms which imposed a hierarchy of genres and the rigid identification of certain forms with certain subjects. These disruptions prompted spectators to question their preconceived ideas regarding stylized theatre and opened up new and diverse means through which they could engage with society and define their own positionality as subjects within it. At the same time, they allowed audiences to work through the legacies of the Stalinist purges and posed difficult questions about the persecution of directors and playwrights within the cultural sphere. The reaction to these productions from critics and audiences offers insight into a society in flux, still riven by the sectarian cultural divisions of the previous era. The 'conspiracy of silence' surrounding Meyerhold up until his official rehabilitation in 1955 and the vilification of his theatrical style, both during and after the Satire Theatre productions, reveal the Thaw as a period still struggling to resolve many of the tensions of Stalinism.

## *The Bathhouse*, 1953

Nikolai Petrov was the Satire Theatre's artistic director when *The Bathhouse* premiered on 5 December 1953, but it was the theatre and film director Sergei Iutkevich who first approached him with the idea to produce the play. Petrov suggested that he collaborate with Valentin Pluchek, another director working at the Satire Theatre and, like Iutkevich, one of Meyerhold's former students. Work began on the production in mid-1953, only a few months after Stalin's death, with Petrov, Pluchek and Iutkevich working together as directors. Iutkevich was also responsible for the set design. As actors under Meyerhold, both Iutkevich and Pluchek had been strongly influenced by his directing style. Iutkevich had been part of the first cohort of students at Meyerhold's State Higher Theatre Workshop in 1921, where he studied biomechanics. Pluchek had also studied under Meyerhold in the mid-1920s before going on to work as an actor at Meyerhold's State Theatre (GOSTIM), playing small roles in the original productions of *The Bedbug* and *The Bathhouse*. After the war he struggled to find permanent work in the hostile climate of the *Zhdanovshchina* but was invited by Petrov to join the Moscow Satire Theatre as a co-director in 1950. Petrov had been Meyerhold's assistant on his productions of *Don Juan* (1910) and *Masquerade* (1917) at the

Aleksandrinskii Theatre before embarking on a meandering career that brought him to the Satire Theatre in 1948. All three directors, therefore, had worked under Meyerhold in some capacity. In the new climate following Stalin's death, they saw an opportunity not only to restore Mayakovsky's legacy as a dramatist but to reacquaint audiences with a style of theatre that had all but disappeared from the major stages over the last two decades.

Mayakovsky wrote *The Bathhouse* as a satire on Soviet bureaucracy, which he believed was hindering the Soviet Union's progress to the communist future. The play features Chudakov, an inventor who has created a time machine but cannot get the funds to complete the project because of red tape. The chief bureaucrat, Pobedonosikov, will not allow the inventor any more money, but in the end, the time machine is completed thanks to the diligence of the young workers, led by Velosipedkin. Once the portal to the future is secured, a delegate from the future, the Phosphorescent Woman, travels to the present day to select the first group of workers who will be privileged to journey in the time machine and live in a society that has become fully communist. Despite having nearly wrecked the project, Pobedonosikov demands to be one of those chosen to travel to the future. However, the Phosphorescent Woman selects only the workers of Chudakov's laboratory, and Pobedonosikov is left behind, along with a crowd of disgruntled bourgeois figures. The play's title is a reference to the Russian bathhouse (*bania*), in which people are traditionally beaten with birch leaves; in the play, the bureaucrats are lampooned, or 'beaten clean'.[11] The original production, which premiered on 16 March 1930, proved unpopular with critics and audiences and was dropped from the repertoire after two seasons due to poor attendance. Meyerhold blamed a hostile preview in *Pravda* written by Vladimir Ermilov, who had formed his opinion having read only part of the text.[12] Other critics followed Ermilov's lead accusing Mayakovsky of harbouring 'a scornful attitude to our reality' and dismissed the play as 'a backward demonstration of agit-prop'.[13]

In order to avoid a similar response from critics, the directors at the Satire Theatre made a conscious decision to temper the original theatricalism of Meyerhold's productions with realistic elements. This began with the layout of the set and the arrangement of Pobedonosikov's office. Rather than being situated open plan on a revolving stage as in the original, the office was located in a three-walled box room, with a portrait of Marx hung above the door for good measure. Behind Pobedonosikov's desk was a large window overlooking a painted vista of Moscow. Echoes of Sergei Vakhtangov's original constructivist set of staircases and platforms could be identified in the zig-zagging steps leading up to Pobedonosikov's apartment in Act Four, but the use of partition walls and door frames to enclose the rooms created a more naturalistic effect.

Another alteration made by the Satire Theatre directors was to project an image of the time machine onto the wall of Chudakov's basement. Mayakovsky had specified that the time machine should be invisible, but that the characters should interact with it anyway in what he called the style of Chinese theatre.[14] Meyerhold had therefore concealed most of the set behind a large screen resembling a Venetian blind, which was removed in the final act as the workers ascended the structure to the time machine located just out of view in the flies. However, the Satire Theatre directors decided that audiences were likely to be unfamiliar with such theatrical 'conventionality' (*uslovnost'*), and so it would be necessary to compromise and at least project the silhouette of the time machine onto a screen, to give the suggestion of what lay behind. Once the time machine took off, a series of images chronicling the life of the Soviet Union over the last twenty-five years was projected on the screen where its outline had been. This three-minute montage, compiled by Iutkevich, contained images of the first tractors at the collective farms, the construction of the Moscow metro, the camp of the Cheliuskin arctic explorers, the building of the Volga-Don canal and the reconstruction of the Dneprostroi Dam after the Second World War. It was intended to show the progress already made along the road to communism since the play's first staging and was accompanied by *komsomol* members singing 'The March of Time', with lyrics by Mayakovsky himself. Immediately afterwards, the entrance of Pobedonosikov's entourage, who in the play have arrived too late to travel to the future, was met with an 'ironic bourgeois melody', in the form of a slow foxtrot played by the orchestra.[15] The conflict between proletarian and bourgeois cultures was thus dramatized by the clash of contrasting musical genres.

One of the key aims of the production was to demonstrate the resonance of Mayakovsky's ideas in the present day, and this was reflected by some of the costume selections the directors made. In the original production of *The Bathhouse*, the delegate from the future, the Phosphorescent Woman, wore a flying helmet and tight-fitting space suit. In the Satire Theatre's production, however, the Phosphorescent Woman (played by Nina Arkhipova) was dressed not in a futuristic outfit but in a grey 1950s suit, resembling many of those seated in the audience. On this decision, Iutkevich noted:

> Her phosphorescence, her glow was not an external effect. First and foremost it was an inner 'radiation', the charming appearance of a morally pure Soviet

person, and the closer her appearance reminded one of the progressive Soviet women of our time . . . then the more convincing and poetically her words on communism would sound.[16]

The intention was to show the potential of the current Soviet generation to become Mayakovsky's utopian vision. The Phosphorescent Woman's advanced morals and psychology, embodied in her composed physiognomy and modest suit, were presented as objectives attainable to all those in the audience. The entrance of the Phosphorescent Woman in the 1930 production was greeted with an array of pyrotechnic effects: explosions, rockets, smoke and fireworks. Her entrance in the Satire Theatre's production was far more reserved, with a bang, blackout and smoke used to indicate her arrival. Rather than dazzle the audience with a multitude of lights, the Satire Theatre production switched to a blackout. Pluchek recalled: 'We did not want to distract the audience's attention with fireworks at that moment, because it seemed more important to observe how the characters reacted to what was going on.'[17] Stylized effects were toned down in order to concentrate attention on the Phosphorescent Woman's 'inner radiation' and the other characters' emotional responses. In this way, the principles of *perezhivanie* were elevated above theatricalism as the most appropriate means to articulate the play's meaning.

Mayakovsky described *The Bathhouse* as 'a drama in six acts with circus and fireworks' and Meyerhold's production had duly combined pyrotechnic effects with acrobatic stunts and choreographed displays.[18] But although they had intended to recreate the style of Meyerhold's circus-like routines, the directors at the Satire Theatre ended up cutting many of the stunts they had worked on in rehearsal just before the performance out of concern that they would be received negatively: something Pluchek, with hindsight, later regretted.[19] This concern that expressive theatricalism might attract negative criticism also led to a number of edits to the play text itself. The ironic third act, which sees the characters enter the stage via the auditorium and review the preceding two acts, was shortened considerably and staged in front of the second curtain as a comedic interlude. One of the sections cut from this act was the pantomime on the theme 'The actors have had their fill of labour and capital.' While Meyerhold had used this scene to showcase his diverse directorial repertoire, from naturalism to dance, the directors at the Satire Theatre felt that such a display would confuse audiences and cut it completely. However, they did retain the sketch in which Pobedonosikov (played by Georgii Menglet) enters the stage through the auditorium and reflects on the authenticity of his own character. This piece of meta-theatre, which

**Figure 3** The Phosphorescent Woman looks down at Pobedonosikov in *The Bathhouse* at the Moscow Satire Theatre, 1953. Courtesy of the Museum of the Moscow Academic Satire Theatre.

in the text also involves the 'director' and other actors entering to discuss the effectiveness of the play, was an exploration of theatrical artifice and a kind of self-referential parody. In their interpretation of this scene, the Satire Theatre directors placed on stage an enlarged version of one of the production's posters depicting Pobedonosikov. Menglet's character then stood in front of this poster and imitated the poster figure's gesture: the symmetry graphically reflecting Mayakovsky's play on theatrical representation. Mayakovsky used the scene to lampoon the views of RAPP, whose members insisted that satire was harmful to the cause of socialism and that art should depict only real life. As Pobedonosikov exclaims: 'We don't have such people [bureaucrats like himself], it's unnatural, not life-like, not the way things are!', the joke is turned on the advocates of realism, as Pobedonosikov's de-familiarized character casts doubt upon himself in their own words. The consequence of this ironic sequence was both the justification of Mayakovsky's satirical target (corrupt bureaucrats *do* exist) and the validation of his theatrical style as an effective mode of satire.

In a review of the Satire Theatre production, one critic noted that the 'deep irony' of this scene was lost on critics back in 1930, as well as their successors, the advocates of 'conflictlessness', twenty years later.[20] Reversing Pobedonosikov's line from the play, the critic insisted that the play was, in fact, 'natural, life-like and the way things are', while also praising the directors for creating 'a sharply satirical performance with grotesque elements'. The critic argued that the production's success arose from its creation of a realistic villain in the figure of Pobedonosikov and blamed Meyerhold's direction for the play's original failure. In the process he recast Mayakovsky's drama as a realistic assault on bureaucratic corruption and re-read Act Three as the moment of the villain's self-unmasking. Overall, the press reaction was positive, with the directors' decision to emphasize the realism in Mayakovsky's drama repeatedly identified as crucial to the production's success. One review in the journal *Ogonek* noted: 'The theatre has managed to overcome the difficulty linked to Mayakovsky's distinctive manner: the combination of satirically-grotesque poster-like forms, with lyrical, romantic, elevated pathos.'[21] The reviewers acknowledged that it would be a mistake to go to a Mayakovsky play expecting the characters to be 'acutely realistic' but insisted that you cannot also reduce their essence to that of a 'conventional mask' (*uslovnaia maska*) and praised the 'life-like warmth' of the Phosphorescent Woman.[22] One critic, writing in *Sovetskaia kul'tura*, dismissed the 'militant-formalist experimentality' of Meyerhold's original production but lauded the Satire Theatre's restaging as a 'major victory', which helped to portray the 'real, visible, life-like basis of Mayakovsky's fantasy'.[23] Essential to this, in the critic's view, was the way the directors gave a realistic depiction of characters such as Velosipedkin (played by Boris Runge) and the Phosphorescent Woman. A review in *Pravda* praised the production for successfully reviving a play that had previously been 'distorted' by 'formalists'.[24] Describing the Satire Theatre production as a 'victory', the critic observed: 'It is good that *The Bathhouse* has reappeared on the stage. It shows how vital the work of satire is for our nation, ridiculing the vulgarity and vices of people.' The true value of the production was considered to be its capacity to weed out bourgeois traits in society. In this sense, satire was understood not as a critique of the system but as a tool with which to consolidate the state's hegemony by identifying and alienating the 'Other'.

Most critics were united in their praise for the Satire Theatre's production because it had diverged from Meyerhold's original (or so they claimed) and enabled the reinterpretation of the text as a classic of socialist realism. Yet although the restaging had moderated many of the most overtly theatrical elements, it was by no means a realistic production of the kind audiences had grown used to in the post-war period. Actors walked through the auditorium, slogans adorned the walls and the directors found their own way of playing with theatrical convention by projecting a giant photograph of Mayakovsky onto the stage backdrop in the final scene. Dwarfed by the looming figure of his author, Pobedonosikov tumbled off the stage to a standing ovation from the audience. The Satire Theatre directors pursued a strategy that would combine the text's potential for theatrical play with a more realistic depiction of characters and scenery. This hybrid approach (or 'Vakhtangov compromise') was undoubtedly a pragmatic decision, taken to appease critics and the censor in order to ensure Mayakovsky's canonization. At the same time, the directors insisted that those stylized elements which had been included were permissible because socialist realism could be considered a broad church that incorporates many different forms and styles.

In justification of their approach, Pluchek argued that although Mayakovsky had been fiercely opposed to psychological realism as practised at the Moscow Art Theatre, dismissing it as 'life through the keyhole', he was in fact also a realist of sorts. Petrov similarly insisted that the more he worked on the text, the more he became sure that Mayakovsky's work was 'deeply realistic', despite being written 'in a sharp satirical and agit-prop form'.[25] After all, Mayakovsky had claimed in his poem 'A letter to Maksim Gorky': 'And we are realists, but not grazing with our snouts thrust downwards – we are in the new reality of the future, multiplied by electricity and communism.'[26] Although Mayakovsky died four years before the official method of socialist realism was unveiled to the public in 1934, his plays share with it a similar teleological obsession with reaching the communist future. Time travel is the central conceit of both *The Bathhouse* and *The Bedbug*. Progression to the communist utopia lies at the heart of their respective dramatic plots, echoing the 'spontaneity-consciousness' dialectic which underpins the 'master plot' of socialist realism.[27] Pluchek and the other directors at the Satire Theatre believed this made Mayakovsky's plays inherently socialist realist and they strove to demonstrate it in all three productions by ensuring that when they used stylized theatrical forms these were always aimed at amplifying the political resonance of the drama, rather than becoming an end in themselves.

In this way the productions contributed to a growing debate that challenged the hierarchical organization of theatre practices that had become entrenched under Stalinism, by arguing that forms previously seen as inferior or taboo could be subsumed under the umbrella of socialist realism. In an essay published in the journal *Teatr* in 1955, the theatre and film scholar Neia Zorkaia argued that the Satire Theatre's restaging of *The Bathhouse* had shown how diverse socialist realism could be.[28] She criticized the 'canonization' of one particular form of performance, that of the 'life-like illusion', which had 'dried out' theatre in places such as the Moscow Art Theatre and insisted that the true nature of socialist realism was 'diversity of form and styles' and 'the free development of creative initiative and fantasy'. She praised the directors at the Satire Theatre for breaking down 'the barriers that had become established and customary on the contemporary stage'. Zorkaia saw *The Bathhouse* as a seminal moment in the Soviet theatre, one that had proved not only that Mayakovsky's drama was socialist realist but that socialist realism could embrace a plurality of theatrical forms. A similar review of the Satire Theatre's restaging of *The Bedbug* in 1955 also criticized the narrowness with which realism was generally interpreted in the theatre, arguing that 'the most expressive means' were needed in order to convey Mayakovsky's blend of 'the grotesque and reality' to audiences.[29] What united these critics was a new impetus to question the rigid definitions of the previous era and the reiteration of the argument that as long as the use of stylized devices furthered the audience's understanding of the play's subject it could be justified. This represented a radical disruption of the representative logic of the Stalinist cultural regime, albeit one that still subordinated avant-garde innovation to the dramatic plot.

## *The Bedbug*, 1955

The Satire Theatre's production of *The Bathhouse* paved the way for other theatres to stage Mayakovsky's drama and even new plays about Mayakovsky himself. In 1954 Vasili Katanian's *They Knew Mayakovsky* was staged at the Aleksandrinskii Theatre in Leningrad, starring Nikolai Cherkasov as the eponymous hero. That same year, the Moscow Drama Theatre (formerly the Theatre of the Revolution) was renamed the Mayakovsky Theatre on the occasion of its thirtieth anniversary. The Satire Theatre had lifted the cloud hanging over Mayakovsky's reputation as a dramatist and opened the door for the restaging of his dramatic works. Determined to capitalize on this, the theatre began rehearsals for Mayakovsky's *The Bedbug*, which premiered on 5 May 1955. By this point, Nikolai Petrov had stepped down as artistic director so the production was left in the hands of Pluchek and Iutkevich. The directors planned a more stylized production than they had achieved with *The Bathhouse*, telling the press: 'We want to create a colourful and lively production that is close in spirit to folk theatre, to spectacular theatre.'[30] This suggested an openness to the style of Meyerhold's original production of 1929, which had combined a range of popular theatrical forms including fairground, circus, and music hall, in the avant-garde spirit of time. Dmitrii Shostakovich was given his first commission in the theatre to write the music for the original, which was based, at Mayakovsky's request, on the popular marches of fire-brigade bands. The play was a success with audiences and although one critic disliked the second half's 'constructivist-futurist spirit of abstraction', there were also favourable reviews.[31]

The play is set in Moscow during the late NEP era. Madame Renaissance, a beautician, has arranged to marry off her daughter El'zevira to a party member, Ivan Prisypkin, in order to take advantage of his union card privileges. Enticed by the petty-bourgeois lifestyle of the Renaissance family, the simple-minded Prisypkin agrees to marry El'zevira. The red wedding organized by the matchmaker Oleg Baian turns into a bacchanalian feast of gluttony and merrymaking, but in the general melee a stove is overturned and a fire burns the building down with everyone inside. The firemen arrive to put out the fire and, in the process, flood the basement where Prisypkin is lying unconscious. The water freezes, entombing his body in ice. The second half of the play is set fifty years in the future. Using the latest technology, scientists manage to revive Prisypkin, who shocks them with his vulgar language and behaviour, his antiquated romanticism and his demands for alcohol. A bedbug that had been living on his body is unfrozen with him and together both 'parasites' begin to infect the society of the future, whose citizens begin to acquire 'bourgeois' habits. The bedbug is finally captured and is secured in a glass dome alongside Prisypkin in the zoo. Crowds flock to see the two parasites, but Prisypkin addresses them as his own people and asks them (and the real audience) why it is only he who has been locked in the cage.

In 1929 Meyerhold had emphasized the contrast between the play's two distinct chronotopes by using different designers for each half. The first half, set in the late 1920s, had a realist design created by the Kukryniksy caricaturists, intended to satirize the vulgar tastes of the petty bourgeoisie, their costumes and *accoutrements* all sourced from local flea markets. The second half, set in 1979, was designed by the constructivist artist Aleksandr Rodchenko as a futuristic vision of the communist utopia, with cold blue and white lighting, and minimalist props and costumes. In their 1955 production Pluchek and Iutkevich also differentiated between the two halves of the play but not in terms of the set design. This remained naturalistic throughout, albeit with certain touches of self-aware theatricality, such as replicas of Mayakovsky's poster designs adorning panels either side of the stage and the use of giant screens during the intervals covered with excerpts from his poetry. Instead, it was the directors' willingness to allow the actors to break the fourth wall that was the main difference between the two halves of the play.

In the first half these occasions, such as the street vendors entering through the auditorium in Act One or the firefighters exiting through the auditorium in Act Four, were cut from the text. The vendors entered the stage via a conveyor belt from the wings, while the firefighters marched on the spot as the fire raged in the background, projected onto a screen behind them. In the second half, however, the actors were allowed to roam about the auditorium and interact with audience members. The hunt for the bedbug was conducted amid the audience with the house lights up, as zookeepers and firefighters ran down the aisles and scaled ladders up to the dress circle in their search. Pluchek noted that, despite their intentions, they were unable to fully replicate the spectacular 'carnival' effect of the original production.[32] Nevertheless, to a public unaccustomed to this level of audience engagement, the scene would have appeared bold and innovative. In Act Five, newspaper vendors descended from the stage to hand out newspapers to members of the audience. In the play, these papers announce the unfreezing of Prisypkin: however, the Satire Theatre created its own in-house gazette which was distributed during each show as an additional programme. It proclaimed the contemporary relevance of the play, particularly its critique of petit-bourgeois consumerism, noting the continuing presence of such traits in modern society in the form of the *stiliagi* (hipsters) who listen to 'boogie-woogie' (*bugi-vugi*) music.[33] Jazz and its derivatives had been outlawed in the Soviet Union since the summer of 1946 as part of Zhdanov's clampdown on the cultural sphere. And although it would gain a degree of social acceptance in 1957, when Moscow hosted international jazz bands for the Sixth World Festival of Youth and Students, at the time of *The Bedbug*'s premiere, jazz was still officially frowned upon, as were the fashionable young people who listened to it.[34]

This attempt to make the play more relevant to contemporary audiences by lampooning the 1950s 'hipster' found its embodiment in the character of Oleg Baian (played by Georgii Menglet), the NEP-man property owner who convinces Prisypkin (Vladimir Lepko) to marry El'zevira (Galina M. Stepanova). The directors were determined to make the character reflect those 'contemporary Baians' who 'work in the variety theatre [*estrada*] . . . corrupting tastes with their bourgeois songs and vulgar lyrics . . . or worse, sell counterfeit film posters, boogie-woogie records, pulp fiction and other ideological poisons'.[35] So they gave Baian long slicked-back red hair, twisted at the ends in the contemporary style and dressed him in modern 'hipster' clothing. In this manner they substituted the new social outcasts of the 1950s for the class enemies of the 1920s. The use of music was crucial in creating the desired effect. In the second half of the play, as the pure citizens of the communist future become infected by Prisypkin's

**Figure 4** The hunt for the bedbug in *The Bedbug* at the Moscow Satire Theatre, 1955. Courtesy of the Museum of the Moscow Academic Satire Theatre.

bourgeois traits, the music switched from Soviet marching bands to saxophones playing 'boogie-woogie'. This transition from orderly marching rhythms to improvised jazz melodies inverted the socialist realist dialectic and its typical movement from spontaneity to order. In the first half, the bourgeois characters had been given leitmotifs from 1920s foxtrots and tangos. In the second, the soundtrack of bourgeois corruption was updated to reflect the dangerous imports from America that Soviet youths were buying on street corners from *stiliagi* who 'work in the variety theatre'. It was, of course, particularly ironic that the Satire Theatre directors should target the humble *estrada* performer while reviving a work that drew particular inspiration from the variety shows and 'small forms' of the 1920s. It was an indication, perhaps, of the pressure the directors were under by a hard-line party establishment, determined to institutionalize Mayakovsky's satire as a means of weeding out undesirables from the body politic.

The 'roasting' of the petty bourgeoisie reached its apogee during the wedding party scene in Act Three. The scene opened with the audience looking into the windows of Madame Renaissance's beauty parlour. Images of featureless mannequins with an assortment of hairstyles were painted onto a lace curtain that hung down to the stage floor. Then the curtain was slowly raised to reveal a long rectangular dining table with the wedding guests seated behind in a row facing the audience in similar mannequin-like poses, frozen and mute. In its stylization, the mise en scène owed an obvious debt to the banquet scene in Meyerhold's 1928 production of *Woe to Wit*, wherein the rumour of Chatskii's madness was passed down the table mechanically from guest to guest, via a series of rhythmic gestures. What followed in *The Bedbug*, though, was a pantomime of a different kind. The guests remained still and silent, awaiting the arrival of Lassal'chenko, the secretary of the factory committee, to start proceedings. Then there was a knock at the door and two unknown men appeared wearing army jackets and jodhpurs. Suddenly, one of them thrust his hands into his pockets and stated in a loud voice 'I have been authorized . . .' but before he could finish, panic broke out among the guests: some made a dash for the door, others raised their hands in the air, while Baian whispered resignedly: 'It's over!'. Finally, the messenger finished his sentence to reveal that he had been authorized merely to report that Lassal'chenko will not be able to attend the wedding today. The guests collapsed in relief. As 'bourgeois profiteers' in the NEP era, Pluchek noted, each one of them would have had their 'fingers in the till' and so 'naturally every knock at the door was a source of panic'.[36] Yet the scene had another resonance which audiences during the Thaw would have been acutely aware of. The sudden knock at the door was a common fear during the Great Purges and, more recently, the anti-cosmopolitan campaign – indeed Meyerhold himself had fallen victim to just such a knock. In this way, the grotesque pantomime poked fun at the bourgeoisie, while also alluding to a more sombre and traumatic collective memory.

Although they failed to fully recreate Meyerhold's spectacular original, the Satire Theatre produced its own innovative interpretation of *The Bedbug*, which combined the use of stylized devices and film animations with realistic sets and costumes. The directors justified this approach, as they had done with *The Bathhouse*, by arguing that the contemporary relevance of Mayakovsky's text legitimized the expressive theatricalism. They insisted that his satire had an important social function in identifying anti-Soviet elements and the final scene was crucial in this regard. At the end of the play, Mayakovsky has Prisypkin led out of the cage to be paraded before the crowd, but on seeing the audience seated in front of him, he rushes over to them joyfully asking his 'brothers' when they got here and why they haven't joined him in the cage. The scene echoes Gogol's ending in *The Government Inspector* when the Mayor turns on the audience and shouts: 'What are you laughing at? You're laughing at yourselves!'[37] In both plays, the spotlight is switched onto the audience, forcing them to question their own culpability in an ironic moment of Brechtian de-familiarization. In the Satire

Theatre production, the directors added their own idiosyncratic finale after Prisypkin has been recaptured and returned to his cage. In a mirror-effect of the play's opening, when the street vendors entered the stage via conveyor belt, the wedding guests from Act Three returned once again, frozen 'like wax-work mannequins from the shop windows of the past', drifting across the stage on the conveyor belt and off again into the wings.[38] Following behind them was Prisypkin, fixed in a similar grotesque pose. The effect was to further strengthen the parallels with Gogol's play, this time with Meyerhold's inspired interpretation of the mute scene in which he replaced living actors with life-sized effigies. In Pluchek and Iutkevich's version, the shock of Prisypkin's address to the audience is reinforced by the ghostly figures of the bourgeoisie gliding past, a warning to spectators of what awaits those who chase materialistic chimeras.

Critics gave the production mixed reviews, with praise for the transformation of one-dimensional characters into believable figures tempered with dissatisfaction at the use of stylized effects. *Pravda* hailed the production as a 'new artistic victory' for the Satire Theatre collective but noted that in some scenes the directors lost their 'sense of proportion' and revealed 'excessive enthusiasm for vivid stage forms'.[39] Writing in *Literaturnaia gazeta*, one critic described

**Figure 5** Vladimir Lepko in *The Bedbug* at the Moscow Satire Theatre, 1955. Courtesy of the Museum of the Moscow Academic Satire Theatre.

the show as 'a complex, uneven production with significant achievements, but also with serious shortcomings'.[40] He observed that, at times, form dominated ideas, complaining that Baian's speech during the wedding scene was buried under 'comedic stunts'. Others disagreed and commended the directors for their original realization of the wedding scene, praising the use of 'sculptured social types' and insisting that 'brave directorial effects' were not the same as 'comedic stunts'.[41] Georgii Menglet's performance as Baian was roundly praised for its 'great temperament' and as a 'brilliant example of the realistic grotesque'.[42] This praise for Baian's life-like portrayal epitomized much of the press reaction to the production. Occasions when the actors had diluted the play's comic theatricalism and created believable character types were lauded. One letter written to the Satire Theatre by A. Dridzo, a theatre-goer from Leningrad, expressed a similar sentiment, noting: 'It's very good that in his external appearance Baian resembles someone from the year 1955, it's as it should be – Baians are still alive today.'[43] Dridzo admitted to having been concerned before he saw both *The Bedbug* and *The Bathhouse* at the Satire Theatre, that much of it would be incomprehensible to a contemporary audience, yet happily informed the theatre how incorrect he had been. The realistic depictions of Baian and Prisypkin, in particular, had made Mayakovsky's play fully intelligible in this spectator's opinion.

The success of the Satire Theatre production was repeatedly measured by critics in terms of its ability to inspire audiences to identify petty-bourgeois imposters in their midst. Reflecting on the play's finale, with its parade of bourgeois figures on the conveyor belt, one critic wished that the theatre had added examples of more contemporary 'parasites' to this 'sinister waxworks show', such as the 'well-groomed and dull-faced "daddy's girl" who dreams of an easy life, sponging off the back of her future "responsible" husband'.[44] In fact, residents of Komsomolsk-on-Amur in the Soviet Far East needed little prompting to denounce 'parasites' of this sort, following a performance of *The Bedbug* by the Satire Theatre on tour there in the summer of 1956. One letter sent to the local newspaper, *Stalinskii Komsomol'sk*, by the inhabitants of House 38 Lenin Avenue complained about the 'bedbug-like existence' (*klopinaia zhizn'*) of one couple, the Solnishkins, in their communal dwelling.[45] The letter, signed by comrades Smirnova, Liutova, Neledova, Tareeva, Kodomtseva and others, stated:

> People in the house live amicably, but it's enough for Solnishkina to enter the room and the mood is ruined. She calls everyone layabouts but doesn't work herself. Solnishkina considers herself a cultured woman and brags about how cultured she is, but she often abuses people with foul language.

The woman's lack of employment and cultural pretentions marked her out as a 'bedbug-like' parasite in the eyes of her neighbours. Her husband, who worked as a rate-setter in the Amur Steel factory, was criticized by the signatories because 'like Prisypkin . . . he is under the thumb of a philistine wife'. A similar letter, signed by the inhabitants of House 2 Chernyshevskii Street, complained to the same newspaper that one of their neighbours, comrade Savostina, was guilty of similar parasitic behaviour, describing her as 'the spitting image of the "bedbug" in Mayakovsky'. Another letter, written by A. P. Sivkov, complained of the 'drunken orgies' conducted by a couple living in House 23 Kalinina Street. Sivkov wrote: 'It is strange that the Prosecutor's Office and police department are not doing anything serious about these "bedbugs". Not only were these concerned citizens following Mayakovsky's appeal and identifying 'parasites' hidden in plain sight, but the phrase 'Mayakovsky's bedbug' was becoming part of their social lexicon. Back in 1929, Mayakovsky had been delighted to overhear on a trolleybus one man attack another with the words 'You scum, you bedbug out of Mayakovsky!'[46] Now, in the wake of the Satire Theatre's restaging, the term appeared to have returned to public usage, indicating not just the success of efforts to demonstrate the relevance of Mayakovsky's work for a new generation but also the extent to which the theatre could shape public discourse. Of course, petty grievances among communal neighbours were a ubiquitous feature of life in this era, but *The Bedbug* gave spectators a particular vocabulary with which to narrate their lived experience: a means of constituting themselves as legitimate subjects of the system by excluding others from it. These kinds of discursive strategies mattered enormously in periods of uncertainty and social upheaval like the Thaw.

What is it, then, that gets unfrozen during a thaw? The historiography of the period would suggest that it was the Soviet cultural system that was unfrozen, as new green shoots of creative possibility broke out intermittently on the stage. The revival of *The Bedbug* undoubtedly reflected this impetus in its reintroduction of avant-garde theatre forms to a mass audience. And yet in its theme, the play offered viewers an intriguing counter-narrative: a reactionary warning not to unfreeze the bourgeois *habitus* of the past and to 'tear off the masks' of imposters in their midst.

## *Mystery Bouffe*, 1957

Two years after the production of *The Bedbug*, Valentin Pluchek, now artistic director of the Moscow Satire Theatre, decided to complete the series and stage

Mayakovsky's *Mystery Bouffe*. Of Mayakovsky's three major plays, *Mystery Bouffe*, written in poetic verse as a parable narrating the story of the revolution, was arguably the least accessible to a contemporary audience.[47] In fact, Mayakovsky had written a note in the second edition of the play requesting that all future directors rewrite the text and bring it up to date before staging it. Regardless of the work's accessibility, though, its iconic status as the 'first Soviet play' ensured that it would be received by officials and the press with a certain level of indulgence.[48] *Mystery Bouffe* is styled as a parody of the biblical story of the Great Flood, when Noah built an ark and preserved two of each animal to start a new world once the flood had washed away the old one. The flood becomes a metaphor for the Revolution, which the Bolsheviks believed would sweep the globe. Those saved in the ark are the 'Clean' (*Chistye*), reactionary figures from the old world, and the 'Unclean' (*Nechistye*) representing the proletariat. In the play, the 'Clean' are deposed from power on the ark by the mutinous 'Unclean', who then journey through Hell, Heaven and the 'Land of Debris' in search of the 'Promised Land', which turns out to be revolutionary Moscow. In Mayakovsky's parable, the Bolshevik capital replaces Heaven as the true utopia founded on earth.

Pluchek's production of *Mystery Bouffe* was prepared in just four months. The premiere was even brought forward by six days to 2 November 1957 so that the production could open a ten-day festival of drama in Moscow celebrating the fortieth anniversary of the October Revolution. As the first play about the Revolution, *Mystery Bouffe* could lay a claim to being the foundation stone of the Soviet dramatic canon. In this sense, it was an obvious choice to headline the anniversary celebrations, and yet the actors had a number of concerns about the feasibility of the production, in particular whether audiences would understand the play. Pluchek had invited the Turkish avant-garde poet Nazim Hikmet to rewrite the play, in line with Mayakovsky's stipulations, but he had been unavailable. Instead, the theatre used the 1918 version as a base and enlisted Vasilii Katanian (author of the play *They Knew Mayakovsky*) to combine it with elements of the 1921 version and extracts from Mayakovsky's unpublished drafts and notes. Parts that would no longer make sense to a contemporary audience, such as the reference to the 'third category' (those citizens who received food rations), were cut, while the lines of the French and German 'imperialists' were altered to make them sound more relevant to the current Cold War context. Mayakovsky's caustic prologue to the 1921 text, in which he had railed against psychological 'theatre through the keyhole', was updated with one less likely to aggravate establishment critics. The new prologue, written by futurist poet Semen Kirsanov, a former apprentice of Mayakovsky's, eschewed any polemical contribution to the debate on theatre style, preferring a more respectful tone that praised the 'valiant path of the Unclean for the last forty years'.[49] Nevertheless, the production of *Mystery Bouffe* could not avoid this debate entirely, because the avant-garde futurist style of its era was encoded into the structure of the text itself.

Pluchek's hybrid approach to the productions of *The Bathhouse* and *The Bedbug* had entailed creating naturalistic scenery, encouraging the actors to explore the psychology of their characters, and cutting the most overtly theatrical elements; while retaining enough stylization to do justice to the works as Mayakovsky had conceived them. However, with a play as conceptual as *Mystery Bouffe* it was clear that this approach would be insufficient. After all, how do you psychologize stock characters that are known only by their job title or nationality? It became clear that for this play, Pluchek was prepared to go further in realizing Mayakovsky's expressive style than he had done in the previous productions, while at the same time ensuring that the form never obscured the content. The director explained his approach in a public discussion at the theatre in November 1957, noting: 'We staged *Mystery Bouffe* inclined not only towards the external effects that give it such a spectacular form, but focusing on the poetry, on the ideas.'[50] This meant that those theatrical devices he used were always in service of the play's revolutionary message.

Meyerhold's 1921 production had crystalized the emerging trends of constructivism and circusization in the theatre, combining a stage set that facilitated the actor's movement across different planes and levels with circus stunts, dancing and fairground (*balagan*) games.[51] The action frequently spilled out into the auditorium; while the opening of the Hell scene saw the circus clown, Vitalii Lazarenko, descend along a wire performing acrobatic tricks dressed as a devil. In his set for the Satire Theatre production, Aleksandr Tyshler paid homage to the *balagan* aesthetic of the original. The set consisted of a large globe encircled by a spiral walkway, which rotated like a fairground carousel. All the scenes in the play utilized this structure except for Act Two when the actors sailed on a wooden ark positioned downstage in front of the globe. Act Two on the ark saw many of the production's most stylized moments. In one pantomime scene the 'Clean', after spending a night on deck with no food, simultaneously put their hands into each other's pockets, creating a chain of dishonest pickpockets. Another improvised episode saw the 'Clean', now deposed from power by the 'Unclean', husk seeds together in a desperate attempt to prove their proletarian credentials. Seated on one side of the deck, the 'Clean' simultaneously threw seeds into their mouths and then spat the husks overboard in unison. After this coordinated action, the Pope (played by Vladimir Lepko) struck up a chorus of the folk song 'The Girl Nadia' and broke into a dance with some of the 'Unclean' in an effort to ingratiate himself with the working class.[52] This episode proved very popular with audiences and was praised by a number of critics for its effective realization of Mayakovsky's satire.[53] The coordination of the actors' gestures and movements to create a specific effect within the mise en scène also gave audiences a reminder of Meyerhold's system of biomechanics.

Act Three, Scene One, set in Hell, provided another opportunity for carnival theatricalism, as the devils, dressed in black body suits with horns and tails, their faces painted, danced to the 'syncopated rhythms of rock and roll'.[54] In March 1957, the former Soviet foreign minister and Politburo member Dmitrii Shepilov had denounced rock and roll music as an 'explosion of the basest instincts and sexual urges', while speaking at the Second Congress of Soviet Composers in Moscow.[55] However, just four months later, rock and roll made an impromptu public debut in the Soviet Union during the Sixth World Festival of Youth and Students. Some of the invited jazz bands from the West included rock and roll numbers in their repertoires, to the consternation of Soviet officials and the delight of the young *stiliagi*.[56] The Satire Theatre's incorporation of a

**Figure 6** Dancing devils in *Mystery Bouffe* at the Moscow Satire Theatre, 1957. Courtesy of the Museum of the Moscow Academic Satire Theatre.

'parodic' rock and roll soundtrack to the Hell scene in *Mystery Bouffe* later that autumn was clearly an attempt to stigmatize this new 'devilish' musical genre: the 'syncopated' rhythms of rock and roll symbolizing the structural decay of the capitalist system. However, the history of the Soviet theatre has shown that the introduction of new cultural forms can have ambiguous and unexpected consequences. When Meyerhold included a jazz band in his production of *The Trust D. E* in 1924, with the intention of lampooning the decadent bourgeois capitalists, the result was not quite what he had expected. The jazz band, led by Valentin Parnakh, brought crowds flocking to the theatre and the political message was somewhat lost under the dazzling energy of the jazz numbers performed.[57] Similarly, Pluchek's use of rock and roll to symbolize the moral corruption of the capitalist West nevertheless gave this music a public platform – a context in which neither the director nor the censor could control how the music was received and interpreted by audiences. Regardless of Pluchek's prior intentions, these first performances of rock and roll in a major Soviet theatre introduced a deviant strain of cultural experience to the theatre-going public and disrupted the norms of performance which prevailed at that time. A year later, writing in *Pravda*, the composer Georgii Sviridov denounced Soviet *estrada* ensembles that had begun to sneak rock and roll numbers into their shows 'in the guise of "parodies"', little realizing, perhaps, that in this regard the Moscow Satire Theatre had inadvertently shown them the way.[58]

Despite Pluchek's willingness to embrace the theatrical spirit of Mayakovsky's drama more readily in *Mystery Bouffe*, than he had done with *The Bathhouse* or *The Bedbug*, the final scene set in the 'Promised Land' proved to be a step too far. In this scene, a parade of giant 'Things' (human-sized tools and goods), representing the fruits of the new utopian society, march out of the city gates to meet the triumphant Unclean. Fearing an adverse response from audiences, Pluchek cut this scene altogether, noting that 'we could not allow ourselves any kind of *balaganism* [*balaganshchina*] during the finale'.[59] In this instance, the term '*balagan*' was used in a pejorative sense to signify carnival excess at the expense of pathos. In place of the parade of 'Things', the Unclean stepped forward together and recited couplets from Mayakovsky's poetry to the music of the 'Internationale'. Then, as the stage went dark, a small red sphere floated high above the stage underneath the gridiron and began to circle the larger globe of the set as the curtain slowly lowered. The Soviet Union had put the first satellite into space only a month before the premiere and this small red *sputnik*, circling on stage, brought a rapturous response from the audience. Pluchek noted:

The satellite was the first envoy from the technology of the future, a trespasser into our today. And what is the 'Promised Land' if not the world of unprecedented technology, which, through social harmony, becomes the solid foundation of communism?[60]

For the director, the red *sputnik* was a symbol of the proximity of the 'Promised Land' and a testament to the progress made since the October Revolution. In this sense, the finale encapsulated the production's Janus-faced nature: both a retrospective classic commemorating the fortieth anniversary of the revolution and, simultaneously, a prospective validation of the communist future – the journey of the proletariat to utopia. The red *sputnik*, like the arrival of the besuited Phosphorescent Woman in *The Bathhouse*, was a messenger from the future but also a link to the present day: a symbol of the socialist realist dialectic for the new space age.

The finale was praised by critics for its power and pathos, validating somewhat Pluchek's decision to alter the ending.[61] Many reviewers noted the warm reception the play received from audiences and praised the Satire Theatre for successfully reviving such a dated play.[62] A number of critics believed the production's success

**Figure 7** The finale of *Mystery Bouffe* at the Moscow Satire Theatre, 1957. Courtesy of the Museum of the Moscow Academic Satire Theatre.

was owed to the director's decision to interpret the play's original theatricalism in a more realistic manner; one critic insisted that this was now the definitive way in which the play should be performed: 'simply and realistically, with rich "earthy" comedy'.[63] Another critic, writing in *Pravda*, noted that 'the director was correct in not trying to show the "Unclean" as some depersonalized "choir", as it was in previous productions'.[64] The inference was that the Satire Theatre had succeeded because it had followed a different course to the one taken by Meyerhold. In fact, Pluchek and cast had been more interested in depicting the 'Unclean' as an ensemble than in drawing each of their individual characters in extensive detail.[65] But some critics seemed determined to interpret the performance in a manner conforming to their preconceptions. They used an established framework that allowed them to praise the production while maintaining the hierarchical ordering of approaches to acting and directing that had been codified in the previous era. However, this was certainly not a universal position. By 1957, the debate on the merits of different theatre styles and forms had become much more open and expansive. In a reflection of this, Irina Vishnevskaia wrote a review of *Mystery Bouffe*, which lamented the decision to cut the parade of 'Things' from the final act.[66] She accused the theatre of watering down the play's contemporary resonance and the 'fruitful tradition of Soviet drama'. Vishnevskaia compared the Satire Theatre production of *Mystery Bouffe* to Ruben Simonov's production of *Kirill the Great* (1957) running concurrently at the Vakhtangov Theatre. What mattered in both of these plays, according to Vishnevskaia, were the key symbols of the party, proletariat and revolution, not detailed psychological analysis of character. Simonov, she argued, had managed to create the type of production that 'turns *conventional* staging into something indisputably life-like, according to the laws of the revolution'. Vishnevskaia gave the example of one scene in *Kirill the Great* in which Lenin entered the stage via the auditorium 'as though emerging from the thick of the people'. Here the technique of breaking the fourth wall seemed entirely logical because it incarnated Lenin's *narodnost'* (being of the people). Echoing what was now becoming a common refrain in the cultural sphere, this critic suggested that there was a place for theatricalism in the Soviet theatre, as long as it reinforced the play's political message.

Vsevolod Meyerhold was officially rehabilitated on 26 November 1955, six months after the premiere of *The Bedbug* at the Moscow Satire Theatre. Following his political rehabilitation, the 'Commission for the Creative Heritage of V. E. Meyerhold' was set up, led by Pavel Markov, which sought to restore his artistic legacy and saw the publication of a number of extracts from Meyerhold's writings in the journal *Teatr* in 1957. As part of Meyerhold's cultural rehabilitation, an event dedicated to his work was held at the House of Culture in the Humanities Faculty of Moscow State University on the evening of 27 March 1961. The event (the last in a trio of commemorative evenings, the first dedicated to Stanislavsky, the second to Vakhtangov) was chaired by Sergei Iutkevich with guests including Valentin Pluchek, Aleksandr Gladkov, Dmitrii Shostakovich and many students from the university. During the event, Meyerhold's former colleagues and pupils gave speeches eulogizing his work. The programme also included performances of selected scenes from his productions, short film clips and music. Iutkevich observed in his opening speech that although there was still 'a hot-tempered struggle' surrounding Meyerhold's name, this event represented the first step towards 'resolving' the director's legacy.[67] He insisted that 'Meyerhold was the first and principal master of revolutionary theatre, and he belongs to us, to our Soviet culture, our socialist state, our Communist Party'. Iutkevich went on to dispel a number of 'lies', which he accused 'our enemies' of spreading in order to discredit the Soviet theatre. And he reserved particular scorn for one former musician at the Vakhtangov Theatre who had emigrated to the United States after the war and written a 'slanderous' book on Meyerhold that painted the director as anti-Soviet.[68] Iutkevich also rejected the idea that Meyerhold was an opponent of Russian realist theatre, insisting that 'Meyerhold loved Stanislavsky' and that it was wrong to pit them against one another. Although simplifying their relationship to a personal level, Iutkevich's argument reflected a desire to look beyond the binary opposition of these two figures and was an advocation of inclusivity and pluralism in the ongoing debate on theatre style. In particular, Iutkevich stressed Meyerhold's contribution to Soviet theatre as the director 'who brought us *Mystery Bouffe*, and who staged, alongside Mayakovsky, *The Bedbug* and *The Bathhouse*'. Of course, it was Iutkevich's production of the latter at the Satire Theatre eight years earlier which had paved the way for Mayakovsky's canonization and Meyerhold's rehabilitation in the first place.

In 1957 the Moscow Satire Theatre won first prize for its work on all three of Mayakovsky's plays at the All-Union Festival of Drama Theatres. It was suggested by one critic that these productions even signalled the rebirth of the Satire Theatre, after it had lost its way during the 1940s, when it staged 'insubstantial vaudevilles, rather than satire that denounced the vices of contemporary life'.[69] Both Akimov at the Lensovet Theatre and Pluchek at the Satire Theatre had answered the call of Georgii Malenkov at the Nineteenth Party Congress for more satires in the Soviet theatre. But while Akimov's productions of Shchedrin and Sukhovo-Kobylin offered veiled critiques of the system to those eyes which were open to see them, Pluchek's restagings of Mayakovsky gave audiences pro-communist satire in the Horatian mode – designed to weed out rogue elements through ridicule and moral lecturing. The Satire Theatre productions were successful, in part, because they fitted the party's definition of satire as a tool to consolidate the hegemony of state power by targeting the anti-Soviet 'Other'. At the same time, their stylized theatricalism remained problematic while society was still 'resolving' the legacy of Meyerhold (the symbolic 'Other' of the Soviet theatre). Thanks to their political theme, Mayakovsky's plays could be moulded into the shape of the party line and were, as a result, relabelled socialist realist. But their meta-political effect was to introduce taboo forms of performance to the stage – breaking the fourth wall, rhythmic choreography, pantomime, rock and roll dancing and so on – interventions which disrupted the theatre's usual tempos and frames of visibility, and which opened up new and alternative experiences for spectators.

One such spectator was Bertolt Brecht, who saw *The Bedbug* and *The Bathhouse* at the Satire Theatre in May 1955 when he was in Moscow to receive the 'Stalin Peace Prize'. Brecht praised both productions highly, noting that the performances of Vladimir Lepko as Prisypkin and Apollon Iachnitskii as Pobedonosikov were 'epic and full of de-familiarization'.[70] At the prize ceremony, Brecht's work was lauded by the director of the Mayakovsky Theatre, Nikolai Okhlopkov, for its 'illumination of the struggle for world peace'.[71] After the ceremony, Brecht returned the compliment and informed Okhlopkov that his production of Nikolai Pogodin's play *Aristocrats* had been the highlight of his visit to Moscow back in 1935, urging the director to revive it with the words: 'Young people need to see what genuine theatricality is.'[72] Okhlopkov took note and a new production of *Aristocrats* opened at the Mayakovsky Theatre a year later, as we will explore in the following chapter.

# 4

# Redefining socialist realism in the era of de-Stalinization

## Tovstonogov and Okhlopkov revive the Soviet classics, 1955–6

On 24 February 1956, the Twentieth Party Congress of the Communist Party of the Soviet Union officially came to an end. Delegates were preparing to leave when they were handed special passes and instructed to return to the Great Hall of the Kremlin for an additional 'closed' session, to which foreign journalists and communists were not invited. It was already past midnight on the morning of the 25 February when Nikita Khrushchev finally took to the stage and delivered a report titled 'On the Cult of Personality and Its Consequences'. Since Stalin's death, the phrase 'cult of personality' had become a metonym for the Stalinist political system in Soviet discourse, employed elliptically as a means to avoid deeper introspection of the previous era. Many of the speeches heard at the congress over the previous days had criticized the cult of personality in abstract terms, but now Khrushchev tore off the mask and denounced Stalin personally. To the disbelief and consternation of his audience, Khrushchev reeled off a list of Stalin's crimes that included the illegal mass incarcerations, tortures and executions he had sanctioned during the Great Purges, his errors of misjudgement during the Second World War and his repressive campaigns in the post-war years. Delegates listened to Khrushchev's iconoclastic performance in stunned silence. Some became unwell and had to be carried out of the hall. When it was over, the delegates left in a state of shock. No discussion was permitted and no stenographic record was kept of the session. Later that day, on the evening of the 25th, delegates from foreign communist parties were invited to the Kremlin to read the 'secret speech', as it became known. On 5 March, the Central Committee printed several thousand copies of the speech and distributed it to party committees across the country. It was then read out at thousands of meetings attended by party members and ordinary citizens.[1]

What at first had seemed like an impromptu and improvised performance by the Soviet premier was in fact carefully planned and coordinated with the backing of the Presidium of the Central Committee. In the year prior to the congress, as the rehabilitation of victims of political repression continued to grow apace, the Presidium set up a commission to study the mass repressions of the 1930s under Stalin. A report of its findings was presented to the Presidium at the beginning of 1956, which implicated Stalin directly in the repressions. Khrushchev based his secret speech on this report and supplemented it with details from his own experience working under Stalin during the war and in the post-war years. Although some members of the Presidium were reluctant to endorse the speech, in particular Molotov and Kaganovich who were personally implicated in the purges, the consensus was that the party needed to address the issue of Stalin's failings head on. By delivering the speech to delegates and then ordinary party members, but prohibiting discussion and general publication of the text, the party hoped to shape public opinion in the direction of its favoured narrative: the reversion from the Stalinist model back to Leninist principles. Unfortunately for the party leadership, these hopes were badly misplaced. Public reactions to the secret speech were varied, unpredictable and often extreme. The majority of letters sent to the authorities and newspapers in the aftermath were from ardent supporters of Stalin who were furious at his defamation. Others used the secret speech as a pretext to commit subversive acts, vandalizing public statues of Stalin or defacing portraits of him in the workplace. Despite the party prohibiting discussion of the speech, this was not always possible. The staged readings at party branches sometimes descended into heated debate, with attendees issuing harsh criticism not only of Stalin but of the entire Soviet system. These impassioned responses alarmed the party hierarchy which was briefed by the KGB on reactions to the speech around the country. In an effort to maintain control over the narrative, Khrushchev himself spoke at many of the meetings of party activists in Moscow and Leningrad. At one such event a note was passed to him from the audience, which read: 'How could you, a member of the Politburo, allow such terrible crimes to take place in our country?' Khrushchev read out the note in a loud voice and then said: 'This note has not been signed. Whoever wrote it, stand up!' No one moved. 'The person who wrote it is afraid', said Khrushchev. 'That's just how it was for us with Stalin.'[2]

Khrushchev gambled that by providing greater transparency over the Stalinist era, the party would earn the trust and support of the public for the building of a new, neo-Leninist society. But by chiselling the first cracks into the Soviet monolith himself, Khrushchev had unwittingly destabilized the entire edifice and what happened next was outside of his control. Alarmed at the escalation of criticisms, subversive acts of vandalism and demands for further reform, by May 1956 the party was beginning to row back. On 30 June the Central Committee issued a resolution 'On Overcoming the Cult of Personality and Its Consequences', which was published in all central newspapers. The resolution attempted to re-establish a definitive party line on the subject of the cult of personality and diffused most of Khrushchev's strident criticism of Stalin from the 'secret speech'. It noted that while the cult of personality was incompatible with Leninist principles of collective leadership, Stalin's 'individual mistakes and failings are overshadowed by his great achievements'.[3] Popular demonstrations and protests simmered in Eastern Europe from the summer to the autumn inspired both by events in Moscow and local concerns. Military action in Poland was averted when Khrushchev came to an agreement with communist reformer Wladyslaw Gomulka in October, but a popular revolution in Hungary led by students and workers was crushed by Soviet tanks after the Kremlin decided that intervention was essential to preserve the integrity of the Soviet bloc.

The revelations of the 'secret speech' had a limited impact on the publication and performance of dramatic texts in the short term, but a greater impact on inspiring forthright debate among cultural critics and the intelligentsia. New plays that were critical of corruption and abuse of power in the party and government, such as Leonid Zorin's *The Guests*, had been published and staged in 1954 during the first wave of the Thaw, before being swiftly banned by the censor.[4] In 1956, dramatists were hesitant to repeat such bold condemnation of the party but plays such as Nikolai Pogodin's *A Petrarchan Sonnet* and Aleksandr Volodin's *The Factory Girl*, both published that year, did criticize party interference in citizens' private lives and the petty superficiality of minor bureaucrats. The period between the mass readings of the 'secret speech' in March and the party's retreat by the end of June was a time of confusion and unease. Like the Thaw era more broadly, it endured as a liminal state of uncertainty between different positions (hard line, liberal, reactionary, progressive), a time when the interactions and negotiations between writers, theatre workers, state officials and journalists (roles and identities that were themselves fluid and changeable) could produce unforeseen and ambiguous outcomes. But while many within the party establishment and the country at large found the months following the secret speech to be unsettling and distressing, many others within the cultural intelligentsia, and the theatre more specifically, discovered a renewed sense of optimism and a willingness to speak out and take risks with their work. One tangible effect of the 'secret speech' was the way it catalysed the debate around the nature of socialist realism in the theatre which had begun back in November 1953 with the *Pravda* article 'The Right and Duty of Theatre', signed by the anonymous 'Spectator'.[5]

Starting in January 1956 and running until June 1957, a lively and at times polemical debate on the identity of Soviet theatre was conducted in the pages of *Teatr*, the Soviet Union's main theatre journal. Stage directors from across the Soviet theatre added their voices to the debate: many questioning the hegemony of the Stanislavsky system, others reasserting its superiority to other methods and some calling for a synthesis between the rival schools. A number of the contributors, such as Valerii Bebutov, had been collaborators or pupils of Meyerhold. In the wake of his rehabilitation, they seized their chance to call for greater tolerance of avant-garde forms in the Soviet theatre. Khrushchev's call in the 'secret speech' for a return to Leninist principles of 'collective leadership' played on a sense of popular nostalgia for the 1920s as a period of greater cultural pluralism and tolerance of diversity. Similarly, in discussions about the theatre, the innovative and experimental practices of the 1920s avant-garde were romanticized and contrasted to the more rigid and restrictive Stalinist 1930s. In fact, this was an over-simplification. Despite the increasing homogenization of theatre in the 1930s, innovation and diverse performance styles continued to be seen frequently on the Soviet stage up until the 1936–7 season, when the anti-formalism campaign and the start of the Great Purges served to ossify the cultural sphere. Two examples of this were Vsevolod Vishnevskii's *An Optimistic Tragedy*, staged at the Kamernyi Theatre by Aleksandr Tairov in 1933, and Nikolai Pogodin's *Aristocrats*, staged at the Realistic Theatre by Nikolai Okhlopkov in 1934. Both productions combined ideologically sound play texts, written in accordance with the blueprint for socialist realism, with expressive and stylized mise en scène that used music, set design and choreography to engage audiences in the action. These iconic productions demonstrated that socialist realism in the theatre could encompass a broad array of styles, genres and devices and need not limit itself to psychological realism of the Moscow Art Theatre variety. In fact, with its use of narrators and musical stage directions, *An Optimistic Tragedy* is an example of generic hybridity within the socialist realist play text itself. The productions by Tairov and Okhlopkov offered proof of the potential for fruitful and productive collaboration between politically committed texts and avant-garde stage craft: a union that became anathema under Stalinism in the 1940s.

It is therefore unsurprising that during the period of increased debate over the identity of socialist realist theatre, both of these plays were revived and performed again. In November 1955, a new production of *An Optimistic Tragedy* opened at the Aleksandrinskii Theatre in Leningrad, staged by Georgii Tovstonogov. A committed follower of Stanislavsky's methods, Tovstonogov brought his own stamp to Vishnevskii's play, combining expressive theatricality with a sharp focus on the psychological make-up of each character. The production was a huge success, and Tovstonogov was awarded a Lenin Prize in recognition of his achievements. Just under a year later, Okhlopkov revived his original production of *Aristocrats*, with much of the same cast, and staged it at the Mayakovsky Theatre in Moscow. A student and actor under Meyerhold in the 1920s, Okhlopkov was widely seen in theatre circles as his heir. He made a name for himself at the Realistic Theatre in the 1930s staging epic productions that rearranged the auditorium and the play text in order to bring spectators closer to the action. But Okhlopkov's decision to revive *Aristocrats* at the Mayakovsky Theatre in 1956 was not simply a nostalgic gesture. It was an artistic statement intended to remind the theatre world just how effective bold theatrical forms could be when harnessed in the service of a political text. It was a further salvo in the campaign to rehabilitate 'conventional' (i.e. stylized) theatre and redefine socialist realism in the process.[6] These two directors, Tovstonogov and Okhlopkov, became reluctant figureheads for their rival schools during the Thaw, an impression cemented by their polemical exchange in the pages of *Teatr* between 1959 and 1960. This exchange revived the debate on theatre style and showed that in the lead up to the Twenty-Second Party Congress, when Khrushchev rejuvenated and expanded the de-Stalinization campaign, such issues remained inflammatory and divisive. The theatre productions analysed here, and the debates they engendered, were some of the processes through which Soviet society reinterpreted itself during the Thaw. In this context, the deconstruction of the Stalinist aesthetic system took place in step with the de-Stalinization of Soviet society as a whole.

## The theatre debate

On 7 January 1956, seven weeks before Khrushchev delivered his 'secret speech', Nikolai Okhlopkov gave an incendiary speech of his own at a plenary session of the council of the All-Russian Theatre Organization (VTO), held at the Central House of the Actor in Moscow. Okhlopkov took to the stage after Mikhail Kedrov, the artistic director of the Moscow Art Theatre, and spoke for just over forty-five minutes. In his speech Okhlopkov criticized the dominance of the MAT and its brand of psychological realism for having 'stifled' Soviet theatre over the last decade and a half. 'The Moscow Art Theatre has taken over everything!', he roared. 'GITIS – taken, VTO – taken ... the only things it hasn't taken over are the Post Office and the Telegraph agency!' The hall erupted into laughter and applause.[7] The MATovites were furious. When Okhlopkov picked on Kedrov's production of *Tartuffe* (1939) at the MAT as proof that the Stanislavsky system does not work for all plays and should not be universally applied, he was shouted down by members of the audience. The chairman had to intervene and appeal for calm. Okhlopkov insisted that he had the greatest respect for Stanislavsky but merely disagreed with the way his system had been interpreted and implemented at the MAT under the guidance of Kedrov and Vasilii Toporkov. 'The Moscow Art Theatre may be our pride and glory but that doesn't mean we have to grovel before it', he reasoned. Some in the audience were outraged. Others were delighted. Okhlopkov had said what many had been thinking for years but had not dared to articulate publicly. That would change over the coming months as a vigorous debate was carried out in the pages of *Teatr*.

It began with an article by Leonid Viv'en, artistic director of the Aleksandrinskii Theatre, entitled 'What Is the Identity of a Theatre?'.[8] In it Viv'en criticized the 'homogenization' of theatre collectives in recent years, noting that they had become copies of one another, rather than finding their own individual identity. In terms similar to Okhlopkov, he blamed this situation on a mistaken and 'scholastic' interpretation of the Stanislavsky system as a set of rules and formulas to be slavishly followed, rather than as a 'source of living and mutable creativity'. For many years, theatres were able to justify dull and monotonous productions by invoking the Stanislavsky system, Viv'en claimed, and he blamed the bureaucratic governance of theatres for pushing collectives to accept a 'smooth easy life'. Theatres must find their own paths and their own identities as quickly as possible, Viv'en insisted; and he warned against confusing the 'unified method of socialist realism' with 'uniformity of creativity'.

In the 1920s, cautious tolerance for a variety of artistic styles and genres had been a feature of Soviet culture. In June 1925, the Central Committee resolution 'On the Party's Policy in the Field of Literature' had stated that although in a class society (as the USSR remained at that point) there cannot be neutral art, the forms of that art are 'infinitely more varied than in politics'.[9] The resolution also confirmed that 'the party can in no way bind itself in adherence to any one direction in the sphere of artistic form', a view that was still being expressed around the time of socialist realism's inception. In 1933, Anatolii Lunacharskii insisted that socialist realism could be a 'broad programme', including 'many different methods'; while Valerii Kirpotin, in his keynote speech on socialist realist drama at the First Soviet Writers' Congress in 1934, told delegates that 'socialist realism grants the writer the freedom to choose their creative path'.[10] However, from the mid-1930s, particularly in the wake of the anti-formalism campaign, socialist realism was defined in increasingly narrow terms and diversity of form was no longer advocated in authoritative discourse. As we saw previously, a hierarchy of acting methods developed, drawing on Stanislavsky's terminology, which placed the school of *perezhivanie* (emotional experiencing) at the top, as the form most suited to depicting the socialist realist subject. Below it came the school of *predstavlenie* (representation), identified with the methods of Diderot and Coquelin, while *remeslo* (stock-in-trade) was at the bottom.[11] Under Kedrov's leadership at the MAT in the 1940s and 1950s, Stanislavsky's ideas were turned into a creed and mandated to other theatres, since the MAT had by that point been turned into the state's favoured and most privileged institution. The school of *perezhivanie* was aligned closely with a naturalistic stage aesthetic based on the early MAT productions, which were themselves influenced by the nineteenth-century Meiningen Company. Under the influence of Nemirovich-Danchenko (also a playwright himself), the author's text was sacrosanct and needed to be treated with complete fidelity and respect by the director. Although Kedrov and Toporkov had worked closely with Stanislavsky while he was developing the Method of Physical Actions at the end of his life, the version of the system practised at other theatres was based predominantly on his earlier (and better-known) ideas of emotional memory and so neglected the late pivot towards physical movement, rhythmic tempo and non-verbal improvisation. Such elements, especially when brought from the rehearsal studio onto the main stage, were labelled formalist and consigned to the bottom of the hierarchy.

The revival of the art of theatrical 'representation' and other styles during the Thaw can be seen as part of a more general call for greater stylistic variation across Soviet art.[12] The party gave tacit endorsement to this revised position via an article published in 1955 in *Kommunist* (the official theoretical organ of the Central Committee), which argued that one of the fundamental conditions of ideological art was the 'struggle against dullness and homogenization in the creative process', insisting that socialist realism 'presupposes diversity in the styles and forms of artistic creation'.[13] This publication undoubtedly gave oxygen to those within the Soviet theatre clamouring for the rehabilitation of 'conventional' theatre practices under the umbrella of socialist realism. One example was Ruben Simonov's contribution to the debate in *Teatr*. In his article, the artistic director of the Vakhtangov Theatre called for a synthesis of the methods of *perezhivanie* and *predstavlenie* (as practised by Vakhtangov) in order to counteract the 'monopoly' of a 'one-sided, narrowly dogmatic understanding and application of the Stanislavsky system'.[14] Simonov's argument was echoed by his colleague and rival at the Vakhtangov Theatre, Boris Zakhava, half a year later in his own contribution titled 'For the Synthesis of the Theatre of *predstavlenie* and *perezhivanie*'.[15] In this piece he claimed that 'there is always form, style, external technique, there is always an element of representation' in the true art of 'experiencing' as long as that art preserves the ability to convey grand ideas. The key point that both Zakhava and Simonov were making was that expressive style and form are integral to theatre when it seeks to communicate an ideological message, which, of course, was the raison d'être of socialist realism. More strident in his argument was Valerii Bebutov, Meyerhold's former assistant. Bebutov called for an end to the pretence that the Stanislavsky system was a 'universal panacea', suitable for all styles of drama, and for an end to the 'abusive label of formalism' targeting directors who chose a different path.[16] Bebutov's strident critique of the Stanislavsky system was, more specifically, an attack on the 'typical framework of perceptions' that ranked the method of *perezhivanie* above those of *predstavlenie* and *remeslo*. 'In fact', Bebutov noted, 'we forget that in the living practice of theatre such delimitations do not exist'. Bebutov's attack on the hierarchy of forms that privileged a simplistic notion of *perezhivanie* over all others was both an appeal for tolerance of diversity and a direct challenge to the aesthetic consensus that had become entrenched in the theatre under Stalinism.

Many contributors to the debate, however, were just as passionate in their counter arguments. Aleksei Popov, artistic director at the Red Army Theatre, insisted that although the 'vulgarization of the Stanislavsky system' across the Soviet theatre, which saw actors ad-libbing and 'losing vividness', had undoubtedly led to stagnation, the call 'back to the 1920s' sounded strange to him.[17] He pointed to examples of recent successful productions in which a 'sharply expressive directorial conception' awakens the real interest of spectators, such as Tovstonogov's *An Optimistic Tragedy*, but warned that it was 'stupid and ignorant to suggest that the battle for realism in the Soviet theatre against aestheticism and formalism has gone away'. Other directors who re-affirmed their support for the school of *perezhivanie*, and tacitly the old status quo, were Anatolii Efros and Maria Knebel', both working at the Moscow Central Children's Theatre. In his article, titled 'Poor Stanislavsky!', Efros rounded on those 'firing critical barbs' at Stanislavsky and accused fellow directors Okhlopkov and Boris

Ravenskikh (another of Meyerhold's proteges) of 'false theatricality'.[18] Like Efros and Popov, Maria Knebel' was also critical of the way the Stanislavsky system had become 'vulgarized and simplified' over the years, something she blamed on the tendency to 'approve bad plays by appealing to the covenants of Stanislavsky' during the time of the cult of personality.[19] A popular teacher and theorist of the system, Knebel' had been pushed out of the MAT by Kedrov in 1950 and so had no loyalty to the MAT administration of recent years. Nevertheless, she insisted that we should not 'throw the baby out with the bath water' and reject the system completely. Knebel' feared that criticizing Stanislavsky had become 'the fashion' and warned that 'nihilism towards the system, towards the school of *perezhivanie* represents a serious threat to the future of Russian realistic art'. Concealed in Knebel''s argument that Stanislavsky needed to be reclaimed there lurked a sectarian impulse to re-affirm the divisions between the different schools. She admitted: 'I much prefer it when Okhlopkov calls himself a student of Meyerhold than when, over the course of many years, he swore allegiance to Stanislavsky', seemingly purblind to the reason why many felt that they had to swear allegiance to Stanislavsky in the first place. In Knebel''s mind the battleground was clear: 'the struggle of the theatre of *perezhivanie*, in the name of the new theatre, with the theatre of *predstavlenie*.' She called on theatre workers to 'repel unjustified attacks on the system' and oppose 'nostalgia' for the theatre of representation. Rather ambiguously, Knebel' expressed support for Meyerhold's rehabilitation, while also appearing keen to erase his influence from the contemporary stage, arguing that 'you can't make him a formalist and at the same time declare him a true believer of socialist realism'. Knebel' went on to insist that the battle between Stanislavsky and Meyerhold was not just a thing of the past but is 'all around us every day'.

The fluctuating positions around Meyerhold, as totemic victim of Stalinist persecution and the homogenization of Soviet theatre, were emblematic of the tug-of-war nature of the Thaw in this period. His official rehabilitation on 26 November 1955 had not led to universal acceptance of his artistic legacy, a fact sharply illustrated by an article published in the newspaper *Izvestiia* almost a year to the day of the Supreme Court's verdict.[20] The article noted that Meyerhold's fate was 'sad and tragic' but attacked his theatre as 'obsolete', insisting that the decision to liquidate the State Meyerhold Theatre in 1938 was merely the fulfilment of 'the needs of the time'. The piece went on to remind readers of the 'ideological and artistic failure of formalism' and the harm it had done to the development of Soviet art. An article in *Pravda* published on the same day, however, was much more conciliatory, including Meyerhold in a list of artists, alongside Aleksandr

Tairov and Solomon Mikhoels, whose work deserved re-evaluation. The article, co-authored by Nikolai Gorchakov, Pavel Markov and Igor Il'insky, struck a very different tone to the anonymous piece in *Izvestiia*, indicating how authoritative pronouncements in the two main news organs of party and government could vary quite significantly depending on the writers in question.[21]

## *An Optimistic Tragedy*, 1955

On 25 November 1955, the day before Meyerhold's sentence was quashed by the Military Collegium of the Supreme Court, a new production of *An Optimistic Tragedy* premiered at the Aleksandrinskii Theatre in Leningrad. The play had not been seen on the Soviet stage since Tairov's Kamernyi Theatre was dissolved in 1949 and the artistic director of the Aleksandrinskii, Leonid Viv'en (whose article had begun the debate in *Teatr*), was required to obtain special permission in order to revive it. Viv'en often brought in directors from outside the theatre to stage productions, and having noticed Georgii Tovstonogov's work at the Lenin Komsomol Theatre (Leningrad), he invited him to direct *An Optimistic Tragedy* in the autumn of 1955. Tovstonogov had experienced mixed success in his time as artistic director of the Lenkom, accused by critics of injecting superfluous theatricality into his productions in order to liven up the plays in the repertoire.[22] Trained in the Stanislavsky system at GITIS rather than at the MAT, Tovstonogov had learned its methods through Aleksei Popov and Andrei Lobanov whose idiosyncratic approaches were close to Vakhtangov's. Tovstonogov's productions, especially early on, varied in style and form as he sought a stage language that would best enable the cast to realize the play's 'supertask'. Nevertheless, he was consistent throughout his career in seeing the role of the director as that of a go-between, facilitating the relationship between text, actor and audience but never taking centre stage himself. His productions tended to have a strong focus on the characters' inner psychology, and he followed Stanislavsky's methods closely when in rehearsal. Tovstonogov's revival of *An Optimistic Tragedy* was no different as he sought to emphasize the play's characters as individuals, rather than as a broad revolutionary chorus.

*An Optimistic Tragedy* was written in 1933 by Vsevolod Vishnevskii, a Red Navy sailor-cum-playwright, who based the plot on the mutiny of the revolutionary Kronstadt sailors who turned on the Bolshevik government in 1921 after it had violently supressed a series of workers' strikes. In real life, the mutiny was brutally put down by the Red Army at the cost of thousands of lives.

In Vishnevskii's re-telling, however, the sailors are led astray by anarchists before being convinced by the example and leadership of a Bolshevik Commissar to rededicate themselves to the party cause. Unusually for Soviet literature of the time, the Commissar is a woman. Vishnevskii modelled his heroine on the real-life Civil War hero Larissa Reisner, whom he encountered when serving with the Red Navy. In the play, the stoic Commissar gradually wins over the support of the sailors and usurps the power of the anarchist Vozhak (Chief). When the ship is captured by German forces, the Commissar refuses to buckle under interrogation, buying time for Red Navy reinforcements to arrive and save the regiment. During the subsequent battle the Commissar is killed: however, her sacrifice only hardens the resolve of the sailors who are now firmly behind the Bolsheviks once again. The tragedy of the Commissar's sacrifice is tempered by the optimism of the revolutionary cause, which continues after her death. The audience is given not a classical tragedy, in which the heroic individual's ambition is acclaimed and their peripetia lamented, but rather a Soviet 'optimistic' tragedy, a new genre in which the tragic hero's sacrifice is redeemed by a struggle more important than their singular individuality.

In his original production in 1933 Tairov envisaged the play's thematic shape as that of a curve, one that led from the chaos of petty-bourgeois individualism and anarchy to the affirmation of a new proletarian class consciousness. He noted that 'all the emotional, visual and rhythmical lines of the staging must be built along a distinct curve leading from negation to affirmation, from death to life, from chaos to harmony, from anarchy to conscious discipline'.[23] In order to realize this concept, the designer Vadim Ryndin created a set in which a central revolve was part encircled by a curved road that banked into three tiers. The curved lines of the set suggested both the trajectory of the plot (the socialist realist 'spontaneity-consciousness dialectic') and the semi-circular banks of an Ancient Greek amphitheatre. The central revolve could sink down or rise upwards to create a platform resembling a ship's deck. Thus in this way, Ryndin's set was mimetic, functional and conceptual.[24]

In their 1955 production, Tovstonogov and designer Anatolii Bosulaev conceived of the play's 'through-action' in similar terms to Tairov, as 'the path of the regiment'.[25] This design concept also entailed a central revolve encircled by an undulating road, except that on the larger stage of the Aleksandrinskii the road passed downstage across the audience's line of sight underneath the proscenium arch, allowing the procession of marching sailors to complete their journey 'from the past into the future'.[26] One main point of departure between the two productions was Tovstonogov's desire to foreground the psychological subtleties of even the minor characters in the cast, rather than allowing them to blend into the general chorus. 'Our task was to show the significance of each of the individual human destinies presented for the destiny of the whole group', Tovstonogov stated.²⁷ This meant depicting the Commissar (played by Ol'ga Lebzak) as an ordinary woman rather than a symbolic figure. Alisa Koonen's Commissar at the Kamernyi Theatre had combined precise movements and lucid speech with bold make-up that resembled a tragic mask. Lebzak's interpretation emphasized the Commissar's fallible human characteristics: her weariness, tenderness and carefully concealed anxiety. Likewise, the anarchist sailors Siply (played by Aleksandr Sokolov) and Aleksei (played by Igor Gorbachev) were depicted as complex and conflicted individuals, 'an organic blend of contradictory human traits', rather than simple outlines.²⁸

Yet alongside this Stanislavskian focus on inner psychology and conflict, Tovstonogov was obliged to introduce theatrical elements necessitated by the text itself. The play is written in an epic style, employing two narrators who break the fourth wall to address the audience directly and musical stage directions which specify the mood and atmosphere of different scenes. Tovstonogov identified two distinct musical layers in the play, which give it qualities of both opera and musical theatre. First, there are the musical and rhythmic descriptions that the author uses to create tension and reveal emotions, often replacing dialogue altogether. Second, there are the specific songs and dances that are performed by the characters themselves to give colour and period detail to the action, which Tovstonogov called the 'internal music'.²⁹ The composer Kara Karayev wrote an original score for the production's first musical layer, while the majority of the 'internal music' was selected from popular sailors' songs, which the actors sang to the accompaniment of guitar, accordion or brass band. Karayev's score included leitmotifs for different themes and groups of characters. For example, the narrators had a theme which was played on their entrance and an 'enemy theme' recurred at various points in the action. The 'enemy theme' first appeared during the night battle scene at the start of Act Two: a 'violent, treacherous theme' played by solo woodwind instruments, which was then taken up by the whole orchestra after Vainonen's murder in Act Three, culminating in 'a frenzied, inhuman din' of trumpets and trombones.³⁰

Perhaps the most important leitmotif was the 'communist party theme' which gradually becomes the Commissar's personal theme. Powerful and strong, it is first heard in Act One when the Commissar tells Vainonen that the party is behind her. It then reoccurs as a 'triumphant brass fanfare' after the successful night battle, and again before the Commissar's fateful confrontation with

Vozhak.³¹ When the 'communist party theme' plays for the last time in the scene of the Commissar's death, it becomes a mournful requiem combining tragic and triumphant notes. Alongside Karayev's leitmotifs, Tovstonogov introduced folk songs at particular moments to create an atmosphere. For example, the melancholy old sailors' song 'The Open Sea' was used once at the start of the play to transmit a general sense of world-weariness and again during the captivity scene in Act Three to convey a spirit of comradeship among the captured sailors. Rather than use a communist or Red Navy song which might have come across as trite or forced, Tovstonogov chose a song that would have been familiar to the condemned sailors since their childhood, allowing the slow crescendo of their voices in unison to articulate the idea of togetherness, rather than the lyrics themselves.

The director also employed contrasting musical tones to add complexity to individual characters. In the scene of his downfall at the hands of the Commissar, Vozhak (played by Iurii Tolubeev) sat centre stage on a gaudy rug, his hulking frame bursting out of his striped sailor's shirt, lazily stirring a great brass samovar filled with spirits and stolen wine. To the strumming of a guitar, he hoarsely droned the lines of a revolutionary 'Varsovienne': 'Left, right, forward march, the workers . . .'.³² The discord between the earnest song and the corrupt tableau was striking and deliberate. Surrounded by his brutish sentries, the allegory was clear for all to see. As Konstantin Rudnitskii recalled:

> Vozhak was the living embodiment of destructive anarchism, unbridled passion for violence and maniacal paranoia. When the revolve dragged into view the fat hulk of this idol, reclining importantly on a flowery carpet surrounded by obsequious henchmen ready to shoot anyone he told them to, the audience was overcome by an acute, if as yet powerless, hatred. Rage swelled in the auditorium. From that moment Tovstonogov and Tolubeev had the audience in the palm of their hands. The play, quickening its pace to a run . . . irrepressibly sped towards the minute of Vozhak's destruction, so longed for by the spectators.³³

The destruction of Vozhak offered spectators a moment of catharsis, particularly those whose loved ones had been repressed at the hands of the *Vozhd' narodov* (Leader of the Peoples). The director's own father had been one of Stalin's victims, shot in 1937 when Tovstonogov was still a student in Moscow. By switching the symbolic focus of the play from the Commissar to Vozhak, Tovstonogov was pouring all his grief, anger and frustration with the regime into the production. Vozhak's execution of summary justice became a critique of the lawlessness of the Great Purges, his cruel power and paranoia – the embodiment of totalitarian dictatorship. Tovstonogov's family tragedy became intertwined with the national tragedy of a people's revolutionary optimism corrupted.

During a public discussion of the production held at the Palace of Culture in Leningrad, the poet Ol'ga Berggol'ts reflected:

> When I go to the theatre, I want the play being performed to speak to me personally. Not only with the whole auditorium at once, but with those latent things that I bring to the theatre myself and which I yearn to be resolved. . . . People have been afraid of the word tragedy for many years. It was said that tragedy carries within it elements of tragic personality. As Vera Mikhailovna Inber said at one of these discussions, forced optimism has been too dominant over art, over poetry and also over the theatre.[34]

Implicit in her speech was a potent idea: not the optimism of a tragedy that serves a noble cause, but the tragedy of optimism when it is forced onto a society. For Berggol'ts, the theatre had a duty to speak directly to individual spectators about their innermost cares, their own personal tragedies which often lie buried, but which might be teased out in the right conditions. The critic Raisa Ben'iash described Vozhak's end in Aesopic terms as 'the spiritual demise of a personality, for which retribution was inevitably coming'.[35] The destruction of Vozhak's (cult of) personality thus became a form of staged retribution for Tovstonogov and many thousands of others who watched the play in the aftermath of Khrushchev's 'secret speech'. As Vozhak was led away by the sailors to be shot, he suddenly turned and cried out: 'Long live the Revolution!' It was an act of desperation that showed both the human fragility beneath the mask of steel and the deceptive nature of Stalinist propaganda. As Anatolii Smelianskii noted, 'the criminal nature of the Stalinist state, dressed up in revolutionary slogans, had been presented by Tovstonogov for all to see'.[36]

In a similar fashion, the director used choreography in order to emphasize the allegorical image created by Tolubeev. He organized the blocking so that everywhere Vozhak went there was always an empty space around him, as though he was separated from the other sailors 'by an invisible but insurmountable barrier'.[37] In the last years of his life, Stalin's mistrust of those around him intensified. One day Khrushchev overheard Stalin mutter: 'I'm finished. I trust no one, not even myself.'[38] On the morning of 1 March 1953, Stalin failed to call for his breakfast at the usual time. He had suffered a massive stroke, but his bodyguards were too afraid of breaking protocol to enter his bedroom to check on him and he was left in a paralysed state until 10.00 pm at night. By the time the doctors arrived, the damage to his brain was irreversible and he died four days

**Figure 8** The Commissar leads the regiment with Vozhak following behind. *An Optimistic Tragedy* at the Aleksandrinskii Theatre, 1955. Courtesy of the Museum of the National Dramatic Theatre of Russia.

later. It was thus through the empty void enclosing Vozhak's slow, heavy gait, that the production of *An Optimistic Tragedy* articulated a sense of the isolation and loneliness of absolute power and the unremitting fear that accompanies it.

The production was met with widespread acclaim from critics and the general public. Reviews in the newspapers hailed it as a 'joyful' and 'significant' event in the theatrical life of Leningrad and praised it as 'deeply instructive for our dramatists and theatres'.[39] Critics applauded the designer Bosulaev for his realistic scenery depicting well-known Leningrad vistas and there was praise for Tovstonogov's 'correct' approach to the staging which aimed 'to reveal the depth of the heroes' inner life, bravely uniting lofty pathos and psychology, straight agit-prop and the authenticity of realistic details'.[40] The decision to introduce realistic elements to both the set design and the characterization was commended as a means of diluting the stylized elements of Vishnevskii's play. Lebzak's performance as the Commissar was acclaimed for its 'great inner restraint of temperament' and simple external features which allowed her to play the role of an 'ordinary' woman.[41] Likewise, Tolubeev's Vozhak was lauded as 'magnificently truthful and convincing', with Ol'ga Berggol'ts noting in *Pravda* that 'you feel physically that you are encountering a great dark force, irreconcilably hostile to the Soviet state and its ideals'.⁴² One reviewer in *Literaturnaia gazeta* observed that Tolubeev played Vozhak 'almost monumentally, as though he is chiselled from stone'.⁴³ When Aleksei Dikii was once asked why, when playing Stalin, his performances were so static, he replied: 'I am playing a monument.'⁴⁴ Tolubeev's 'monumental' Vozhak was undoubtedly hewn from the same rock. Tovstonogov had wanted the play to speak to a contemporary audience, 'to reflect the spiritual experience, outlook, thoughts and views of Soviet people today'.⁴⁵ By toppling the figure of the violent autocrat from his perch, the director's production achieved just that. In the uncertain and uneasy climate of the Thaw, memories of the long Stalinist tragedy merged with a cautious optimism for change. And it was a sense of this precarious union that Tovstonogov's *An Optimistic Tragedy* captured. At the Twentieth Party Congress in February 1956, delegates were treated to a performance of the production brought over from Leningrad specially for their benefit. The symbolism could not have been any clearer.

## *Aristocrats*, 1956

On 27 October 1956, Nikolai Pogodin's socialist realist classic *Aristocrats* opened at the Mayakovsky Theatre in Moscow. The production, directed by Nikolai Okhlopkov, was in many respects the same that had run twenty-two years earlier at his Realistic Theatre. It even contained much of the original cast who had followed Okhlopkov to the Mayakovsky Theatre, including Pavel Arzhanov who reprised his role as the young captain Kostia at the ripe old age of fifty-five. Okhlopkov's *Aristocrats*, like Tairov's *An Optimistic Tragedy*, was an example of the versatility of socialist realist theatre in the 1930s before the anti-formalism campaign and the Stalinist freeze on stylistic innovation. Its revival in 1956 formed part of Okhlopkov's efforts to rehabilitate expressive theatricalism, offered up to the public as evidence of the way realism and stylization could successfully combine and inform one another. Growing up in Irkutsk Siberia, Okhlopkov had made his entrance onto the theatrical scene in 1921 when he staged a mass spectacle in the town's Tikhvinskii Square for the May Day celebrations in front of 30,000 people. Recognized as a precocious talent, he was sent to Moscow to study at GITIS where he was spotted by Meyerhold and cast in a number of his seminal productions of the period, including *Tarelkin's Death* (1922) and *Bubus the Teacher* (1925). When he returned to the theatre in 1931 after a stint working in cinema, Okhlopkov took over as artistic director at the Realistic Theatre, formerly the Fourth MAT studio, situated on the north-east corner of Moscow's Triumfal'naia Square. Despite its small scale (seating around 325 people), Okhlopkov brought to this theatre the lessons in stage craft he had learned from Meyerhold and his own ideas of theatre as a form of mass spectacle. Through his use of music to structure the performance, his reconfiguration of the stage space and his insistence on the vital role of the mise en scène, Okhlopkov continued the legacy of the avant-garde into the post-Stalinist era. But Okhlopkov was also convinced that directorial innovation should be used to reinforce the ideological impact of a production. He believed in creating a unity between actor, play text and audience that would reflect the communal spirit of a new egalitarian society. It is no surprise, therefore, that his favourite poet was Walt Whitman, whose free verse and frenetic rhythms sought the 'potential for infinitization' in every sensible form: the egalitarian identification of everything in life as a part of one whole and therefore equally worthy of literary attention.[46] In his theatre, Okhlopkov sought to create this sense of wholeness by enveloping the spectator in the action so they became a part of its story. In a dramatization of Vladimir Stavskii's collectivization novella *Running Start* (1931), Okhlopkov placed a stage in the middle of the audience with a spiral walkway leading off one end that raked up over the spectators' heads in a circle before descending to the opposite end of the stage platform. The mise en scène was fragmented into individual units of action that took place either consecutively or simultaneously, at different places in the auditorium with different sets of actors. At one point, a peasant wounded in a fight crawled for ten minutes along the walkway while the action on the stage platform below shifted to a different scene altogether.[47] This created an immersive experience for spectators, who could choose which part of the action to follow at any given moment. Out of these montages Okhlopkov created a sense of life freed from the chronology of a plot, a Whitmanian symbol of the incessant incompleteness of the whole.

In his production of *Aristocrats*, which first premiered on 30 December 1934, Okhlopkov drew on the traditions of popular folk theatre to give form to what he called a 'carnival play'.[48] The action takes place in a forced labour camp on the White Sea-Baltic Canal, which was constructed by Gulag prisoners between 1931 and 1933. The play follows the lives of a number of former 'aristocrats' such as the captain Kostia Dorokhov, a petty-bourgeois thief, who has been interred in the camp for re-education (*perekovka*). At the time of the first Five-Year Plan, the Gulag was still seen by the party as a means of transforming criminals into socially productive members of society by educating them in socialist ideals. However, by the late 1930s this reformist agenda had been dropped and the Gulag became a place to extract maximum slave labour with little hope for re-entry into society. Nevertheless, at the end of Pogodin's play, many of the 'aristocrats', including Kostia, have been successfully converted into loyal Soviet citizens and they renounce their former bourgeois ways. The play is a clear example of how the 'spontaneity-consciousness dialectic' began to underlie all works of socialist realism in the 1930s. The aristocrats are transformed from a 'spontaneous' or unenlightened existence into socialist 'consciousness' through hard labour.

Okhlopkov's conceit was to draw on the traditions of Japanese Kabuki theatre and the Commedia dell'arte to bring out the comic elements of the text and engage spectators in the action by stimulating their imagination. In the original production, the stage consisted of two raised oblong platforms rounded at one end, which were stretched across the centre of the auditorium so that the top right corner of one was connected to the bottom left corner of the other. The audience was seated around this central structure which was covered in canvas but otherwise bare. In the 1956 restaging, however, the two connected platforms were positioned diagonally from stage right upstage to stage left downstage so that the bottom platform extended over the orchestra pit and the first few rows of seating. The majority of the audience was seated in the auditorium facing the proscenium arch: however, around a hundred spectators were seated on the stage behind the platforms, facing downstage. In both configurations, the spectators were seated in the round and brought up close to the action. One of the most striking details of Okhlopkov's production was the use of proscenium servants or *zanni*, a device that both Meyerhold and Tairov had used in the past. Dressed in masks and blue overalls, the *zanni* assisted the actors, brought on properties or created scenic effects, in a manner similar to the black-cladded *kurogo* of Kabuki theatre.

The play began with the sound of a gong. The audience watched as a dozen *zanni* entered the stage and started throwing clouds of white confetti in the air, creating a blizzard of snow that filled the entire auditorium. In the next scene the *zanni* ran past a stationary skier while holding branches to create the impression of forward movement. A table was represented by two kneeling *zanni* stretching a piece of green baize between them. And whenever Gromov, the camp commander, made a telephone call, a masked servant brought the phone to him, before carrying it offstage again once he was finished. During the knife fight scene in the canal between Kostia and Limon, the *zanni* stretched a large canvas cloth, painted with a wave design, across one of the stage platforms with holes cut into it. As Kostia and his adversary struggled in and out of these holes, the *zanni* rippled the cloth to create the effect of moving water, accompanied by tense music.[49] These stylized devices were intended to spark the spectators' creative imagination, allowing them to develop the hint provided by the staging and transform it into a complete picture themselves. 'This is an attempt to express theatrically the real essence of facts, events, people, to express it positively', argued one critic in 1935. 'This type of theatricality is fruitful. That is why an Okhlopkov play is a celebration.'[50] It was this kind of 'fruitful' theatricality that Okhlopkov would later describe in 1959 as 'realistic conventionality' (*realisticheskaia uslovnost'*), a form of stylization (i.e. the embracing of stage convention) which serves a realistic goal and therefore belongs under the umbrella of socialist realism.[51]

A public discussion of the play was held in March 1935 at the Masters of Arts' Club in Moscow, chaired by the newly appointed Procurator General of the USSR Andrei Vyshinskii. Refusing to play the role of a neutral chair, Vyshinskii denounced the play for romanticizing criminals, presaging in both severity and lack of impartiality his later performances presiding over the Moscow show trials of the Great Purges.[52] In spite of Vyshinskii's criticisms, however, Okhlopkov and Pogodin defended the work so passionately that soon afterwards *Pravda* gave the production at the Realistic Theatre its official seal of approval.[53] But if reviews of the original production of *Aristocrats* had been generally positive, in 1956 the critics were less charitable. One review in *Sovetskaia kul'tura* criticized the use of stage devices which 'contradict the spirit of verisimilitude'

**Figure 9** Kapitolina Pugacheva as Lady Niurka in *Aristocrats* at the Mayakovsky Theatre, 1956. Courtesy of the Archive of the Moscow Academic Vladimir Mayakovsky Theatre.

and singled out the *zanni* as evidence of Okhlopkov's questionable emphasis on 'style and sensationalism'.[54] The reviewer also found fault with the play text itself, bemoaning its 'unrealistic and clichéd events', such as the surprising speed with which the former criminals are remade into dutiful citizens. This had been one of Vladimir Pomerantsev's main criticisms of socialist realism as a genre in his controversial essay 'On Sincerity in Literature' published in December 1953 during the first wave of the Thaw.[55] In the essay, Pomerantsev decried the 'varnishing of reality' in many Soviet literary works which led to far-fetched characters and events that lacked sincerity. One of the problems the Vakhtangov Theatre encountered in 1935 when it staged its own production of *Aristocrats* in a realistic manner was the incompatibility between the method of *perezhivanie* on the one hand and Pogodin's schematic character types, with their implausible ideological transformation, on the other. The director Boris Zakhava placed the focus of the production on the inner psychological conversion of Kostia, but the lead actor Ruben Simonov struggled to extract a convincing psychological portrait from the character's clichéd dialogue.[56] By contrast, Okhlopkov used 'conventional' devices to dramatize the *physical* process of the transformation via a series of connected events and actions; a mode of staging more in tune with the style and structure of many socialist realist dramas, including *Aristocrats*. It is arguably one of the great ironies of the homogenization of Soviet theatre under Stalin that the method of psychological realism became the privileged mode of stage interpretation for a literary genre that tended to lack psychological continuity in character development.[57]

One example of Okhlopkov's approach to the *perekovka* theme was the scene in which the prostitute Sonia (Tat'iana Karpova) is won over by the ideological arguments of Gromov (Evgenii Samoilov). After her conversation with the camp commander, who has been convincing her to abandon her past ways, Sonia goes for a walk to mull over Gromov's words. As she strolled about the platform, strewn with flowers to suggest a meadow, she was followed by a masked violinist who played a seductive tune full of the promise of a new life. At first Sonia ran away from the violinist's tune, but he kept re-appearing, following her around the platform, the melody increasing in intensity and emotion as she began to listen. Finally, Sonia laughed with joy and threw herself onto the ground, stretching out happily to touch the flowers as the music swelled to a climax.[58] The character's inner psychological conversion was depicted by purely external means through movement and music. In this way, Okhlopkov replaced Pogodin's stilted dialogue with the poetry of mise en scène and solved the problem of the play's artistic sincerity in the process. By 1956, reform of the Gulag system was one of

Khrushchev's key priorities. He idealized the Soviet penitentiary system of the 1920s and hoped to make re-education by labour the focus of penal detention once again.[59] On 25 October 1956, two days before the premiere of *Aristocrats*, a Central Committee decree reorganized the Gulag system and made re-education a priority – the *perekovka* narrative was back on the Moscow stage and up the social agenda. But such naïve idealism appeared in stark contrast to the private testimonies of returning Gulag prisoners and the public rehabilitation of those silenced in the camps. Their stories brought a different kind of sincerity to the *perekovka* theme, which no amount of theatrical ingenuity could redeem any more.

## Okhlopkov and Tovstonogov

In late 1959, Okhlopkov continued his mission to rehabilitate stylized theatre by publishing a long essay titled 'On Conventionality' spread over the November and December editions of *Teatr*.[60] This intervention and the reaction it provoked marked a resumption of the debate on theatrical identity which had dominated the pages of the journal between 1956 and 1957. In the essay, Okhlopkov noted that 'interest towards conventionality as an organic element of realism' had undoubtedly increased in recent years 'as the concept of socialist realism in the theatre broadens'.[61] He went on to argue the case for what he called 'realistic conventionality', a type of conventionality derived from national traditions, as opposed to 'formalist' or 'aesthetic' conventionality. This oxymoron would act as a kind of discursive placeholder, Okhlopkov suggested, until the time when everyone agreed that conventionality is 'organically included in the broad understanding of realism'. To prove his point, Okhlopkov pointed to the impossibility of depicting certain events on stage without recourse to 'conventional' means. How can a director enact Shakespeare's stage directions at the start of *The Tempest*, he asked, with naturalistic methods alone? Are you supposed to flood the stage and sink a ship? 'Life demands from art, artistic forms of life', he argued, not a 'simple mirror'. And he insisted that the truth of the theatre is an artistic truth which appeals to the imagination of the spectator: 'the spectator should finish that which the theatre creates', he reasoned. Like Meyerhold, Okhlopkov imagined the art of the actor as a kind of unfinished equation, an incomplete performance that requires the creative input of the spectator to complete the picture. If an actor 'experiences' the role in an ultra-realistic manner, then their performance will be closed off to the imagination of the spectator who will lose interest. 'This is what conventionality can do in the service of genuine realism', he insisted. 'It is a flame brought to the gunpowder store of the spectator's imagination.' Okhlopkov's aim in this essay was to make the case for conventional stage devices as an integral element within socialist realist theatre. In the process, he was dismantling the hierarchical organization of styles and methods that had enshrined the school of *perezhivanie* and stage realism above all others. But if Okhlopkov's main hypothesis seemed logical, then the essay's renewed attack on Kedrov and the MAT – criticizing a recent production of *The Winter's Tale* as overburdened with 'primitive everyday logic' – was bound to raise the hackles of the establishment.

A response came two months later, in the form of Tovstonogov's 'Open Letter to Nikolai Okhlopkov' also published in *Teatr*.[62] Whether Tovstonogov felt duty bound to refute Okhlopkov's argument purely on artistic grounds or whether he was leaned on by those higher up is unknown. Certainly, his insistence that 'no one has ordered us to speak a certain way' and his claim that having unease over the state of Soviet theatre 'is a personal matter for every director, as it is for the Minister of Culture' suggest that he may not have been the sole author of the piece.[63] Tovstonogov's main bone of contention was that Okhlopkov had 'broadened the concept of "realism" to such an extreme that it could encompass absolutely anything'. While not disagreeing that the theatre requires a degree of conventionality, he disputed whether the kind of conventionality Okhlopkov was eager to rehabilitate was in fact realistic: 'You are in favour of conventionality which is above truth of life', he insisted, a conventionality 'which we don't need'. 'Your conventionality, Nikolai Pavlovich, is based only on your imagination. Your conventionality exists separate from the dramatist, the actor and the spectator.' Here Tovstonogov laid out the central thesis of his directorial philosophy, the triumvirate of dramatist – actor – spectator. The role of the director is to cement the power of this triad, he claimed, but never to overshadow it. He went on to explain further:

> Our work is like that of a chef's. Delicate work. We decide on which tray the human fates, characters and conflicts should be served to the audience and with which 'garnish'. It must be served in a way that preserves the individual, unrepeatable aroma and taste of the author's work.

This was one of Tovstonogov's main criticisms of Okhlopkov's productions, the fact that he failed to respect the inviolability of the author's creation and considered himself a creator on an equal footing. Insisting that the art of the director lies in self-limitation, Tovstonogov maintained that 'the limits of our imagination are set by the author and crossing over these [limits] should be punished as betrayal and treachery to the author'. The sanctity of the dramatist and the word was one of Nemirovich-Danchenko's key tenets at the MAT and it was no surprise that this was one credo the party was particularly keen to establish as axiomatic across the Soviet theatre. Having imposed strict controls on the way play texts were conceived, written and edited for performance, the party was always likely to baulk at directors riding roughshod over the carefully prepared manuscripts, interpreting them in unforeseen and potentially subversive ways. Under Stalinism, controlling the insurgent and spontaneous potential of live theatre performance often meant shackling the capricious urges of the director-demiurge.

One of the persistent accusations levelled at Meyerhold had always been his disregard for the authority of the dramatists he staged. In his open letter, Tovstonogov also singled out Meyerhold's (and by implication Okhlopkov's) use of the devices of the Commedia dell'arte as an example of decadent 'aesthetic formalism' rather than 'realistic conventionality'. His point was that while the Commedia dell'arte was a popular form of national theatre in Italy, in Soviet Russia it was foreign and therefore decadent. He went on to elaborate:

> The Chinese theatre is also conventional by its nature. Conventional in a completely different way to European theatre. For the Chinese people everything in their theatre is understandable, truthful and realistic. But if you, me or someone else tried to transfer the devices of Chinese national theatre to the Soviet theatre then we will not escape charges of aestheticism and formalism. And it would serve us right!

Running through Tovstonogov's argument was both a sense of parochial orientalism and the same strain of chauvinism that had underlined the Stalinist campaigns against formalism and cosmopolitanism. The inherent stylization of Chinese or Japanese theatre may be acceptable on their own national stages, but once brought over to Soviet Russia it becomes alien and formalist. The transnational merger of cultural forms that was such a feature of the early Soviet avant-garde is viewed with hostility, as a transgression of Soviet nationalism embodied by *Moscow's* Art Theatre.

When the renowned Chinese actor Mei Lanfang had performed in Moscow in the spring of 1935 it influenced not only Soviet directors like Okhlopkov and Meyerhold but also the watching Bertolt Brecht, crystallizing his ideas on the 'Verfremdungseffekt' which he wrote down soon after. But under Stalinism such cultural internationalism was increasingly viewed with suspicion, as the policy of 'socialism in one country' dominated and the influence of the Comintern waned. It was not until after Stalin's death that the Soviet Union cautiously opened up to the world once again under Khrushchev's (inconsistent) internationalist policies. Coincidentally, the same month that Okhlopkov's *Aristocrats* opened in 1956, an exhibition of Japanese artwork was held at the Pushkin Museum of Fine Art in Moscow, displaying wood block prints designed by artists such as Harunobu and Hokusai from the Edo period. Condemnation of Okhlopkov's experiments with Japanese Kabuki stage devices circulated in the same publications that were praising Japanese artworks, many of which had been sent over from France on the initiative of UNESCO.[64] In this manner, the ironic collision of chauvinism and internationalism, which became a feature of Khrushchev's approach to foreign culture during the Thaw, was played out in the back pages of the newspapers for all to see.

The dispute between Okhlopkov and Tovstonogov made clear that the fault lines of the Stalinist era remained active beneath the boards of the Soviet stage during the Thaw. Although softened by de-Stalinization, the sectarian divisions of the past were still exerting influence over critical discourse, government policy and stage practices. As a consequence, responses to de-Stalinization in the theatre were often ambiguous and unpredictable. In 1955 Tovstonogov took on the challenge of a play such as *An Optimistic Tragedy*, diluting its inherent theatricality with realistic details, while at the same time denouncing the lawless corruption of the cult of personality through targeted symbolism. Yet a few years later he could attack Okhlopkov's efforts to rehabilitate conventional theatre (and subvert the Stalinist aesthetic hierarchy), accusing him of feeding the 'nihilism' of contemporary directors.[65] Okhlopkov also refused to shy away from polemical confrontation, as evidenced by his repeated attacks on Kedrov and the MAT. But while Tovstonogov's intervention put the brakes on efforts to open up Soviet theatre to a diverse array of approaches, Okhlopkov's was aimed at encouraging theatrical pluralism and righting the injustices of the past. True, his revival of *Aristocrats*, with its stylized mise en scène but Gulag-apologist plot line, enabled the former rather than the latter. However, Okhlopkov had already contributed his own stinging critique of the Stalinist state during the first wave of the Thaw. Undoubtedly drawing inspiration from Nikolai Akimov's productions at the Lensovet Theatre, Okhlopkov's iconic staging of *Hamlet* in 1954 offered audiences one of the most enduring metaphors of Stalinism. With its monumental set constructed in the form of two massive bronze gates, the director turned Elsinore into a vast labyrinthine prison. In this way, criticism of Stalinism as a political phenomenon and the deconstruction of the Stalinist aesthetic system took place concurrently in his productions.

The argument for greater tolerance of diversity in the Soviet theatre centred on a redefinition of socialist realism to encompass a greater array of styles and forms. As such, these arguments were always a form of compromise with the past and with the regime. In contrast to Pomerantsev's essay which condemned the insincerity of socialist realism directly, the debate on theatrical identity took a trojan-horse approach, attacking the assumptions and prejudices of socialist realism from within. In some ways, this made it a far more effective method of critique. After all, de-Stalinization of the theatre was always about more than rehabilitating victims of repression; it was about dismantling the entire system of representation that codified norms, values and practices within a hierarchy that privileged some forms and anathemized others; an aesthetic system that mirrored Stalin's methods of political dictatorship and social control. But while the first critiques of this system came from directors of the *predstavlenie* school, in 1956 a new challenge to the MAT consensus emerged from within the MAT itself. In his essay on conventionality, Okhlopkov had hailed the appearance of the fledgling Sovremennik Theatre-Studio, set up by a group of former MAT School students, who were determined to restore the true ideals of Stanislavsky and Nemirovich-Danchenko to the Soviet stage. 'They act truthfully, without affectation, but not naturalistically, not simply copying life', Okhlopkov observed. 'This brings the imagination of the spectator to life.'[66] As we will see in the following chapter, the Sovremennik Theatre-Studio would go on to revitalize the understanding of socialist realism in the theatre, staging a new wave of plays by contemporary dramatists that spoke to the concerns and experiences of the thaw generation.

5

# New writers for new times

## Moscow realism at the Sovremennik Theatre-Studio, 1956–9

At midnight on 15 April 1956, the curtain finally rose at the Moscow Art Theatre's subsidiary stage on Moskvin Street. The auditorium was packed with directors, actors and critics from across the Moscow theatre scene, who were gathered to witness a ground-breaking event: the debut of the first new theatre-studio in Moscow for eighteen years. This new theatre-studio was comprised almost entirely of students and recent graduates of the Moscow Art Theatre School, led by Oleg Efremov, an idealistic director who had been teaching at the School since graduating there in 1949. Efremov and the young cast were helped with their new initiative by Aleksandr Solodovnikov, the new administrator of the MAT, who agreed to provide funding and affiliation to the Theatre-Studio. It was also Solodovnikov who suggested the name 'Sovremennik', meaning 'contemporary', which epitomized the youthful ethos of the collective. Giving their debut performance only a few months after Khrushchev's 'secret speech' at the Twentieth Party Congress, the Sovremennik Theatre-Studio embodied for many the desire for change and new beginnings that had been released in its wake. With a modern repertoire consisting of plays by a new vanguard of Soviet dramatists who preferred to focus on themes of moral sincerity and integrity, rather than party ideology, the Sovremennik spoke directly to a new generation of young people who had come of age after the war. By the mid-1960s, 70 per cent of the Sovremennik's audience was aged between twenty and forty years old, with 94 per cent identifying themselves as students, white collar workers or the 'intelligentsia'.[1]

Over the course of its early history, the MAT had a complex relationship with its studios – both resisting their innovations and being rejuvenated by them. Ever since his first aborted attempt at establishing a theatre-studio with Meyerhold in 1905, Stanislavsky had invested most of his creative energy in the MAT studios, leaving the main theatre to Nemirovich-Danchenko. But by 1937 only the Vakhtangov Theatre had survived of the four original MAT studios, as theatre became homogenized around the model of the Gorky MAT and a simplified Stanislavsky system. Later in his career, Oleg Efremov reflected on the MAT's stagnation in the post-war period:

> People simply stopped going. Theatres became deserted and so did the Moscow Art Theatre. . . . Every year the theatre received a Stalin Prize and quite a few actors and directors lived 'from prize to prize'. It was with a view to the prize that the repertoire was planned and roles were assigned. It was, if you like, the surrender of all principles.[2]

Efremov's dissatisfaction with the MAT stemmed from what he saw as its sacrifice of creative independence through collusion with the bureaucratic apparatus and its reward system. This had led to a crisis of legitimacy in the theatre and the betrayal of the tradition of Stanislavsky and Nemirovich-Danchenko who, Efremov believed, had always put artistic concerns ahead of financial reward and patronage. By the start of the Thaw, the MAT was firmly tied to the Soviet state. Efremov noted that 'there were people then who gauged one's attitude to Soviet power by one's attitude to the Art Theatre'.[3] It was therefore the Sovremennik Theatre-Studio's self-prescribed mission to revive the 'lost values' of the MAT by restoring a sense of civic responsibility and artistic integrity to the theatre. Stanislavsky had always looked to the MAT studios as sources of innovation and experimentation which could be used to freshen up the main theatre. Now a group of MAT graduates were following in this tradition, replanting the core principles of the Stanislavsky system into fresh soil. In response to the revival of stylized theatre, these young actors were determined to prove that psychological realism could also be inventive and original. Rejecting the prevalent nostalgia for the 1920s avant-garde, they popularized instead a nostalgia for the old MAT values which would bring to life a new contemporary dramaturgy. But if the Sovremennik Theatre-Studio was dogmatic in its adherence to the acting school of *perezhivanie*, in which the actor experiences emotions akin to those of the character in the moment of creation onstage, it was far more ambivalent towards the naturalistic stage aesthetic of the Russian realist tradition. Many of the Sovremennik's productions combined psychologically truthful acting with a minimalist and even abstract set design, creating a new interpretation of stage realism for a new generation of young theatregoers.

It became commonplace during the Thaw to describe this new kind of realism with a term borrowed from Italian cinema: 'neorealism'.[4] As a short-lived national cinematic practice and a longer-lasting transnational theoretical approach, neorealism is often perceived to be the prioritization of authenticity over stylization.⁵ Emerging in 1945 from a desire to show the true social conditions of post-war Italy, this cinematic movement was typified by a documentary format, location filming away from the studio, a lack of complex editing and the use of non-professional actors. Italian neorealist films by Roberto Rossellini, Vittorio De Sica and Giuseppe De Santis were popular among Soviet audiences in the 1950s, and the movement had a great deal of influence on the emerging Soviet filmmakers of the Thaw. Notwithstanding the problems transposing a cinematic term into the theatre, there were evident similarities between the plays staged by the Sovremennik, with their visceral focus on post-war Soviet life, and the Italian neorealists' depictions of war-torn Italy. In addition, the Sovremennik's emphasis on the truthful depiction of everyday experience echoed the neorealist concern for authenticity. Perhaps inevitably, the label 'neorealist' was also appropriated by officials in the Ministry of Culture and used to criticize the Sovremennik's productions as an unacceptable deviation from official socialist realism. There were frequent run-ins between the Sovremennik and the party establishment during the first decade of its existence, based not so much on disagreement over theatre style but over repertoire selection. The emergence of the Sovremennik Theatre-Studio indicated that reform could come from within as well as outside the spatial hierarchy that placed the MAT at the centre of the Soviet theatrical universe. The Sovremennik achieved this by combining truthful acting with non-naturalistic stage designs and by giving a platform to some of the new literary voices that emerged during the Thaw: writers such as Viktor Rozov, Aleksandr Volodin and Anatolii Kuznetsov, who reimagined the limits of what it was possible to say on stage and the manner in which it could be said.

## *Alive Forever*, 1956

Oleg Efremov joined the MAT School in 1945, however on graduating four years later he failed to be accepted into the main theatre. Instead, he joined the Moscow Central Children's Theatre, led by Ol'ga Pyzhova, while at the same time returning to the MAT School to teach. In the early 1950s, the Central Children's Theatre became one of Moscow's creative hubs, drawing in audiences who came to see new plays by writers such as Viktor Rozov that were not being staged elsewhere. Efremov's first role at the Children's Theatre was the lead in Rozov's play *Her Friends* (1948). Two years later, the Stanislavskian director Maria

Knebel' was kicked out of the MAT and she joined the Children's Theatre, later inviting one of her students from the director's course at GITIS, Anatolii Efros, to join her. In 1954 Efros directed the premiere of Rozov's play *Good Luck* (1954) with Efremov playing the lead role of Aleksei. A year later, in 1955, Efremov began rehearsing the same play with his students at the MAT School, setting in train the events that would lead to the Sovremennik being formed. After watching the first act, the School directors were so impressed that they agreed to include the production in the students' end-of-year diploma performance. Efremov was then given permission to stage another production, but this time he brought in a group of young actors from various theatres across Moscow to work with him. Among this group were the MAT School graduates Galina Volchek, Oleg Tabakov, Lilia Tolmacheva, Igor Kvasha, Evgenii Evstigneev and Svetlana Mizeri – names that would become famous in the Soviet theatre. In the winter of 1955, they began rehearsing another play by Rozov, *Alive Forever* (1943) at the MAT School, practising at night time when the School's hall was not in use. The outcome was the performance on 15 April 1956, which created a buzz around Moscow and convinced the young actors to continue with their project.[6]

Efremov sought to implement Stanislavsky's idea of the 'theatre house' in which the actors would live and eat together as a collective, making joint decisions on the selection of the repertoire and who they worked with. Together the group drew up a manifesto which promised to continue the creative legacy of Stanislavsky and Nemirovich-Danchenko. Although later on his career, Efremov was much more critical of the stagnation of the MAT, the Sovremennik's manifesto of 1956 condemned those who took a 'revisionist' approach to the MAT and described conversations about the MAT's obsolescence as 'masked attacks on the foundational principles of the realist theatre as a whole'.[7] The document left no room for doubt as to the young collective's allegiances and their determination to defend the 'spirit of Stanislavsky' from 'the restorers of the aesthetics of Meyerhold', 'supporters of the dogmatism of "conventionality"' and those calling for the union of the theatre of *predstavlenie* (representation) with the theatre of *perezhivanie* (emotion-experiencing).

As an actor Efremov followed the precepts of the Stanislavsky system closely, while as a director he sought to facilitate the actor's creative process, always putting them at the centre of a production.[8] Trained in the system by Mikhail Kedrov and Vasilii Toporkov, Efremov was an early advocate of the Method of Physical Actions and placed great importance on the construction of the 'through-action' and the use of *études* (improvisations) to work out the building blocks of a scene. Nevertheless, Efremov maintained a sceptical attitude towards stylized theatre throughout his career, believing that, more often than not, the use of theatrical devices and shocks tended to impede a meaningful connection between actor and spectator. Instead, Efremov maintained that the actor must evoke the empathy of the audience and in doing so draw it into the creative process. This relationship between actor and spectator was rooted in what Efremov (following Stanislavsky) called the 'confessional principle'.[9] This meant that the actor should enrich their performance with their own personal theme, their own identity and their own experience. In this way, the actor forms an emotional connection with the audience based on honesty and openness and taps into feelings that the spectator usually keeps hidden. This was one of the performance techniques that distinguished the young actors of the Sovremennik Theatre-Studio from the very beginning.

On 4 April 1958, the 'studio of young actors', as it was initially called, was officially renamed the Sovremennik Theatre-Studio, under the Gorky MAT, by decree of the Ministry of Culture. On the choice of this name, Efremov noted: 'In this name the principal direction of the theatre is made clear. On our stage we want to resolve the burning issues of our day, raise those questions that concern people.'[10] This desire to represent the concerns of a new generation was reflected in the Sovremennik's choice of repertoire from the very beginning. Its debut production, Rozov's *Alive Forever*, was written in 1943 but had been rejected by the censor for its unorthodox depiction of Soviet war-time experience. Now in the wake of the revelations of Khrushchev's 'secret speech', a new openness to alternate narratives of the past saw the play finally accepted for performance.

*Alive Forever* concerns those who are left behind during war and how they find a sense of purpose in their lives. It centres on the experience of Veronika, a young woman who is devastated when her fiancée Boris, an engineer, refuses to apply for deferment and insists that it is his duty to join up and fight. Boris is placed in stark contrast to his cousin Mark, a gifted pianist, who manages to avoid the draft and tells Veronika that talented artists and musicians should resist the 'mass hypnosis' which pressurizes them to enlist. Veronika is evacuated with Boris's father, sister and Mark whom she reluctantly marries. Boris is reported missing in action and his death is eventually confirmed when the soldier whose life he saved in battle pays them a visit. Veronika's character arc shows her development from a young, self-centred individual into a mature member of society. By the end of the play, she has left Mark and is about to enter an electromechanical institute in Moscow to help rebuild the country after the war. Mark, who hangs around with a crowd of petty-bourgeois types, is vilified as a coward and eventually exposed for faking his draft exemption. The play contains the rite of passage plot, so familiar to socialist realism, as well as the typical conflict between Soviet patriotism and bourgeois materialism. However, it also broke new ground by focusing on an ambiguous heroine, Veronika, and in the way it dealt with notions of party ideology and the clichés of building socialism. In Act One, Scene Two, Boris's father, Dr Borozdin, makes fun of the girls from Boris's factory who have come to give him leaving presents on behalf of the factory's *komsomol* branch. Borozdin cuts them off before they can recite their rehearsed speech and parodies the official rhetoric, declaring: 'Our factory here in the rear will fulfil and overfulfil . . . we know all this already, don't worry.'[11] When one of the girls, Dasha, says that she cried for her brother when he left, Borozdin asks her whether she cried for him on behalf of the local party committee or as a member of his family. She laughs and replies as a family member, of course. The emphasis is shifted onto the importance of family ties, rather than political ones, and the clichéd language of *komsomol* branches and party committees is made to look hollow and out of place.

Rozov was part of a group of Soviet playwrights who came to prominence after the war by foregrounding the relationships of ordinary, unremarkable people, rather than the heroic protagonists of Stalinist socialist realism. The ordinariness of these characters was embodied not only in the trajectories of their lives but in the way they spoke – reproducing the patterns and lexicons of ordinary speech, shorn of the rhetorical clichés of party propaganda. In the production of *Alive Forever*, the Sovremennik actors approached Rozov's dramatic dialogue with a down-to-earth style of delivery that was labelled 'whispering realism' by critics.[12] This marriage of realistic script writing and natural speech delivery proved to be highly influential in the Soviet theatre, as 'authenticity' (*dostovernost'*) became the buzzword of the times. But although the actors embodied their roles with the utmost truth of feeling, the set design for the production broke with the naturalistic tradition of the MAT. The stage was bare, with the exception of a few items of furniture, and the director used lighting to demarcate rooms rather than partition walls, windows and doors. This minimalist stage design was partly a result of financial constraints, but it was subsequently repeated in later productions and eventually became known as part of the Sovremennik's signature aesthetic, justified as a means of foregrounding the characters in the play. Efremov believed that by stripping away unnecessary stage detail the audience's attention would be drawn to the actors and the subtleties of their characters would be better perceived.

**Figure 10** Oleg Efremov and Viktor Rozov at the premiere of *Alive Forever* at the Sovremennik Theatre-Studio, 1956. Courtesy of the Moscow Sovremennik Theatre.

On the whole, critics greeted the birth of the new theatre-studio warmly and gave encouragement to the young collective, while remaining critical of some of the actors' performances.[13] Writing in *Moskovskaia pravda*, the actor Boris Babochkin praised the cast for their sincere and professional acting, but at the same time criticized the 'ordinary' and 'uninteresting' characters they had created.[14] Babochkin felt that the cast, 'in a manner characteristic of the cinema', had failed to elevate the idea of the play to the 'heights of civic pathos' and had 'set its ambitions too low'. In the 1930s Babochkin had been immortalized on the cinema screen as the Red Army soldier Chapaev, who became an archetype for the swashbuckling positive hero of socialist realism. In comparison to Chapaev, however, Rozov's characters were far more mundane, a fact that clearly troubled Babochkin who felt that the 'cinematic' manner of acting lacked pathos and dwelt on the humdrum rather than the heroic. At a public discussion of the play, held on 26 June 1956, Efremov responded to a letter that he had received which complained that his production failed to make the characters appear special. 'Boris may be talented or untalented', Efremov countered, 'but what is important is that he is a very decent person, he is a hero because for him social interests are always more important that personal ones.'[15] It was an important distinction and a recalibration of what was expected of characters created on the stage: from idealized role models to more authentic reflections. While Babochkin was suspicious of the 'low ambitions' of contemporary cinema, Efremov saw 'authenticity' as an unmistakable quality shared between Rozov's play and Italian neorealist cinema.[16] It was a theme picked up by the playwright Aleksei Arbuzov in an article published in January 1957 titled 'In Defence of the Little Man'.[17] Arbuzov saw in the prosaic characters of Italian neorealism a return to the spirit of the 'little man', a nineteenth-century trope that had re-emerged at the start of the first Five-Year Plan to venerate the everyday and the egalitarian in Soviet literature. Those spectators who had been expecting the positive heroes of Stalinist socialist realism were disappointed with the Sovremennik's production of *Alive Forever*, which instead presented imperfect, ambiguous characters and acclaimed the underachieving 'ordinary person' as the new dramatic subject of the Thaw.

This character type was exemplified by Veronika (played by Svetlana Mizeri) who divided the opinion of critics and spectators. Writing in *Sovetskaia kul'tura*, one reviewer insisted that Boris should in fact be considered the 'true hero' of the play and that, despite only appearing in two scenes in the first act, Ivan Gubanov had created a 'vibrant, charming image of youth that . . . runs through the whole play as a symbol of heroism, selflessness and human beauty'.[18] Rather than acknowledge the morally ambiguous Veronika as the hero, the critic preferred to valorize Boris, the fallen soldier, as the play's heroic symbol. A similar sentiment was expressed in a letter sent to the Sovremennik by Mark Naumov, a student in Moscow, who disagreed strongly with the Theatre-Studio's portrayal of Veronika. 'Your production loves Veronika, understands and forgives her', he wrote, 'but you absolve her of all responsibility to answer for her mistakes.'[19] Naumov thought that Veronika should answer for her 'betrayal' of Boris and was due all the suffering that came her way.

The idealized figure of the loyal woman who waits for her love to return from the front was enshrined during the Second World War in Konstantin Simonov's much-loved poem 'Wait for Me, and I Shall Return' (1941). The lyrical 'I' of the poem appeals to the addressee to wait, even when everyone else has given up hope; a sentiment that resonated with front-line soldiers, many of whom knew the poem by heart, or carried a copy of it on their person.[20] In contrast to Simonov's romantic stereotype, Rozov's Veronika was a far more complex character: a woman struggling with her conscience and the patriarchal social conditions, which saw women often compelled to accept marriage for their own survival. But while some critics of the Sovremennik's production seemed impervious to this nuance, many spectators responded to Veronika in an altogether different manner when she was brought to life on the big screen in October 1957.

Mikhail Kalatozov's film *The Cranes Are Flying* was based on Rozov's play, which he adapted into a film script himself, albeit with some changes to the plot. Perhaps the most significant of these was a scene implying a more coercive relationship between Mark and Veronika, intended to make the latter appear more sympathetic. The film proved extremely popular with the Soviet public and with international audiences, winning the *Palme d'Or* at the Cannes Film Festival in 1958. The role of Veronika was played by Tatiana Samoilova, who inspired widespread admiration from audiences and became an unlikely icon for young women across the country.[21] Both Rozov's play and Kalatozov's film popularized a new ambivalent character type whose life trajectory was uncertain yet ultimately filled with purpose and hope. And although this focus on flawed, ordinary people was seen by many as a neorealist trend, the Italian film director Pier Paolo Pasolini would later dub Soviet thaw cinema 'neoromanticist' on account of this lingering sense of optimism.[22]

## Problems with the repertoire, 1957–9

*Alive Forever* opened for another season on the MAT's subsidiary stage on 15 April 1957 and continued to be performed that spring and summer. Then on 10 August that year, the Sovremennik signed a contract with the MAT to stage a new play by Rozov called *In Search of Happiness* (1957) as part of its first full season. The production premiered on 6 December 1957 at the MAT's subsidiary. The play is set in an overcrowded Moscow apartment inhabited by Klavdiia Savina, a widow, and her four children. Rozov uses one of his favourite devices, the arrival of relatives from the countryside, to develop the plot as the children struggle to balance family responsibilities with an awakening desire for personal independence. The iconic scene in the play sees fifteen-year-old Oleg (played by Oleg Tabakov in the Sovremennik's production) grab his deceased father's army sabre from the wall and start hacking up his sister-in-law's expensive furniture – a distinctly anti-bourgeois act of defiance. The Sovremennik's production was well received by the press with one reviewer praising the Studio-Theatre for 'listening closely to the pulse of contemporary life' and continuing the fight against 'banality' (*poshlost'*) that had been waged in the MAT's productions in the early 1900s.[23] In the spring of 1958, the Sovremennik's production of *In Search of Happiness* won a prize at the Moscow spring theatre festival, a new initiative that was already in its second year. The festival heralded a fresh drive to encourage new plays on contemporary life: according to the festival rules, each theatre entering had to stage one play on a modern Soviet theme. In 1958 theatres took part in Moscow, Leningrad, Ukraine, the Baltic countries, the Caucasus and the Soviet Far East. The Moscow event saw forty productions staged, of which half had been prepared specially for the festival.

The Sovremennik's first production of the 1957–8 season had been declared a success, but two further productions were beset by difficulties. Its second production was a never-before staged script by Aleksandr Galich titled *Sailor's Silence*, the name of one of Moscow's most infamous prisons. The play chronicles the life of a Soviet Jewish family, the Shvartses, from 1929 to 1955, as they live through the first Five-Year Plan, the Great Purges, the Second World War and the Gulag. The first general run-through was attended by around 500 people, but the next day a scandal broke out. 'How did you dare to stage that! Who authorized you?!' Solodovnikov raged.[24] There were problems with the text and rumours that it would be banned. A dress-rehearsal was held at the Palace of Culture on 16 January 1958, but this time Solodovnikov ensured that entry was restricted to those named on a special list. On the day of the dress-rehearsal only fifteen people were seated in the audience, consisting of MAT administrators, bureaucrats from the Ministry of Culture and representatives from the Ministry of Internal Affairs. The production was banned after the rehearsal. At a meeting with an official from the Ministry of Culture, Galich and Efremov were told: 'What do you want, comrade Galich, that in the centre of Moscow, in one of the capital's young theatres, a play is staged which tells the story of how the Jews won the war? These are the Jews we're talking about!'[25] It was clear that the anti-Semitism which had scythed down theatre critics and other Jewish cultural figures at the tail end of the Stalinist era remained a malign and toxic presence within Soviet society during the Thaw.

The banning of *Sailor's Silence* increased the pressure on the Sovremennik's third production of the season – Eduardo De Filippo's *Vincenzo De Pretore* (staged under the title *No One*). The play was guest directed by Anatolii Efros and starred Efremov as the thief Vincenzo and Lilia Tolmacheva as Ninuccia. Rehearsals coincided with a two-week visit by De Filippo to Moscow in March 1958, at the invitation of the Ministry of Culture, to watch the one-hundredth performance of his play *My Family* (1955) at the Red Army Theatre.[26] While he was in Moscow, it was arranged for De Filippo to attend one of the Sovremennik's rehearsals, where he demonstrated to the cast an expressive form of acting, full of sudden, exaggerated movements and dramatic utterances. It was an introduction to a kind of theatricalism that the Sovremennik actors were 'strongly apprehensive' of at the time.[27] Perhaps influenced by their meeting with

De Filippo, Efros and Efremov commissioned a bold, 'conventional' backdrop for the production from the artist Lev-Feliks Zbarskii. The painter's design contained stylized and asymmetrical depictions of Italian religious statues, inspired by an exhibition of folk art that Efros had seen in a museum in Perm. For a final flourish, Zbarskii donned a pair of old boots, filled basins with different coloured paints and then jumped in and out of the basins, stomping across the canvas which was spread out on the floor.[28] *No One* premiered on 16 April 1958 and played for two more shows, before the MAT cancelled performances at their subsidiary on Moskvin Street. The management was unhappy that such an 'abstract' looking backdrop was being used on their stage. The Sovremennik was forced to move the production elsewhere and the play was eventually performed at the State Literature Museum on a stage only 4 metres wide. The production was later criticized by the Ministry of Culture for being staged 'in the spirit of Italian neorealism'.[29]

The MAT's party bureau reprimanded Solodovnikov for his part in enabling the production and prohibited the Sovremennik from staging any further performances at the MAT's subsidiary stage.[30] From September 1958, the Sovremennik was forced to rent the concert hall in the Sovetskaia Hotel, paying 3,000 roubles per performance and 500 roubles per rehearsal, although it continued to receive state funding channelled through the MAT.[31] The Sovremennik was ordered by the Ministry to set up an artistic council to oversee its productions, consisting of representatives of the Art Theatre, the MAT School and its own collective. Artistic councils were in turn supervised by Glavk, the central directorate of culture of the Moscow City Council and the Ministry of Culture. However, the studio failed to carry out the directive and filled the artistic council exclusively with its own members, with Igor Kvasha as chairman and Galina Volchek as chair of the union committee.[32] This reflected both the collective's desire to retain full responsibility over its repertoire, in the spirit of the 'theatre house', and the MAT's reluctance to associate itself too closely with its progeny. The lack of outside representation on the Sovremennik's artistic council was later criticized by the Ministry of Culture as one of the main reasons for the Theatre-Studio's problematic choice of plays.[33]

For the 1958–9 season, the Sovremennik turned to less contentious material, beginning with a dramatization of Anatolii Kuznetsov's 'youth novel' *Sequel to a Legend* (1957). The play premiered at the Sovetskaia Hotel on 24 October 1958 and was directed jointly by Efremov and Margarita Mikaelian. The 'youth novel' was a new variant of socialist realist literature that emerged during the Thaw, featuring young idealistic protagonists who leave the cities to find work and a sense of purpose in the countryside. In this way it reversed the trajectory of Stalinist literature that saw protagonists leave the backward provinces to find meaning and enlightenment in Moscow/Leningrad.[34] Instead, 'youth prose' depicted the big city as a false space of petty-bourgeois materialism, bureaucracy and cronyism. The dramatic analogue to the 'youth novel' was Rozov's 'youth play' *Good Luck*, in which the protagonist Aleksei returns to his home in Siberia after failing the entrance exams to a prestigious college in Moscow. When he leaves, Aleksei is accompanied by his cousin Andrei who has grown disenchanted with his family's bourgeois lifestyle in the city. In *Sequel to a Legend*, the hero Tolia (played by Oleg Tabakov) also travels from Moscow to Siberia in search of work after failing to get into university. He stops off in Irkutsk where he is convinced to join in the construction of the Irkutsk power station by Leonid, the story's mentor figure. Tolia finds the work testing but eventually resolves to stay in Irkutsk rather than returning to Moscow after hearing reports from his friend Viktor about a new craze for rock and roll which is polluting his hometown. In preparation for the production, Efremov took the troupe on a field trip to the Irkutsk region, where the work is set, in order to gather impressions that the actors could draw on later when creating their roles. It was a technique that Stanislavsky had used at the MAT, famously sending his cast to visit the Khitrov market in Moscow to study society's underbelly prior to staging Maksim Gorky's *The Lower Depths* in 1902. The result was a much-needed hit for the Sovremennik and was followed by another success with the play *Two Colours* by Avenir Zak and Isai Kuznetsov. However, the Sovremennik's next two productions, Oleg Skachkov's *Breakers of the Silence* (1959) and Aleksandr Volodin's *Five Evenings* (1959), were both criticized by the Ministry of Culture, which accused the Sovremennik of trying to be 'fashionable' in pursuit of 'easy success'.[35]

The three or so years that followed the Twentieth Party Congress, from February 1956 to the end of 1958, saw Khrushchev's leadership pursue an inconsistent and ambiguous cultural policy, as the ebb and flow of relaxation and restriction, thaw and frost, formed an unstable backdrop to people's lives. At times the clampdown and the liberalization even appeared to occur simultaneously. In late November 1956, as the party was reeling from events in Hungary, a reaction against Vladimir Dudintsev's inflammatory novel *Not by Bread Alone* (serialized in *Novyi mir* from August to October) began in the press.[36] However, that same month saw the publication of the second volume of the almanac *Literaturnaia Moskva*, which contained Nikolai Pogodin's play *A Petrarchan Sonnet*, poetry by Marina Tsvetaeva and many works of literary criticism.³⁷ One essay in the volume, written by critic Mark Shcheglov, praised the 'unmistakable step forward from the poor dramatic productions of the era of conflictlessness' made in the last few years.³⁸ Shcheglov commended plays such as Rozov's *Good Luck* and Aleksei Arbuzov's *Years of Wandering* (1954) for bringing a new focus on incisive, real-life themes rather than delivering 'a thesis from the political-agricultural sector'. Another essay, by dramatist Aleksandr Kron, blamed the 'cult of personality' for creating a 'bureaucratic hierarchy in art' which had led to stagnation in the theatre.³⁹ The fact that these bold interventions were published at the same time that official organs were attacking Dudintsev draws a picture of a dysfunctional and post hoc approach to censorship; a period when shifts in party messaging could occur so rapidly that the time lag between censor approval and printing could be enough to render a new publication like *Literaturnaia Moskva* out of step with the current party line. The almanac was subsequently criticized in the press four months later, with Kron's essay singled out for its 'biased and false generalizations'.⁴⁰ Then on 13 May 1957, Khrushchev and other party leaders held a meeting with the literary intelligentsia in Moscow. In his speech, Khrushchev attacked Dudintsev's novel as 'false at its base' and claimed that *Literaturnaia Moskva* contained 'ideologically fallacious' work.⁴¹

However, the reining in of liberal elements in the intelligentsia that spring and summer took place alongside a revival of outward-looking cultural exchange and the embrace of Soviet internationalism. In May and June, the Berliner Ensemble toured Moscow and Leningrad for the first time, although without Brecht who had died the previous summer.⁴² Then in July and August, Moscow experienced a carnivalesque suspension of the status quo as the city hosted the Sixth World Festival of Youth and Students. In all, 34,000 young people from 131 countries descended on the city, which responded with an outpouring of joyful elation and communal celebration. Miniature foreign cities sprung up across Moscow, exhibitions of Western modernist and abstract art were displayed in galleries, public transport vehicles were painted with bright colours, live jazz was played in the streets and circus clowns gave impromptu performances as Soviet citizens and foreigners conversed, sang and danced together in spontaneous outbreaks of festive revelry. Many of the planned safeguards put in place by the authorities to regulate interactions between Muscovites and foreigners collapsed in the mayhem. After the guests had departed and the stages were taken down, criticism of the excesses witnessed at the festival became commonplace in the press. However, the impact of the festival on a generation of Soviet youths would prove to be long lasting.⁴³

In June 1957, Khrushchev had successfully defeated an attempt to oust him by the 'anti-party group' of disgruntled Stalinists, and he continued to consolidate his position at the top of the party over the course of the next year. Khrushchev also made a number of cultural concessions in an attempt to gain intelligentsia support for his de-Stalinization campaign and to create a counterweight to conservative forces in the party apparatus. On 28 May 1958, the Central Committee issued a decree correcting its 'mistakes' regarding criticism of the composers Vano Muradeli, Dmitrii Shostakovich and Sergei Prokofiev for 'formalism' a decade earlier. It was the first time that the Central Committee had formally corrected itself in the cultural sphere since Stalin's death.[44] Then in July that year, Aleksandr Tvardovskii was reinstated as the editor of *Novyi mir*, having been sacked four years earlier for publishing controversial essays, including Vladimir Pomerantsev's 'On Sincerity in Literature'. Tvardovskii would go on to play a vital role in the publication of Aleksandr Solzhenitsyn's revelatory novella about the Gulag, *One Day in the Life of Ivan Denisovich*, in *Novyi mir* four years later. In October 1958 the All-Union Conference of Theatre Workers, Dramatists and Critics was held in Moscow, the first such conference of the post-Stalin era. The conference ran without incident until Aleksei Arbuzov took to the stage and delivered an impassioned defence of Aleksandr Volodin's play *The Factory Girl*, which had been criticized by Anatolii Sofronov (one of the three officially promoted dramatists of the Zhdanov era). Arbuzov's speech caused uproar in the hall. Delegates cheered and laughed at this unexpected act of insubordination, until the police had to be called in to restore order. That night at the conference reception, Arbuzov was warmly congratulated by delegates. It felt like a changing of the guard.[45]

## *Five Evenings*, 1959

Aleksandr Volodin's next play, *Five Evenings*, premiered at the Leningrad Bolshoi Dramatic Theatre on 6 March 1959, directed by Georgii Tovstonogov who had taken over as the theatre's artistic director in 1956. The production received positive reviews in the Leningrad press, with one critic praising 'the fine acting' and 'the light, lyrical atmosphere'.[46] The critic also noted that in the play 'It is not the table of ranks, not official posts or diplomas that determine the social-moral value of a person. Any job, any work can be honourable and bring one joy'.[47] *Five Evenings*, like the plays of Viktor Rozov, shifted focus away from the Stakhanovite overachiever and onto the 'ordinary person'. The plot unfolds over the course of five evenings and is divided into five acts, with each act corresponding to a particular evening. Sasha Il'in and Tamara were young sweethearts in Leningrad before the war. Il'in studied at an institute and rented a room from Tamara's sister. He was an excellent student and was expected to become a scientist, but then the war came and the young couple were split up when Il'in was sent to the front. After the war, Il'in never returned to the institute to finish his studies and ended up in the Far North, apparently working as a driver. Seventeen years have passed when the play begins and Il'in has finally returned to Leningrad. He decides to look in on Tamara at her old flat, which she now shares with her nephew Slava. Tamara is shocked to see Il'in but finally agrees to let him in and they talk. Il'in cannot bring himself to reveal his mundane job to her and lies that he is the head engineer of a large chemical plant, in fact the job of one of his old classmates, Timofeev, who later makes an appearance. Over the next four evenings the couple tentatively begin to warm to each other again and old feelings are reawakened, before Il'in panics as a result of the lie he has told Tamara and decides he must leave. Sitting in a railway station café, on the fifth evening, Il'in is visited by Slava's friend Katia. She convinces him to go back to Tamara and tell her the truth about his job. Il'in realizes that what matters is not who he is but that he still loves Tamara. They are reconciled again but still uncertain about what the future will bring.

The critic Vadim Gaevskii noted many years later that the production was staged 'at a time when disappeared people and forgotten names were returning from non-being, when a sense of humanity that had seemed vanished forever was brought back to life'.[48] The play's subtext, then, is the release of thousands of prisoners from the Gulag during the Thaw and the interrupted lives they attempted to resume. Il'in's seventeen-year absence is glossed over in the play, but the pointed reference to the Far North was an allusion that many, although not all, spectators interpreted in relation to the labour camps. Il'in was possibly one of the many Red Army soldiers who, after being captured by the Germans, was sent to the Gulag after the war, accused of collaborating with the enemy. In 1955 an amnesty was awarded to almost 60,000 Soviet citizens who had been sentenced for collaboration. Further amnesties, including one in the summer of 1959, meant that by the start of 1960 the number of prisoners in the Gulag had fallen to its lowest level since 1935, numbering around half a million.[49] However, the reintroduction of former convicts into society was a complex and unsettling process as families and friends tried to pick up the pieces of fragmented relationships and disrupted lives. Il'in and Tamara's reunion mirrored thousands of similar private reconciliations across the country and turned the couple into unlikely figureheads for a particular collective experience that until then had remained unaddressed in cultural life. One review of Tovstonogov's production observed that the roles of main character and subordinate appeared to have been reversed in the play. The critic noted that the character of Timofeev (played by Vsevolod Kuznetsov), who as a head engineer with 'progressive ideas' would normally be the hero of the play, is in Volodin's drama merely a peripheral figure.[50] By contrast, the 'ordinary' Il'in (played by Efim Kopelian) and Tamara (played by Zinaida Sharko), who would 'usually appear in our plays and productions as minor characters', were elevated to the level of central figures. This allowed the audience to relate more closely to their thoughts and feelings, the reviewer argued.[51] Although Leningrad critics were surprised at the shift in focalization away from idealistic heroes, they treated the change as a positive development, with one suggesting 'the play could become a banner for the "direction" of Soviet drama'.[52]

*Five Evenings* was subsequently staged by the Sovremennik Theatre-Studio, premiering on 3 July 1959 at the Mayakovsky Theatre, where the Sovremennik

**Figure 11** Zinaida Sharko and Efim Kopelian in *Five Evenings* at the Leningrad Bolshoi Dramatic Theatre, 1959. Courtesy of the St Petersburg State Museum of Theatre and Music.

had a month-long residency. This production received mixed reviews, with elements of the Moscow press turning out to be more critical than their Leningrad counterparts. One review praised the production for managing to find 'deposits of gold in the souls' of these 'most ordinary people', noting the 'authentic' and 'life-like' depiction of 'human psychology' achieved by the actors.[53] But another reviewer criticized the production for turning the play into a 'hopeless drama of human relations' and found fault with the characterization of Il'in for failing to show the 'pure soul' of a 'man who dreams of home'.[54] These were sentiments shared by other audience members who seemed to struggle with the play's apparent lack of ideas and the heroes' negative traits. At a public conference for spectators held after a performance of the play on 8 February 1960, Kekin, a geologist by profession, said:

> Maybe there are correct observations of life here, correct characterizations by the actors, everything is life-like, everything is accurate, but for many years we have been taught, whether the staging is good or bad . . . (*laughter*) . . . that a play should have an idea. But here I don't get it. If it's any consolation you could say that I just didn't understand it.[55]

This audience member had grown used to watching plays that conveyed clear ideas and now seemed perplexed at the absence of an overt message. In fact, the open-ended plot and indecisive characters appeared to have confused a number of those at the conference. Trofimov, a worker at a car factory in Moscow, found it hard to accept that Tamara (played by Lilia Tolmacheva) could be a party member, insisting that in that case she should have 'strong convictions', whereas Tamara's character was 'kind of fragile and even negative'. Bril'iantshikova, a teacher from Moscow, was similarly unsatisfied and admitted that she did not like the play. Addressing Oleg Efremov, who played the role of Il'in, she asked him: 'And what prevented you from showing your feelings to the woman you idolized? Did the author prevent you?' Her dissatisfaction with the hero's inertia led her to question whether Efremov might have misinterpreted the playwright's script. It seemed as though many in the audience found it hard to comprehend the ambiguous characterization. One spectator, Chopenko, told those in attendance that he could not understand what stopped Il'in from doing what he really wanted (i.e. become a scientist) and accused him of not giving enough back to the state:

> A person doesn't go to an institute just like that, he is enticed by the profession. After the war, what ruined his life? What prevented him from devoting his life to that which he loved? And why suddenly become a driver? It turns out that he could have given a lot back to the state but gave less than he was capable of.

This spectator seemed genuinely at a loss to explain Il'in's seventeen-year absence and, unlike the critic Gaevskii, evidently saw no allusion to the Gulag in the character's vague account of his past. Moreover, the play seemed to have confounded many of the stereotypes about work and personal achievement that had become culturally embedded through traditional socialist realist dramas. Having grown accustomed to the dialectical narrative of the master plot, in which dreams are realized, Chopenko felt that Il'in's underachievement was incongruous and even selfish.

The depiction of flawed heroes on the stage seemed to have surprised a number of spectators. This fact was even commented on by one unnamed audience member who noted: 'The audience has become so used to the standard formula, to the division of characters into positive and negative, that from the start of the play many people could not comprehend it, they didn't know who was supposed to be positive and who was supposed to be negative.' This suggests that while some audience members struggled to interpret the play, others were keenly aware that it represented a break with the socialist realist canon. In one review, Nikolai Okhlopkov (artistic director of the Mayakovsky Theatre) praised the play, observing that the characters are not 'cardboard figures' but 'one's acquaintances and that's all'.[56] The sharp contrast between Okhlopkov's review and the views of conference participants such as Chopenko were based

**Figure 12** Oleg Efremov and Lilia Tolmacheva in *Five Evenings* at the Sovremennik Theatre-Studio, 1959. Courtesy of the Moscow Sovremennik Theatre.

on differing interpretations of realism. While Chopenko believed that Il'in's underachievement was illogical and therefore unrealistic, Okhlopkov believed that the characters' imperfections made them more believable and therefore highly realistic. Indeed, some spectators appreciated the proximity of the plot to their own personal experience. One anonymous speaker at the conference stated that the play was 'very close' to them, to the extent that they could almost see themself on the stage and found it difficult to talk about it without emotion. Perhaps the most articulate contribution to the public discussion came from a scriptwriter, Ganelina, who observed:

> Over the course of many years we have become used to being shown completely identical situations: a whole act would be taken up by a party meeting where everyone would be good without exception; if someone embraced a woman then it could only be his own wife. In this play the theatre gives the spectator a chance to think for themself, it knows that the spectator is not a fool and can work out themself who is positive, who is negative and what the main idea is.

In voicing her dissatisfaction with the homogeneity of a certain type of socialist realist drama in which the action was limited to staid party events (and strictly observed monogamy), Ganelina also articulated what she felt was contemporary about the play: it allowed audiences the space to think for themselves. It was a change in emphasis that she believed defined the Sovremennik as an institution. 'I come to this theatre like to my own home', she reflected. 'I am drawn here, whereas I am not drawn to the Art Theatre.' While the MAT had become suffocated by its ties to the party establishment, the Sovremennik was providing audiences with a kind of confessional performance that resonated with their experiences and gave them space to interpret those experiences in diverse and multiform ways.

This contrast between the Sovremennik and the MAT was also reflected in the production's stage design. The set was arranged in a minimalist style with a lack of naturalistic detail. Only a few necessary props were positioned on stage, with the space delineated by spotlights and the juxtaposition of plain scenery flats set at irregular angles and contrasting heights. Blue lighting made the floors and furniture appear cold and uncanny. One critic noted that the production showed the search for 'a new means of stage expression', while 'never giving the impression of a lack of realism'.[57] He observed that 'even when the stage is practically bare, you can tell immediately that it is a small station outside Moscow, or a workers dormitory, or the room of a young lawyer, all it takes is two or three details to create the atmosphere'.[58] This type of associative set design was very different from the one used in the play's first production at the Bolshoi Dramatic Theatre. In Leningrad, Tovstonogov's set observed a full naturalistic scheme, with Tamara's apartment recreated with three walls, connecting doors and all the expected furnishings. The curtain was lowered to the apartment's ceiling height to remove the empty space above the actors' heads. By contrast, the Sovremennik's embrace of open space and minimal properties provided another example of the merger of realistic acting with a more conventional design, part of the 'Vakhtangov compromise' which Akimov had utilized in his productions at the Lensovet Theatre; Pluchek and Iutkevich had embraced in their restagings of Mayakovsky; and which Tovstonogov had employed in his production of *An Optimistic Tragedy* at the Aleksandrinskii Theatre.

The Sovremennik's austere design was both a rejection of the MAT model and a deliberate attempt to foreground the characters in the play. The fluid and open nature of the set shifted the focus onto the actors, requiring them to demarcate the stage space through their movement and interactions with one other. Although different from what many theatregoers were used to, this production style was generally well received by audiences. Rozenberg, an engineer from Kiev, noted at the public conference on 8 February that it was the first time he had seen such a staging 'where a chair is not a chair, and a door is not a door' and that it was difficult for him but he 'got there' in the end. The Sovremennik's use of realist acting methods perhaps encouraged audiences to grant the more abstract stage aesthetic greater latitude. However, the press response to the staging was less amenable. One critic argued that the 'stage conventionality' obscured that which was 'concrete' and 'living' in the play.[59] She described the furniture as 'resembling that of a hospital' and complained that its 'unexpected blueness' made the production 'cold' and hindered the true depiction of the characters. The critic was unhappy that the Sovremennik had interpreted Volodin's play in such a downbeat manner and felt that the non-naturalistic set design had contributed to this misreading. Reminding her readers that the cast were 'recent students' of the MAT School, where they had been taught a 'sense of truth', the critic suggested caustically that the actors were finding the transition to professional work a little difficult.[60] The Sovremennik's links to the MAT ensured that its treatment in the press was often demanding and inconsistent. As part of the heralded lineage of the MAT, the Sovremennik was accepted into the cultural mainstream. But this meant that when it deviated from the MAT tradition in terms of stage interpretation or aesthetic, the Sovremennik was often accused of recalcitrance and chastised like a wayward son.

The Sovremennik's production of *Five Evenings* was particularly unpopular with the Ministry of Culture. One report accused the Sovremennik of 'propagandizing petit-bourgeois ideology from the stage' with a hero who has 'no note-worthy qualities' and is 'intentionally down-to-earth'.[61] The play's ambiguous, unremarkable characters and its pessimistic portrayal of the war and its aftermath presented an undesirable image of Soviet life that the Ministry was at pains to reject. Reflecting on the difference between his play and others of that time, Volodin noted:

> On the stage in those days were girls in bright dresses. In the last act they would be rewarded with the love of an innovator who had discovered a new tool angle. Tamara, though, was an unmarried woman not in the prime of her youth. Someone, I recall, asked me: 'What are you trying to say? That after the war there were fewer men?' It was still a serious accusation: the interrupted fates.[62]

While most Soviet plays of the post-war period mythologized the conflict and enshrined its legacy as one of patriotic glory and noble sacrifice, *Five Evenings* gestured towards a different kind of legacy: the catastrophic death tolls, the bereaved loved ones who could not move on, the incarceration of loyal soldiers in the camps and all the other 'interrupted fates'. In this sense, the debate over realism was not just a dispute over correct theatre practice and acting methods but also a battle over the narrative of people's experiences: over what was considered a realistic, authentic representation of Soviet life. For many audience members, Volodin's play was realistic because it depicted a reality that was similar to their own. However, for other spectators, and officials in the Ministry of Culture, the play's bleakness represented a 'neorealism' that was no more authentic than any other narrative and much less desirable. One ministry report from September 1959 claimed that Volodin was talented, but that in *Five Evenings* 'he has shown ordinary Soviet people not at their best, but in the backyards of their private lives, he has deprived them of the fresh air of modernity'.[63] In the eyes of the Ministry, Volodin's mistake was to focus on the 'private' aspect of his character's lives rather than the communal. Volodin's exposure of Soviet people 'not at their best' was seen as invasive, because it allowed private suffering to intrude into the state's idealistic public narrative. The documentary feel of Volodin's close-ups of post-war Soviet life led to the interpretation of this form of drama in cinematic terms and allowed the Ministry to see in this 'neorealism' a threat to official socialist realism.

By the end of the decade, the Sovremennik was coming under increasing pressure from officials in the Ministry of Culture on account of productions such as *Five Evenings*. In an open letter to the Ministry of Culture and the editors of *Pravda* and *Sovetskaia kul'tura* published on 2 February 1960, a group of directors, writers and editors, including Ruben Simonov, Viktor Rozov and Ilia Ehrenburg, offered their support to the Sovremennik, stressing its good work and asking the Ministry to help it find a permanent home.[64] The Theatre-Studio's lack of a reliable rehearsal and performance space was described as one of the main factors hindering its progress. By the beginning of 1960 the Sovremennik's arrangement with the Sovetskaia Hotel was becoming untenable as the hotel management would cancel advertised performances at short notice if foreign delegations were arriving. In January 1960 the Sovremennik was prevented from staging eight of its scheduled performances and had not been allocated a single day in April and only six days for May.[65] Concerns about its ability to stage productions and criticism of its repertoire had put the Sovremennik in a difficult position. At a two-day conference to discuss the work of drama theatres, organized by the Ministry of Culture's theatre department on 14 and 15 March 1960, the artistic director of the Moscow Satire Theatre, Valentin Pluchek, stated that he was worried for the Sovremennik's future on account of the furore surrounding its production of Skachkov's *Breakers of the Silence*, noting that the play had been a 'big mistake'.[66] According to one report, the production was withdrawn from the repertoire for displaying 'political immaturity' and 'a conciliatory attitude towards bourgeois philosophy'.[67] In response, the Sovremennik's artistic council wrote to the first secretary of the party's Moscow City Committee, Vladimir Ustinov, defending both this production and *Five Evenings*, but it did little to ease the pressure.[68] The Presidium of the artistic council for dramatic theatres of the Ministry of Culture met on 20 March, specifically to discuss the work of the Sovremennik Theatre-Studio and commissioned a report on its activities.[69] However, rather than acquiescing to the pressure, the Sovremennik took a bold and risky step. Four days later, on 24 March 1960, it staged a production of Evgenii Shvarts's fairy-tale satire *The Naked King*, which had been banned since 1934. As we will see in the following chapter, it was an act of defiance that would see the Theatre-Studio threatened with closure, but which also established an enduring legacy with audiences as one of the most memorable theatrical events of the Thaw.

6

# The fairy tale that would not come true
## Staging Evgenii Shvarts, 1960–3

Following the defeat of the 'anti-party group' in June 1957, Khrushchev became the undisputed leader of the Soviet Union. When Nikolai Bulganin was forced to step down as prime minister in March 1958, Khrushchev took the role for himself. This put him in charge of both the party and the government, despite having previously criticized Stalin for combining the two roles himself. With no one left to challenge him, Khrushchev's style of leadership changed. Whereas before he would consult with his peers in the Presidium, now he became increasingly autocratic, arrogant and aloof. At the Twenty-First Party Congress held in late January 1959, members of the Presidium flattered and fawned over Khrushchev. Aleksei Kirichenko, at that time the second-highest ranking figure in the party, lauded Khrushchev for his 'outstanding activity, Leninist firmness, devotion to principle, initiative [...] and enormous organizational work'.[1] Despite having been the man responsible for exposing Stalin's 'cult of personality' back in 1956, now a new cult was developing around Khrushchev, which he did little to supress.

In Evgenii Shvarts's fairy-tale satire *The Dragon* (1943), after the hero Lancelot has killed the Dragon and freed the townspeople from his iron rule, something unexpected happens. The Mayor, who had been meekly serving the Dragon while he was alive, spots his chance after the Dragon's death and seizes power for himself. The Mayor spreads the lie that he killed the Dragon, not Lancelot, and imprisons anyone who disagrees: one tyrant is replaced by another and the cycle continues. Although when he wrote the play Shvarts could not have foreseen how Stalin's succession would play out, *The Dragon* appeared remarkably prescient when it was finally given a stage run in 1962 at the Leningrad Comedy Theatre. Audiences saw in Pavel Sukhanov's Mayor an allusion to Khrushchev and flocked to see the play before it was axed a year later, as another cultural frost set in. *The Dragon* at the Comedy Theatre was the last in a series of productions of Shvarts's work that sprung up during the Thaw. After a number of his plays were banned by the Committee for Artistic Affairs in the 1940s, Shvarts went into self-imposed hibernation during the last years of Stalin's rule. However, the Thaw brought with it new opportunities to stage his work and a renewed interest in the fairy-tale genre as a vehicle for satire and social critique. The popular Soviet anthem 'The Aviators' March' (1923) proclaimed: 'We were born to make fairy tales come true.'[2] But if the revelations of Khrushchev's 'secret speech' and the harrowing private narratives of Gulag returnees attested to anything, then it was the realization that the Soviet fairy tale had somehow turned sour. In this light, Shvarts's plays epitomized the spirit of the Thaw with their allegorical critiques of authoritarian power, corruption and bureaucracy; and in their playful, grotesque style which demanded a non-realist mise en scène. Therefore in both theme and form, Shvarts's plays broke with the norms of Stalinist socialist realism and offered audiences a new lens with which to consider the society around them: through the discerning, prelapsarian eyes of a child.

## Evgenii Shvarts and the fairy-tale play

Before he began writing plays in the late 1920s, Evgenii Shvarts worked in children's literature, serving as personal secretary to the children's author Kornei Chukovskii and in the children's department of the state publishing house in Leningrad. Shvarts's first plays for children were staged at the Leningrad Theatre for Young People, with works such as *Little Red Riding Hood* (1936) and *The Snow Queen* (1938) becoming firmly established in the repertoire. These plays adopt story lines and motifs from literary fairy tales by writers such as Hans Christian Andersen and Charles Perrault but combine them with references to everyday life to achieve a blend of fantasy and realism. Shvarts recognized that the fairy tale was a useful genre for writing about contemporary issues as it allows the writer to cloak allusions to contemporary society within the familiar backdrop of the struggle between good and evil (which is the master plot of all fairy tales).[3]

The social value of fairy tales had been a topic of fierce debate for the Bolsheviks during the 1920s. One of the most vehement critics of the genre was Lenin's widow Nadezhda Krupskaia who, as chair of Glavpolitprosvet (Central Committee on Political Education), had overseen the removal of fairy tales from Soviet libraries along with other texts considered to have an adverse influence on child development. Krupskaia was supported by Soviet child psychologists and literary theorists who believed that fairy tales were harmful remnants of bourgeois ideology that impacted negatively on children's developing minds.⁴ However, Maksim Gorky's return to the Soviet Union in 1931 and his role in the formulation of socialist realism saw folklore and fairy tales return to favour. In his speech at the First Soviet Writers' Congress in 1934, Gorky praised the folktale as a genre that belonged to the working classes and called on Soviet writers to model their characters on epic folk heroes.⁵ This call was repeated by the children's author Samuil Marshak who gave a speech at the congress in which he advocated for new Soviet fairy tales that would combine the heroic and utopian elements of folk tradition with Marxist-Leninist ideology.⁶ Following the congress, the fairy tale was promoted as a literary genre capable of conveying the idealized Soviet worldview to readers and audiences.⁷

In the era of Stakhanovite record-breakers and the heroic feats of Soviet aviators and explorers, the fairy tale seemed not just a suitable conduit for such narratives but a means of inspiring others to turn their ordinary reality into something extraordinary. Marina Balina has argued that the socialist realist fairy tale 'extended the normal limits of fairy tale temporality into a contemporary Soviet reality [. . .] Soviet life becomes the embodiment of the fairy tale utopian dream that finally comes true'.⁸ One popular example of the socialist realist fairy tale was the musical comedy *The Radiant Path* (1940), based on a play by Viktor Ardov and directed by Grigorii Aleksandrov. Originally titled *Cinderella*, but renamed at Stalin's suggestion, the film tells the rags-to-riches story of a humble maid turned Stakhanovite weaver who eventually becomes a deputy to the Supreme Soviet. The film depicted the life of its heroine Tanya Morozova (played by Liubov' Orlova) as a fairy tale come true in contemporary Moscow. But while socialist realist fairy tales transposed fantasy tropes into a realistic setting, Shvarts's fairy-tale plays did the opposite. Shvarts takes contemporary issues and places them in a fantastical setting which accentuates and parodies them in a grotesque manner. Shvarts's fairy-tale plays are grotesque not only because they juxtapose opposites (i.e. they combine the real and the fantastical), but because they defamiliarize the spectator by repeatedly switching back and forth between these genres: between contemporary details and the clichés of the fairy-tale tradition.⁹ This generic ambiguity creates the space for a variety of interpretations and improvisations which actors took advantage of when tailoring their roles for performance.

The first fairy-tale play that Shvarts wrote for adults was *The Princess and the Swineherd* (1934), which Nikolai Akimov began rehearsing at the Leningrad Comedy Theatre in 1935, before it was banned by Glavrepertkom in the wake of the anti-formalism campaign. The play combines three fairy tales by Hans Christian Anderson into a two-act play: 'The Princess and the Swineherd', 'The Princess and the Pea' and 'The Emperor's New Clothes'. Shvarts wrote it ostensibly as a satire on Hitler's rise to power and the militarization of Nazi Germany. However, parallels could be drawn with the bureaucracy of Soviet society and Stalin's emerging cult of personality – which led the censor to ban it while it was still in preliminary rehearsals. The play would eventually be staged twenty-five years later by the Sovremennik Theatre-Studio under the title *The Naked King*.

The first of Shvarts's adult fairy-tale plays to be staged publicly was *The Shadow* (1940), based on a story by Hans Christian Andersen, which premiered at the Leningrad Comedy Theatre on 11 April 1940, directed by Akimov. In Shvarts's version an idealistic Scholar visits a kingdom and falls in love with a Princess. At the same time, the Scholar loses his shadow, which returns as a cunning and ruthless figure who steals the Princess from him and takes the throne. Eventually the Scholar triumphs and the Shadow flees: however, the Scholar decides to reject the Princess and the throne, departing instead to track down the Shadow and erase its presence from the earth. Despite extensive changes to the plot, characters and setting, Shvarts's rendering of the story keeps intact its fundamental idea: that all people are capable of evil, symbolized in the doubling of the Scholar and his shadow. The Scholar's decision to reject the throne at the end suggests a general disillusionment with autocratic leaders in favour of the slow process of tracking down and eliminating the shadow (the evil) inside everyone, a recurring motif in Shvarts's plays. In his production, Akimov paid particular attention to comic details and utilized an array of slapstick episodes and pyrotechnic effects, drawing on the acrobatic skills of actors such as Aleksandr Beniaminov, who played the Minister of Finance, and Erast Garin who played the Shadow.[10] Garin had made his name as an actor at the Meyerhold Theatre, playing Khlestakov in *The Government Inspector* (1926) and Chatskii in *Woe to Wit* (1928); here he brought his grotesque style to Shvarts's fantastical drama.

During the Second World War, Shvarts was airlifted out of besieged Leningrad in December 1941 and eventually found his way to Dushanbe, the capital of the Tajik Soviet Socialist Republic, where the Leningrad Comedy Theatre had also been evacuated. It was here that he completed his play *The Dragon*, a re-telling of the myth of 'St George and the Dragon' with topical references to Nazi Germany. The play was rehearsed by Akimov and the Comedy Theatre while in Dushanbe and received approval by Glavrepertkom. In June 1944 the Comedy Theatre moved from Soviet Tajikistan to Moscow, where *The Dragon* premiered on 4 August in the Moscow Operetta Theatre.[11] However, soon afterwards Akimov was summoned by the chair of the Committee for Artistic Affairs, who informed him that the play would not be allowed any further performances. Much later Akimov learned that some high-ranking official 'had seen something in the play that wasn't there'.[12] Or was it there? The broad allegorical resonance of Shvarts's play meant that audiences could make their own inference as to its meaning. While one spectator might view the Dragon's eradication of gypsies from the town's population as an obvious reference to Nazi racial persecution, another might regard the Mayor's usurpation of power after the Dragon's death as a critique of the Soviet one-party state. This ambiguity certainly troubled one reviewer of the play, which was published in a collotype edition of 500 copies in the spring of 1944. In a hostile article, the critic condemned *The Dragon* as nothing more than a 'lampoon of the heroic liberation struggle of peoples against Hitlerism'.[13] What really riled the critic was the fact that the townspeople are 'in awe of their dragon' and he complained that the people seem like 'hopelessly crippled egotistical philistines'.[14] At a time when the patriotic fighting spirit of the people was being eulogized in the press, any suggestion that societies may become complicit in their own suppression was anathema. The play would not be performed again until 1962, when it was revived by Akimov at the Comedy Theatre in Leningrad.

On returning to the Comedy Theatre in 1956, Akimov began his second tenure with another play by Shvarts, *An Ordinary Miracle*, which premiered on 30 April that year. As the playwright notes in the prologue, the 'ordinary miracle' described by the title is love; the play's underlying idea is that love is more powerful than magic. To illustrate this, Shvarts inverts the fairy-tale trope in which an evil wizard transforms a person into an animal, a curse that can only be broken by true love, usually embodied by a kiss which returns them to human form. *An Ordinary Miracle*, however, tells the tale of a good wizard who turns a bear into a man. Although the young man believes that if he kisses the Princess he will turn back into a bear, in fact when he does so he remains a man to the surprise of everyone, including the wizard – the only possible conclusion being that true love triumphs over magic. Although sentimental in its theme, the play premiered only a few months after the Twentieth Party Congress and so resonated with the expressions of optimism recalled by many who lived through that period.[15] In Akimov's set design a large panel in the roof of the wizard's house was missing, which allowed a branch of Japanese cherry blossom to protrude into the room from outside – an obvious symbol of the coming spring and of the Thaw. A year later, Akimov staged Shvarts's play *The Story of a Young Couple*, which he had written while evacuated in Dushanbe under the title *One Year*. Like most of his works the play blends realism with fairy-tale theatricality. The young newlyweds Marusia and Sergei argue over everyday problems, quickly make up, then start arguing again, all the while being observed by a pair of puppet narrators – a teddy bear and a doll – who comment on the action to the audience, like a Greek chorus. The play premiered on 30 December 1957, but Shvarts died only a few weeks afterwards and never saw it performed. Three years later, Akimov revived *The Shadow*, which premiered for a second time on 19 November 1960. The role of the Shadow was played by Lev Milinder, who echoed Garin's original performance with his acrobatic technique and lithe plasticity, creating a hostile and inhuman figure.[16]

Garin and his wife Khesia Lokshina had, in fact, been the first directors to stage Shvarts's *An Ordinary Miracle*, which premiered at the Moscow Theatre of Cinema Actors on 18 January 1956. The production was designed by Boris Erdman and played to full houses throughout the year. The theatre marked the occasion of Shvarts's sixtieth birthday with its sixtieth production of the play on 21 October 1956. Not long afterwards, however, the theatre company was liquidated by the Ministry of Culture and Erdman's sets were burned so as not to take up any space.[17] Garin directed and acted in the play, performing the role of the King (the Princess's father) as an 'ordinary despot', both wicked and mediocre. To illustrate this character type, Garin created a skit around the King's initial entrance. At first the audience only saw the head of the monarch, which greeted them with the words: 'I am the King my dears!' Everything below the head needed to be imagined: the regal poise, the royal mantle and so on, but then the King took a step forward and his naked legs came into view. The audience laughed, its expectations confounded, as the King walked towards them dressed in a Scottish kilt. Sitting down on a chair, toying with the pleats of his kilt, the King declared: 'I am a terrible man, I am a tyrant.'[18] The play of foreignness and femininity was both comical and defamiliarizing for Soviet audiences; while the contrast between imagined robes and real nudity was a device that the Sovremennik Theatre-Studio would exploit fully in its production of Shvarts's *The Naked King* four years later.

## *The Naked King*, 1960

At the start of the 1959–60 season, the Sovremennik Theatre-Studio was under pressure due a number of recent controversial productions.[19] Nevertheless, that autumn it requested permission from the Ministry of Culture to stage Shvarts's play *The Princess and the Swineherd*, renaming it *The Naked King*. Earlier that year, Margarita Mikaelian had successfully co-directed Anatolii Kuznetsov's *Sequel to a Legend* at the Sovremennik with Oleg Efremov. Mikaelian was then invited back by the Theatre-Studio to direct a children's play that could be staged during the school holidays. At a general meeting of the Sovremennik company, held on 17 October 1959, the actors discussed Mikaelian's proposal to stage *The Naked King*.[20] Mikaelian noted that the play was a parody of Nazi Germany and suggested that they could stage two versions: one for adults and another for children. Most of those present agreed that the text was excellent but argued that it would have to be a play for adults rather than children, with a number of actors questioning the play's ideological meaning. The actor Igor Kvasha noted cautiously that 'if it is going to be a production about the cult of personality then no one wants that'.[21] Efremov also expressed grave doubts due to the play's 'double meaning', the fact that 'it simultaneously exposes the evils of fascist society and our own society during the time of the cult of personality'.[22] Efremov insisted that if they were to stage the play then they would have to drop all references to Soviet Russia, but that as long as it was approved by the Ministry he was happy to proceed. After this endorsement, a majority of the troupe voted in favour of rehearsing the play.

Before rehearsals could start, however, the Sovremennik had to obtain permission from the Ministry of Culture. The play was included in a repertoire plan for the season which was sent to the deputy head of the theatre department at the Ministry of Culture, Boris Pokarzhevskii, on 28 November 1959.[23] Mikaelian also went to see Pokarzhevskii in order to obtain permission to start rehearsals, recalling that he was 'overcautious' but gave the authorization.[24] As was the protocol, a representative from the Ministry then came to watch a run-through of the play, held on 6 February 1960, which was also attended by critics, after which, to Mikaelian's surprise, the Ministry gave approval for the production without further comment.[25] After the run-through, the theatre held a discussion with the actors, staff and critics. This discussion indicated that the issues concerning the play's 'double meaning' had still not been resolved and that many were worried about possible ramifications.[26] The actor Vladlen Paulus revealed that he was 'afraid of the ideological resonance of the play'.[27] Vladimir Kumanin, the Sovremennik's government-appointed administrative director, also questioned whether the production was suitable, arguing that he could not see the allusion to contemporary West Germany, which would be the only basis on which to stage it. Igor Kvasha, who played the King's First Minister, confirmed that the play would surely evoke associations with Russia, rather than with the

West, but insisted that he did not want to impersonate someone specific, but rather a general caricature of a Russian bureaucrat. In spite of these doubts some at the meeting also spoke in support of the play. Theatre critic Vladimir Sappak praised the quality of the acting and the wit of the production, insisting that what they needed was 'hardly a play directed at West Germany but one directed at the auditorium'.[28] The actress Liliia Tolmacheva agreed with him and noted that it was not important if the production 'evokes associations with our recent past'.[29] The critic Maiia Turovskaia, a close friend of Mikaelian, similarly argued that fears over the play's ideological tone were unfounded, suggesting that the play could be directed at both the West and at targets closer to home. A number of the actors called for Efremov to take over control of the directing from Mikaelian to resolve some of the issues they were discussing. However, Efremov tried to calm the doubters, arguing that even though there was 'visible hatred towards the cult of personality' in the play, today's run-through had proved that they could stage a different interpretation of the text. The way to do this, he said, was through the acting style, ensuring that the associations were complex, rather than direct. Efremov insisted that it was important for the theatre to show it could be 'sincere' and 'life-like' in this genre but equally not end up with a production that 'sticks a finger up at the past'.[30] Whether Efremov and the other actors genuinely believed that the production could be staged in a way that avoided allusions to Soviet society is unclear. Knowing that the meeting was being recorded, there may have been a certain amount of 'playing to the camera' going on, with the actors covering their backs in case of censure further down the line.

The play premiered on 24 March 1960 while the Sovremennik was on tour in Leningrad and was billed underneath the established productions of *Two Colours* and *Sequel to a Legend*.[31] Leningrad officials and press were caught off guard by *The Naked King* and, assuming that it must have been fully approved of in Moscow, local critics wrote glowing reviews praising the daringness of the production. This consequently made it much harder for the authorities in Moscow to ban the play outright once the Sovremennik returned home.[32] One Leningrad critic writing in *Smena* commended the play's 'irony' and 'wit', insisting that 'one could go and see it once, thrice, and probably even more times with the same sense of joy and fun'.[33] The critic lauded the theatre's new creative direction, claiming that 'in front of the director and actors a whole sea has opened up for brave swimming', and he stressed how important it was that humour is able to expose 'the terrible power of banality, stupidity and falsity'.[34] Another review in *Leningradskaia pravda* praised the 'life-like, contemporary intonation' of the actors, noting the likeness of the First Minister and the Minister of Tender

Feelings to contemporary personalities, and stated that the play could 'go on to become a classic'.³⁵ Despite Efremov's earlier insistence that the character associations should be complex and not direct, by the time the production reached the stage some of the cast had modelled their characters on well-known public individuals. For example, audiences were said to have recognized in Viktor Sergachev's Minister of Tender Feelings, a likeness to the sycophantic Vasilii Zakharchenko, chief editor of the journal *Tekhnika molodezhi* (Technology for Young People). Zakharchenko wrote the script for a fawning documentary in honour of Khrushchev, released in June 1961, entitled *Our Nikita Sergeevich*.³⁶ By the time the Ministry of Culture in Moscow realized what was happening, the play had already sold out. In fact, tickets for the play were bought up on the very first day of the tour, with people queuing through the night to get hold of them.³⁷ 'All of Leningrad' attended the premiere at the Palace of Culture of the Five-Year Plan, including directors Georgii Tovstonogov, Grigorii Kozintsev and Nikolai Akimov.³⁸ Leningrad artist Valentin Dorrer designed the sets and costumes for the production, using soft pastel colours to create a childlike effect. The podiums on the stage floor were turquoise, the streetlamps wore bowties and the impressionistic dwellings painted on the backdrop were coloured in pink, mauve and light blue. Edik Kolmanovskii composed the music and the poet Mikhail Svetlov was commissioned to write lyrics for the songs. When choreographing the scenes, Mikaelian encouraged the actors to use grotesque and eccentric movements that befitted Dorrer's extravagantly stylized costumes. The sudden movements and unnatural poses of the Princess's foreign governess (played by Ol'ga Stanitsyna), who wore a checked dress and bowler hat with bull's horns, reminded one critic of the style of Tairov or Meyerhold 'whose name appeared to hover in the air above the absent curtain'.³⁹

In Act One, Genrikh the swineherd falls in love with Princess Genrietta. However, she is due to marry a neighbouring King, a feared despot who rules over his kingdom with an iron fist. Genrikh devises a plan with his friend Khristian the weaver to disrupt the wedding so that he can marry Genrietta instead. In Act Two they travel to the King's castle and promise to make the monarch the most beautiful suit in the world for his wedding day. In a re-working of the story of 'The Emperor's New Clothes', they tell the King that the cloth they will use for the suit is so pure and subtle that only the most intelligent people in the kingdom can see it. Of course, in reality, there is no such cloth. Evgenii Evstigneev's portrayal of the King was Janus-faced, switching abruptly between comic silliness and the rages of a tyrant. Mid-way through the rehearsal process, Evstigneev had changed his approach to the role so that his character was no longer simply a caricature but at times appeared realistic and plausible. To help create this split persona, Evstigneev's appearance was full of contradictions: he wore resplendent pink robes with an ermine trim, a black bow tie and gold shoes, but would throw his cloak over his shoulder casually like a bath towel and wore his flimsy crown (made out of papier-mâché) jauntily at an angle like a flat cap.[40] Critics noted that Evstigneev's King was both a 'narrow-minded dunce' and a 'monster with a glassy appearance'.[41] Mikaelian recalled that he played the role so that 'behind the visible silliness from time to time there appeared [. . .] flashes of rage and displays of cruelty'.[42] In this way, Evstigneev's character ridiculed the cult of personality by reducing it to a kind of infantile egomania, while also remembering its impulsive outbursts of violence.

In Shvarts's fairy-tale world, the King inspires fear throughout the kingdom: a militarized land where the birds fly in formation, racial purity is obsessed over and books are burned in public squares. But alongside these allusions towards Nazi Germany, Shvarts included scenes that resonated closer to home, ones in which the King is fawned on by his terrified courtiers. In one scene, particularly beloved by audiences, the First Minister would shamelessly flatter the King and in the process parody the sycophancy endemic within the Soviet bureaucracy.

> **First Minister:** Your majesty! You know that I'm an honest old man, an absolutely straight old man. I tell the truth straight to a man's face even when the truth happens to be unpleasant. You see, I've been standing here all the time, I saw you waking up, I heard you – to put it crudely – laughing at things, and so on. Allow me to tell you straight, Your majesty . . .
>
> **King:** Yes, yes, go on, tell me. You know I'm never cross with you.
>
> **First Minister:** Permit me to tell you straight to your face, brutally, in my old man's way – you're a great man, Sire!
>
> **King:** (*Very pleased*) Now, now . . . why should you?
>
> **First Minister:** No, Your majesty, no, I just can't contain myself! I must repeat this – forgive my lack of self-control – you're a giant! A blinding light!
>
> **King:** Oh-oh! What a fellow! You really mustn't . . . ![43]

Members of the cast recalled nostalgically that during these scenes the audience would applaud practically every line, until the atmosphere felt like a concert.[44] During one performance, Evstigneev improvised and went off-script, inviting the First Minister to sit on the throne with him. Kvasha's First Minister looked terrified at first but eventually perched gingerly on the edge of the throne. Then the King went further and took off his crown and placed it on his minister's head. The First Minister squirmed but soon became accustomed to it and settled down

**Figure 13** Evgenii Evstigneev and Igor Kvasha in *The Naked King* at the Sovremennik Theatre-Studio, 1960. Courtesy of the Moscow Sovremennik Theatre.

on the throne, even putting his arm around the King's shoulders. The audience watched with bated breath to see what would happen next, perhaps recalling Stalin's habit of chopping down his favourites whenever they got too powerful. Then as quick as a flash, the King grabbed the First Minister by the scruff of the neck and booted him onto the floor.[45]

The brazen obsequiousness of the King's courtiers also provides the key to the play's dramatic peripeteia, for when the King sends his servants to view the suit they are too scared to admit that they cannot see it and so return glowing reports of its beauty. When the suit is finally revealed to him, the King is forced to play along with the lie in order to avoid humiliation in front of his subordinates. On his wedding day, the King parades naked in front of the people who remain silent until a little boy points out the truth and the crowd finally descends into uproar. The role of the child, unencumbered by the compliant *habitus* of adulthood and so uniquely able to speak out, is therefore crucial to the play. The King is dethroned and the cult of personality is metaphorically disrobed. When staging the final scene, the Sovremennik decided not to show the King completely in the nude but carried him around in a sedan chair with only his naked upper body visible to the audience. To show full nudity on the stage was taboo in the Soviet Union but leaving something to the spectators' imagination was, perhaps, even more effective: daring them to complete the image for themselves in their heads. Evstigneev's bare torso, floating above the stage, was a suitably grotesque image with which to close the show.

In his well-known study of Rabelais, Mikhail Bakhtin observed that the grotesque concept was central to the spirit of carnival in the Middle Ages, when 'carnival celebrated temporary liberation from the prevailing truth of the established order; marked the suspension of all hierarchical rank, privileges, norms and prohibitions'.[46] In many ways, the tremendous popularity of *The Naked King* stemmed from a similar sense of temporary liberation that it brought to the auditorium. Within the fictionalized world of the performance, just as in the medieval carnival, life was turned upside down for a moment, hierarchies were inverted and the symbol of power belittled through 'carnival laughter'.[47] By laughing at the characters on stage, and through them the system of patronage and privilege they represented, the spectator is 'emancipated', in Rancière's terms, connecting their own experience to the performance and using it to interpret the world for themself.[48] It was this 'sovereignty of the audience' that led Plato to denounce the ancient theatre as a dangerous 'theatrocracy', a designation, Rancière notes, that gestures to theatre's subversive potential for political disruption.[49] The split world of the theatre stage, in which actors can be two people at once, implicitly contradicted Plato's orderly distribution of functions and places in the *Republic*, by challenging the principle that people can only have one role in life, assigned at birth. For Rancière, the theatre is 'a place that suspends conventional relations of obedience or deference'.[50] With a production such as *The Naked King*, this kind of *dissensus* was doubly enacted: both in the muddling of identities and temporalities common to all theatre performance and in the carnivalesque satire of the play itself.

The experience for audiences was, in many ways, cathartic. Spectators revelled in a performance that temporarily subverted the established order and spoke to a collective experience that was overlooked by mainstream discourse. In one piece of improvisation, Oleg Tabakov, in his role as the Conductor, carried around a small knapsack with him that suggested a change of clothes in case he was suddenly arrested.[51] During the purges, many people had carried these bundles around with them, not knowing when they might be taken away abruptly to prison. At the moment in the play when the soldiers lead away the Conductor, Tabakov would clutch the bundle tightly to his chest, a gesture which, he recalled, always drew a strong reaction from the audience.[52] In this respect, the production took part in the process of de-Stalinization that had been set in motion by the 'secret speech' four years earlier. Within Shvarts's

**Figure 14** Evgenii Evstigneev in *The Naked King* at the Sovremennik Theatre-Studio, 1960. Courtesy of the Moscow Sovremennik Theatre.

upside-down fairy-tale world, the actors parodied the cult of personality and its continued legacy in Soviet society. Although Khrushchev had performed the initial disrobing of Stalin himself in February 1956, the party's strict response to public displays of dissent and unfettered criticism of its record had led to confusion in the years that followed. Perpetually afraid of precipitating a domino effect by ceding too much control, the party leadership clamped down hard on independent acts of de-Stalinization that took place outside of its purview. Moreover, the emergence after 1957 of Khrushchev's own burgeoning cult of personality and his increasingly autocratic leadership made the party highly sensitive to criticism of leader cults, both past and present.

The Sovremennik arrived back in Moscow after its tour in Leningrad at the beginning of April 1960. Immediately on arrival, the Sovremennik's artistic council, including Efremov and Mikaelian, was summoned to appear before the board of the Ministry of Culture. The Minister for Culture Nikolai Mikhailov was furious and demanded to know who had sanctioned the play.[53] It was revealed to be Pokarzhevskii, the deputy head of the Ministry's theatre department, who was consequently fired. During the meeting an aide to the minister entered and read the Theatre-Studio a resolution from the Sovetskaia Hotel on the cancellation of its contract, making it homeless. A report on the Sovremennik's activities had already been commissioned prior to the premiere of *The Naked King*, and this report now formed the basis of an investigation into how the production had reached the stage. The report, issued on 18 April, stated that the Theatre-Studio's board had declared the play to be 'educational work' to be used only as 'training material for improving acting techniques'.[54] According to the report, the Ministry had been given assurances that the play would not be transferred to the main stage as part of the theatre's forthcoming repertoire. However, this claim is contradicted by the repertoire plan sent to Pokarzhevskii on 28 November, which had listed *The Naked King* first in its planned performances for the second half of the season, with the premiere date set for 25 January 1960. The report went on to insist that the Sovremennik had failed to interpret the play as Shvarts had intended, 'as a direct response to Hitler's rise in Germany', and claimed that the production would have been justified only if it had targeted 'current West-German militarism and revanchism'.[55] The report demanded that the Theatre-Studio's artistic council be dissolved and a new one set up that included representatives from the Moscow Art Theatre, the Ministry of Culture's theatre department, the Writers' Union and the Central Committee.[56] Much of the blame for the production was subsequently directed towards the heads of the MAT, who were accused of failing to provide sufficient guidance and neglecting their responsibilities to the young collective.[57]

On 2 November the Ministry of Culture issued a decree which noted 'serious failings' in the work of theatres' artistic councils and announced that these councils could no longer be formed autonomously by theatre's themselves but only on application to the Minister of Culture.[58] Following this, on 14 December 1960, the Ministry of Culture issued another decree which criticized the lack of plays on 'the great themes of modernity' in current theatre repertoires and stated that the Ministry of Culture would now intervene more rigorously in decisions over repertoire selection.[59] Although not referring to the Sovremennik Theatre-Studio explicitly, it was clear that these decrees were issued in order to prevent a play such as *The Naked King* slipping through the net again.

After the cancellation of its contract with the Sovetskaia Hotel, the Sovremennik managed to book the Moscow Pushkin Theatre, where *The Naked King* premiered on 5 April and immediately sold out, along with tickets for all of the Sovremennik's other productions. Ticket queues stretched half a kilometre down the street and were overseen by the police, who drove away people carrying signs offering to buy spare tickets to the show. Not knowing when they might be shut down, the Sovremennik performed *The Naked King* nearly every day over the summer, thirty times a month at the Pushkin Theatre and then at the Theatre of Cinema Actors. Mikhail Kozakov, who played the role of the Chamberlain, suggested that the play was not banned outright because it was already too late: 'the bird had flown the nest'.[60] Rather than risking a public outcry by cancelling the production and having to refund tickets, the Ministry of Culture let it continue. All the same, it sent out a warning that such productions were unacceptable by allowing rumours to spread that it might close down the Sovremennik completely. *The Naked King* was also condemned harshly by sections of the Moscow press. One review published in *Teatral'naia zhizn'* (an official organ of the Ministry of Culture) assured readers that, in spite of all the fuss, those who go and see the play are 'disappointed'.[61] The critic described the production as a simple '*kapustnik*' and a 'dubious theatrical game' that has 'a dishonourable attitude towards life'.[62] She went on to explain that the production was 'bankrupt' because 'at the blossoming of Soviet democracy it gives insinuation to facts about our society which the party has already spoken of long ago at the top of its voice, clearly and directly'. This was clearly a reference to the disclosures made in the 'secret speech' and suggested that one of the Ministry of Culture's main objections to *The Naked King* was that its performative iconoclasm was being staged in public outside the control of party and government.

In April, when rumours that the authorities would shut down the Sovremennik were rife, Khrushchev had invited the Soviet intelligentsia to a party at his dacha in Semenovskoe (formerly one of Stalin's residences). The creative elite of Moscow was in attendance: film directors, actors, ballet stars. All the major Moscow theatre directors had been invited, with the exception of Efremov. However, Nina Doroshina, the Sovremennik actress who played Princess Genrietta, was scheduled to perform as part of a variety concert put on for the guests. Efremov told Doroshina to find Khrushchev at the party and beg him not to shut down the Sovremennik. During a break in the concert, Doroshina went to look for Khrushchev but bumped into Ruben Simonov, director at the Vakhtangov Theatre, who immediately stopped her. 'Don't look for Khrushchev', he told her, 'what are you to him. He doesn't know about your theatre or about the play, it would be useless.'[63] Instead, Simonov directed her towards a lady standing nearby talking to Anastas Mikoyan, the deputy head of the government. It was Elena Furtseva, who would shortly replace Mikhailov as the Minister of Culture. Under Furtseva's leadership, the Sovremennik received a stay of execution, although she insisted on certain cuts being made to the script of *The Naked King* to remove lines which suggested anti-Semitism was prevalent in Soviet society.[64]

One prominent show of support for the Sovremennik came from the literary critic Aleksandr Karaganov in an article titled 'Be True to Your Name'. Karaganov reminded readers that at a time when Soviet theatre was undergoing a process of 'aesthetic demarcation', a time when many productions emphasized the 'conventionality' of the performance, through the 'rejection of the curtain and backdrop' or by having 'actors walking through the auditorium', the Sovremennik had bravely fought for the Stanislavskian way and a return to the values of the MAT.[65] The critic was clear that in the perennial debate over theatre style, the Sovremennik was part of the school of *perezhivanie* and that this should count in its favour. With regard to the production itself, the critic argued that those who had interpreted the play as a 'simple allegory, [with] direct allusions to the present day' were mistaken.[66] The critic refuted the idea that *The Naked King* was a critique of the Soviet Union and insisted that it was targeted only at Germany. Karaganov's defence of the Sovremennik consisted of reforging the links between the Theatre-Studio and the establishment by referencing the Stanislavskian values that had given the theatre success in its early years.

In the autumn of 1960, as if taking its lead from Karaganov, the Sovremennik revived its much-loved first production *Alive Forever* by Viktor Rozov, in an attempt to placate its critics. Mikhail Kozakov recalled:

> After the 'scandalous' success of *The Naked King* the theatre needed to demonstrate loyalty. The aesthetics of Shvarts's play were considered a kind of formal extravagance. In some way it was certainly closer to the Vakhtangov tradition, a shift away from the declarations of the former Moscow Art Theatre students.[67]

It was hoped that a return to the familiar psychological realism of Rozov's play, away from the grotesque stylization of *The Naked King*, would convince the authorities that the Theatre-Studio was ready to atone for its sins. In spite of this, the Sovremennik managed to stage *The Naked King* a total of 89 times during the year and the production was seen by around 78,900 spectators.[68] Largely due to the play's success the theatre ended the year in profit to the sum of 1,000 roubles.[69] The production went on to celebrate its 300th performance on 22 September 1966, and the play ran at the Sovremennik until Evgenii Evstigneev's departure in 1970. *The Naked King* became one of the Sovremennik's most renowned productions, widely regarded as the show from which much of the Theatre-Studio's success and popularity derived.[70] The Sovremennik was eventually granted full theatre status on 9 August 1965 but did not find a permanent home until April 1974, when it moved from the former Al'kazar Variety Theatre on

Triumfal'naia Square into the premises of the former Coliseum Cinema opposite Moscow's *Chistye prudy*.

## *The Dragon*, 1962

On 17 October 1961, the Twenty-Second Communist Party Congress convened at the Kremlin in Moscow. By now the principle of 'collective leadership' had long been abandoned and Khrushchev's position at the top of the party was irrefutable. In their speeches, members of the Politburo went even further in their flattery of Khrushchev than they had done at the previous congress in 1959. As the Moscow city party boss Petr Demichev later recalled, the Twenty-Second Congress was Khrushchev's 'time in the sun'.[71] Khrushchev delivered the Central Committee's general report and revealed the Third Party Programme, which declared that the communist fairy tale would be achieved by 1980. But the unveiling of the new programme was overshadowed by Khrushchev's decision to revive the de-Stalinization campaign that he had first begun in 1956. Whether this was a planned move or spontaneous grand standing is unclear. Khrushchev was well known for going off-script, but public discussions of the Third Party Programme had also thrown up suggestions that it should set out a definitive party line on the 'cult of personality' once and for all.[72] Regardless of the motivation, the effect was electrifying. Khrushchev denounced Stalin and his 'accomplices' Molotov, Kaganovich and Voroshilov with a venom that had never been heard in public before. His remarks released a torrent of anti-Stalin rhetoric from other delegates and the press, which scrambled to follow the Soviet premier's lead. On its penultimate day, the congress voted unanimously to remove Stalin's sarcophagus from the mausoleum where it had lain alongside Lenin for eight years, receiving pilgrims in silent performances of hushed reverie. Later that night, under the cover of darkness, Stalin's body was carried out of the marble stage-set on Red Square and buried a few metres away by the wall of the Kremlin. It was a watershed moment of the Thaw and in the history of the Soviet Union.

The months after the congress are often described as the liberal peak of the third wave of the Thaw, a brief window of increased cultural freedoms and opportunities. A report by the Ministry of Culture on the 'Problems of the Soviet theatre' issued in March the following year claimed that 'the restoration of Leninist norms in party and social life had helped to unmask and eradicate the harmful consequences of the cult of personality within the theatre and drama'.[73]

The report argued that the rehabilitation of 'such eminent masters of Soviet theatre' as Meyerhold and Solomon Mikhoels (the Jewish actor assassinated during the anti-cosmopolitan campaign) had demonstrated the progress made by the party in correcting the past errors of Stalinism in the theatrical sphere. However, the report also complained about 'absurd statements in newspapers suggesting that the 1930s and 1940s were a kind of dead zone in the history of the Soviet theatre' and insisted that returning to 'the directorial practices of the 1920s' would be a mistake. This was a rebuke to those critics who had argued for avant-garde theatre forms to be included under the umbrella of socialist realism and suggested that even at the peak of de-Stalinization there was still strong resistance to ceding control over the cultural narrative to progressive voices.

On 7 December 1961, a month or so after the Twenty-Second Party Congress, Shvarts's play *The Dragon* went into rehearsal again at the Leningrad Comedy Theatre. The director Akimov insisted that they would stage the play 'as a fairy tale' and try to avoid contemporary references. 'We will not allude to the past, because that's cheap and dissipates the theme, which is important and meant for tomorrow', he told the cast. 'The Dragon will not have a Georgian accent.'[74] The play begins with the hero Lancelot (a mix of Arthurian knight, Saint George and Russian *bogatyr*) arriving in a nameless kingdom at the house of Charlemagne, the Keeper of Public Records. The kingdom has been ruled by a Dragon for 400 years and the townspeople have drifted into apathy: accepting without a murmur the Dragon's tyrannous rule, which he executes with the help of puppet officials such as the Mayor and his son Genrikh. Charlemagne reveals to Lancelot that his daughter Elsa has been selected as the Dragon's annual tribute and will be sacrificed the next day. On hearing this, Lancelot vows to defeat the Dragon and save Elsa's life. The Mayor and his son Genrikh try to dissuade Lancelot from fighting the Dragon but he cannot be swayed. In Act Two, Lancelot presents himself in the town square awaiting the weapons the townspeople are obliged to provide him with according to an ancient treaty, but the weapons turn out to be useless. Instead of a lance, he is given a certificate that the lance is currently being repaired – convenient for the Dragon but also a satirical swipe at bureaucracies where nothing works but there is always a signed and stamped certificate. Instead, the cat (one of the play's heroes) arranges for some local tradespeople to provide Lancelot with useful accessories: a magic carpet, a cap of invisibility and a sword. With the help of these resources, Lancelot manages to defeat the dragon and cut off each of his three heads, much to the bewilderment of the crowd watching down below who have been bombarded with misinformation from Genrikh's propaganda bulletins throughout the battle. The only person who questions these bulletins is a little boy who can't understand their logic – here once again we see the crucial role of the child who dares to state what he sees, thereby rendering propaganda narratives absurd. After the Dragon is defeated the crowd disperses in confusion. Lancelot, badly wounded, is carried to safety in the Black Mountains by the cat and a donkey. Act Three begins a year later, but instead of a happy thriving town, a new autocrat is in charge. The Mayor, with the support of Genrikh, has taken the Dragon's place and is about to wed Elsa. But Lancelot returns just in time to disrupt the wedding and banish the Mayor and his supporters. The citizens side with Lancelot, and he and Elsa are reunited. The audience is given the happy ending that the fairy-tale genre demands, but Lancelot and Elsa acknowledge that the hard work is only just beginning. In order for the townspeople to live happily ever after, they will have to 'kill the dragon in each and every one of them'.[75]

*The Dragon* premiered on 29 May 1962 at the Leningrad Comedy Theatre with Lancelot played by Gennadii Voropaev and the Dragon by Lev Kolesov. Akimov's sets were designed to create the look of a medieval town with stone castle, inner square, pointed roofs and narrow alleyways. This design even made its way onto the costumes of the sentries who wore tunics covered in a brickwork pattern, as if to camouflage them against the castle walls. In general, the costumes had a medieval-era style, with the exception of the Dragon who in Act Two wore a painted mask with hooked nose and a military-looking tunic covered with small, pointed spikes. The Dragon's first entrance in the previous act is one of the play's great de-familiarizing shocks – after the sky roars and the windows vibrate, the figure who enters Charlemagne's house is just a middle-aged man in 'plain clothes'. Shvarts confounds expectations and suggests to the audience that dragons can look remarkably similar to the person sitting next to you. In Akimov's production, the Dragon entered in painted mask but wearing a smart black-and-white morning suit – creating a jarring visual impression that juxtaposed the fantastical and the realistic.

Despite Akimov's stated intentions, the similarities between Khrushchev and the Mayor, who serves the Dragon dutifully while he is alive but opportunistically takes power after his death, were too obvious for audiences to ignore. In Act Three, the Mayor hosts a wedding feast to celebrate his impending marriage to Elsa (Nelli Korneva), but fearing that Lancelot might still disrupt proceedings, he orders Genrikh (Iosif Khanzel') to gain Elsa's confidence and ascertain whether Lancelot is still alive. Elsa reveals to Genrikh that Lancelot died after the battle, while the Mayor listens in to their conversation. To facilitate this scene, Akimov placed a large statue of the Mayor (modelled on the actor Sukhanov) in the centre of the banqueting hall, dressed in a Roman toga, top hat and standing on a high pedestal. The space below the pedestal was encircled by a curtain, like a confessional booth, and functioned as a secret listening post. With this device, Akimov brought the trappings of Soviet state surveillance into Shvarts's fairy-tale world, as the Mayor hides in the booth and eavesdrops on Elsa and Genrikh. The final *coup de theatre* came, however, with Lancelot's triumphant return. As the Mayor and Genrikh were led away to prison and Lancelot pronounced his final words promising happiness to all, the toga suddenly dropped from the Mayor's statue to reveal, instead of a mighty torso, a 'thin and scraggy carcass, with a heavy plaster head wobbling absurdly above it'.[76] It was both a striking visual metaphor for the unmasking of a cult of personality and a playful nod to the Sovremennik's trail-blazing production of *The Naked King*.

A few days after *The Dragon* premiered at the Comedy Theatre, retail prices for basic goods were increased which led to protests and strikes around the country. On 2 June, in the southern Russian city of Novocherkassk, a demonstration of around 10,000 workers was brutally supressed by the military with 26 killed and 87 wounded.[77] Thus while Leningrad audiences were experiencing the thrill of political insubordination from the comfort of their cushioned seats at the

**Figure 15** Nelli Korneva and Lev Kolesov in *The Dragon* at the Leningrad Comedy Theatre, 1962. Courtesy of the Akimov Comedy Theatre.

Comedy Theatre, the bodies of protesters in Novocherkassk (including two women and one schoolboy) were being buried in secret and the streets where their blood had been spilt were hastily repaved. But this striking disconnect between staged dissent in the theatre and real protest on the streets should not negate the political significance of the former. The productions of Shvarts's plays at the Leningrad Comedy Theatre and the Sovremennik Theatre-Studio enacted a carnival-like suspension of conventional relations of power, a grotesque liberation that satirized the 'cult of personality' and participated in the process of de-Stalinization through 'carnival laughter': the ambivalent laughter of the people directed at everyone, including themselves.[78] Whether or not this experience led any spectators to commit acts of political *dissensus*, in the form of strikes or protests, would be almost impossible to ascertain. But if in the process of watching and interpreting a play the spectator is compelled to think, to constitute itself as a thinking subject with a stake in the world, then this is a form of subjectivation which may become political. And politics, as Rancière has argued compellingly, is itself a form of theatrical spectacle because it consists in the staging of a reality that has not yet been achieved.[79] The protester in the street creates a spectacle, builds a stage on which its voice can be heard and performs the role of the empowered, thereby dissociating themself from the existing system of places and hierarchies which denies them that very empowerment. In Soviet historiography, the period lasting from autumn 1961 to autumn 1962 is often described as the apex of the Thaw. However, the reaction of the Soviet regime to demonstrations of dissent, such as those in Novocherkassk, during this period indicated that while limited concessions were made to the liberal intelligentsia in the cultural sphere, any attempts to destabilize the administration of power would be met with brutal resistance in the streets. This was the lesson of the Hungarian Revolution in 1956 and one that would be repeated in Prague in 1968. Nevertheless, in their satirical swipes at the Communist Party apparatus and in their grotesque stylization, which broke with the norms of MAT realism, these productions of Shvarts's plays offered a political critique of Soviet power while also effecting a meta-political disruption of the Stalinist aesthetic hierarchy.

In late November 1962, following the publication of Aleksandr Solzhenitsyn's Gulag novella *One Day in the Life of Ivan Denisovich*, conservatives within the cultural apparatus began scheming to get Khrushchev to reverse the latest cultural Thaw. On 1 December Khrushchev and other members of the party leadership visited Moscow's Central Exhibition Hall (known as the Manege) to view an art exhibition marking 'Thirty Years of the Moscow Artist's Union'. Just prior to Khrushchev's visit, the head of the Artist's Union, Vladimir Serov, had arranged for a small exhibit of avant-garde artworks, which had been displayed in the Moscow studio of a local art teacher, to be transferred to the Manege for display alongside the large exhibit of traditional socialist realist works. The set-up worked perfectly. Khrushchev looked at the avant-garde works with indignation and began swearing at the artists, calling them 'pederasts' and their work 'dog shit', concluding with the words 'gentlemen, we are waging war on you'.[80] On 7 March 1963 the creative intelligentsia was invited to a meeting held in the Sverdlovsk Hall at the Kremlin. There were over 600 people gathered, including party, *komsomol* and KGB officials. 'The Thaw is over!' Khrushchev told the attendees. 'This is not even a light morning frost. For you and your likes it will be the arctic frost.'[81] Oleg Efremov, who was in the audience, described it as one of the most depressing experiences of his life.[82] In the ensuing cultural freeze, the Comedy Theatre's production of *The Dragon* was accused of having an 'ambiguous ideological message' by Vasilii Tolstikov, the First Secretary of the Leningrad Obkom.[83] *The Dragon* was staged only three more times that season (the last performance was on 18 May) with a number of lines deleted, before it was axed from the repertoire for good. That spring, a student production of *The Dragon* directed by Mark Zakharov at the Moscow State University House of Culture was also banned.[84] *The Dragon* would not be performed again in the Soviet Union until 1979.

While holidaying in his villa by the Black Sea in October 1964, Khrushchev received a telephone call from Leonid Brezhnev, calling him to an urgent meeting of the Presidium back in Moscow. At the meeting, held on 13 October, Brezhnev spoke first and began denouncing Khrushchev for acting 'unilaterally and ignoring the Presidium'.[85] The Presidium's expert on agriculture, Gennady Voronov, followed up the attack, claiming 'it's become impossible to get anything done in the Presidium. Instead of the Stalin cult we have the cult of Khrushchev'.[86] According to Aleksandr Shelepin, the Central Committee secretary, Khrushchev had become 'Bonapartist' in his use of 'crude threats' and had surrounded himself with 'sycophants'.[87] The next day, the Presidium voted unanimously to 'retire' Khrushchev and he was deposed from power. The Twenty-Second Party Congress had witnessed Khrushchev at the height of his career. However, the intervening three years saw a series of missteps which alarmed and alienated his colleagues at the top of the party. Khrushchev's blunders over agricultural policy had led to food shortages across the country, while his embarrassing climbdown over the Cuban Missile Crisis and the Sino-Soviet split had weakened the USSR's international standing. Within the party, Khrushchev's attempts to weed out nepotism and his threats to replace the entire Presidium with fresh blood alarmed those who owed their careers to his patronage. Khrushchev's most significant legacy was the de-Stalinization programme, but this was typically far better appreciated by the liberal cultural intelligentsia than it was by those within the party apparatus, who were fearful of sudden shifts in party messaging. In his approach to cultural matters, Khrushchev also had a mixed record: at times making concessions which cultivated greater openness (*glasnost'*) and tolerance of diversity; on other occasions, reimposing harsh restrictions and sanctions seemingly on a whim. Khrushchev had an underlying respect for the intelligentsia, while also feeling perennially insecure about his own lack of formal education and so was prone to lash out if he felt his authority was being challenged. In the end, these insecurities were manipulated by conservatives within the cultural apparatus who in 1963 incited him to withdraw the freedoms he had only recently granted.

The Khrushchev Thaw was thus an uncertain period in which the party's approach to culture was inconsistent and contested, when relations between editors and writers, artistic councils and directors, theatres and audiences were complex, unpredictable and yet pregnant with possibility. If the Thaw was characterized by its liminality between fixed positions, neither fully liberal nor reactionary, then its position within Soviet history also came to be defined as a transition between the homogenized Stalinist and stagnant Brezhnevian eras. Still working out the legacies of the former while looking ahead with misplaced hope to the latter, the Thaw was marked by bursts of youthful optimism reflected in the emergence of youth literature and new young theatre collectives. In this sense, it was apt that the spirit of the Thaw would find its sharpest expression on the Soviet stage in the space between youth and adult theatre – in the fairy-tale satires of Evgenii Shvarts. In Shvarts's work, the role of making networks of power visible is invariably played by children. He has a great utopian faith in the child not only as the future of humanity but in the idea of childishness itself: the uncorrupted, playful and imaginative childishness that asks difficult questions and refuses to accept falsehood. Just as Shvarts used the literary genre of the fairy tale to hold societies to account, so the figure of the child in his plays holds the powerful accountable. The child who makes visible that which others refuse to see becomes a simulacrum for the fairy-tale play itself. Both function as a political device to shape the world for the better. Oleg Efremov recalled that as soon as top Central Committee members were kicked out of office they would go and see *The Naked King* at the Sovremennik almost as a ritual.[88] The former Minister of Foreign Affairs Dmitrii Shepilov was one such attendee, as was former Minister of Defence Marshal Georgii Zhukov. And, after his fall from power, in between tending his garden at the dacha, Khrushchev too liked to go and watch *The Naked King* and laugh at the absurdity of it all.

# Epilogue

In 1977 the building of the former Al'kazar Variety Theatre on Moscow's Triumfal'naia Square was demolished. By then the Satire Theatre had moved into the premises of the former Nikitin Circus on the opposite side of the square and the Sovremennik Theatre had moved into the former Coliseum Cinema by *Chistye prudy*. By this point too, Oleg Efremov had left the Sovremennik and taken over as artistic director at the Moscow Art Theatre. Nevertheless, as he approached the square and saw the pile of rubble that used to house his theatre, Efremov was hit by a wave of sadness: 'We drove into the square and there. . . . They'd demolished it for no reason. I'd tried to defend it in various ways. They were supposed to knock it down for some kind of anniversary of the revolution.'[1] The revolution was sixty years old and the Soviet theatre had changed significantly since the Thaw. That same year, Iurii Liubimov directed the capital's first stage production of Mikhail Bulgakov's novel *The Master and Margarita*, set in Stalinist Moscow and depicting a writer's struggle with censorship as the devil wreaks havoc across the city. Liubimov's production contained an array of stylized devices: a Brechtian author-narrator, actors walking through the auditorium and Woland's variety show, recreated with cabaret, acrobatics, and the release of hundreds of fake banknotes from the ceiling onto the audience below.[2] Avant-garde devices had become far more prevalent on the stage since the early 1950s, a consequence, in part, of the revival of these forms in productions during the Thaw and the debates on theatre style which had questioned the hegemony of a simplified MAT realism.

Liubimov had been a successful actor at the Vakhtangov Theatre for many years before he turned to pedagogy in his mid-forties and began teaching at the Shchukin Drama School. In the spring of 1963 Liubimov staged a production of Brecht's *The Good Person of Szechwan* with his third-year degree students, which caused a sensation in Moscow.[3] Much like the birth of the Sovremennik Theatre-Studio seven years earlier, out of this student production sprang the Taganka Theatre. Within a year, Liubimov was appointed artistic director at the small, relatively unknown Theatre of Drama and Comedy on Taganka Square and his production of *The Good Person of Szechwan* opened on 23 April 1964 with a new cast, including some of his students from the Shchukin School. During the 1960s and 1970s the Taganka Theatre became a haven for expressive, stylized theatre, continuing the legacy of the Soviet avant-garde into the late twentieth century. In his open letter criticizing the directorial excesses of Nikolai Okhlopkov, published in 1960, Georgii Tovstonogov observed that 'the twentieth century is the century of the atom, satellite, cybernetics and directors'.[4] For better or worse, the role of the theatre director had been transformed from wardrobe keeper in the nineteenth century to omnipotent demiurge in the next. And it was in this tradition of the director-creator that Liubimov cultivated a 'poetic theatre' at the Taganka, wherein the production was organized around a central metaphor rather than the dramatic text.[5]

In spite of his previous attacks on Okhlopkov's 'conventionality', Tovstonogov also evolved his directorial practice at the Leningrad Bolshoi Dramatic Theatre in the years after the Thaw. In 1972 he staged a production of Gogol's *The Government Inspector* that abandoned comedy in favour of 'fantastical realism'.[6] The key concept of the production was fear. Men in black coats and dark glasses lurked in the background, issuing instructions to the local police. While a carriage containing a dummy inspector floated high above the stage as though a figment of the townspeople's nightmares. When the real inspector was announced at the end, Khlestakov himself returned, to the consternation of the audience. Any lingering hope of getting at the truth was crushed under the weight of an endlessly repeating chain of simulacra. It was a trick that the futurist director Igor' Terent'ev had pulled in his version of the play back in 1927.

In the late 1960s, even sworn disciples of the Stanislavsky system such as Oleg Efremov and Anatolii Efros experimented with stylized devices. In a production of Viktor Rozov's *The Traditional Reunion* at the Sovremennik Theatre in 1966, Efremov used shadow theatre to clever effect.[7] Young people danced behind transparent screens at the back of the stage, bringing to life in a play of silhouettes the youthful memories of those taking part in the reunion of old school friends. The director also broke the fourth wall for the first time in his career by having some famous members of the audience called up spontaneously onto the stage, as if they too had been invited to the reunion.

That same year, Efros staged an irreverent production of Chekhov's *The Seagull* at the Lenin Komsomol Theatre which dispensed with the traditional naturalistic setting in favour of a bare, neutral design. The small stage within a stage, made of unpainted wooden boards, on which Treplev's play is performed was imagined as the writer's own scaffold. Efros was dismissed from his post a year later, accused of 'ideological shortcomings'.[8] Since the trial of Andrei

Siniavskii and Iulii Daniel in the winter of 1965–6, the government had become particularly sensitive to allegations that writers were being persecuted for their art.[9]

The legacy of the Thaw was also apparent in the work of new dramatists that emerged in the late 1960s. The obsession of thaw writers with authenticity and truthfulness gave way to themes of disillusionment and apathy as the 1960s generation (*shestidesiatniki*) became frustrated with the lack of meaningful reform. The failure of Soviet prime minister Aleksei Kosygin's attempts at diversifying the economy in 1965 and the consolidation of the *nomenklatura* under Brezhnev led to an era of stagnation. Corruption and the black market became normalized for ordinary citizens who participated in the empty rituals and ceremonies of work and state politics to ensure a quiet life. At the same time, they would invest their time and labour into other pursuits and lifestyles, creating what Alexei Yurchak has called 'deterritorialized realities' outside of the binary categories of support or opposition to the state.[10] In the 1960s and 1970s, these realities were captured by playwrights such as Liudmila Petrushevskaia and Aleksandr Vampilov who wrote dramas that were neither pro-Soviet nor explicitly dissident. Petrushevskaia is a journalist-turned writer who completed her first play *Music Lessons* in 1973. Her work combines absurdist themes of moral disintegration and a loss of faith with dramatic realism in character and setting. Her most acclaimed play, *Three Girls in Blue* (1980), was first staged at the Lenin Komsomol Theatre in Leningrad in 1985 and uses the metaphor of a leaking roof in a damp cottage as an allegory for social decay.[11]

Aleksandr Vampilov began writing plays in the early 1960s but was only just coming to prominence when his life was tragically cut short in an accident in 1972 at the age of only thirty-four.[12] Vampilov's best-known play *Duck Hunting* (1967) was banned until 1976 for its negative portrayal of Soviet everyday life. The play's anti-hero Viktor Zilov, a prototype of the 1970s *homo sovieticus*, wakes up one morning with a hangover and receives delivery of a funeral wreath addressed in his name.[13] Slowly he pieces together what has led to this point via a series of flashbacks, creatively realized on stage through the use of lighting spots and blackouts. Vampilov was likely influenced by a production of John Osborne's *Look Back in Anger* staged in 1965 at the Sovremennik Theatre, directed by Oleg Efremov. Like Jimmy Porter, Zilov represents a new generation of disillusioned young men who take out their anger on those around them, destroying relationships in the process. The play was first staged in Riga in 1976 before Efremov directed a production in 1978 at the Moscow Art Theatre, casting himself as the anti-hero Zilov. The director interpreted the play as a lament for the 1960s generation and the lost idealism of the Thaw, when change still seemed possible.[14]

Oleg Efremov had been invited to take over as artistic director of the Moscow Art Theatre in 1970: a Sisyphean task but one he considered it his duty to fulfil. With a bloated payroll and a cast list numbering around 150, Efremov struggled to reform the culture within the theatre. Many senior actors did little work and just sat around collecting their large salaries, taking advantage of the generous benefits available to them as members of the Soviet Union's premier drama theatre. Eventually, after fifteen years, Efremov forced through his long-held ambition to divide the MAT in half so as to make the cast size more manageable. The splitting up of the MAT into two separate companies, completed in 1987, was the most contentious event in its history, with acrimony and rancour lasting for years. Efremov took half the troupe to form the Chekhov Moscow Art Theatre based on Kamergerskii Lane, while the other half, led by Tatiana Doronina, retained the name the Gorky Moscow Art Theatre and was based a short walk up the street on Tverskaia Boulevard. It was a rupture that in many ways epitomized the underlying tensions within the Soviet theatre: the conflict between official culture, with its cosy relation to power, and the desire for new creative directions, embodied in the idealistic director who set up the Sovremennik Theatre-Studio during the heady days of the Thaw.

These divergent paths were evident in two productions staged as the Soviet Union was disintegrating. In 1988 the Chekhov MAT produced Bulgakov's play about Molière, *A Cabal of Hypocrites*, which had been banned by Stalin in the 1930s.[15] Efremov played the role of Molière as a tired and browbeaten artist, trampled on by the autocrat King. Four years later, the Gorky MAT staged a production of Bulgakov's play *Batum*, about Stalin's early years, written in 1939 but never performed. The production, directed by political hardliner Sergei Kurginian, premiered for its one and only performance on 7 November 1992, the seventy-fifth anniversary of the revolution.[16] By that point, the Soviet Union was no more, but the event turned into a rally for the old regime. At the grand finale, Stalin in his white uniform stood on the stage surveying the audience as a giant red banner bearing the hammer and sickle unfurled behind him. The crowd rose to its feet applauding as the banned Soviet anthem swelled. That is, the few that were left rose to their feet. As one critic recalled, people had started walking out just half an hour into the performance.[17] None of the actors returned for the curtain call.

# Notes

## Introduction

1 Iurii Fedosiuk, *Moskva v kol'tse sadovykh* (Moscow: Moskovskii rabochii, 1983), 385.
2 P. Sytin, *Proshloe Moskvy v nazvaniiakh ulits* (Moscow: Moskovskii rabochii, 1948), 43–4, 78–80.
3 Anatolii Skorik in discussion with the author, May 2011. On responses to Stalin's death, see also Iurii Aksiutin, 'Popular Responses to Khrushchev', in *Nikita Khrushchev*, ed. William Taubman et al. (New Haven: Yale University Press, 2000), 178–80.
4 Stephen V. Bittner, *The Many Lives of Khrushchev's Thaw: Experience and Memory in Moscow's Arbat* (Ithaca: Cornell University Press, 2008), 3–4; Denis Kozlov and Eleonory Gilburd, 'The Thaw as an Event in Russian History', in *The Thaw: Soviet Society and Culture during the 1950s and 1960s*, ed. Denis Kozlov and Eleonory Gilburd (Toronto: University of Toronto Press, 2013), 32.
5 Il'ia Erenburg, *Ottepel'* (Moscow: Sovetskii pisatel', 1956).
6 On the thaw metaphor, see Kozlov and Gilburd, 'The Thaw as an Event in Russian History', 18–23.
7 Bittner, *The Many Lives of Khrushchev's Thaw*, 7.
8 Katerina Clark, 'Rethinking the Past and Current Thaw', in *Glasnost' in Context: On the Recurrence of Liberalizations in Central and East European Literatures and Cultures*, ed. Marko Pavlyshyn (New York: Berg, 1990).
9 For an overview of these approaches, see Polly Jones, 'Introduction: The Dilemmas of de–Stalinization', in *The Dilemmas of De-Stalinization: Negotiating Cultural and Social Change in the Khrushchev Era*, ed. Polly Jones (Oxon: Routledge, 2006), 1–18; Kozlov and Gilburd, 'The Thaw as an Event in Russian History', 23–8.
10 Golfo Alexopoulos, 'Amnesty 1945: The Revolving Door of Stalin's Gulag', *Slavic Review* 64, no. 2 (Summer 2005): 274–306.
11 Elena Zubkova, *Russia after the War: Hopes, Illusions, and Disappointments, 1945–1957*, trans. Hugh Ragsdale, 2nd edn. (1998; London: Routledge, 2015).
12 Nancy Condee, 'Cultural Codes of the Thaw', in *Nikita Khrushchev*, 162.
13 On the emerging consumer culture during the Thaw, see Susan E. Reid, 'Cold War in the Kitchen: Gender and the De-Stalinization of Consumer Taste in the Soviet Union under Khrushchev', *Slavic Review* 61, no. 2 (Summer 2002): 211–52.

14 See, for example, Condee, 'Cultural Codes of the Thaw', 160–1; Jones, 'Introduction: The Dilemmas of de-Stalinization', 11–12; Katerina Clark, *The Soviet Novel: History as Ritual*, 3rd edn. (1981; Bloomington: Indiana University Press, 2000), 211.
15 On this point see Miriam Dobson, *Khrushchev's Cold Summer: Gulag Returnees, Crime, and the Fate of Reform after Stalin* (Ithaca: Cornell University Press, 2009), 15.
16 On the Gulag amnesty, see Miriam Dobson, '"Show the Bandit-Enemies No Mercy!": Amnesty, Criminality and Public Response in 1953', in *The Dilemmas of De-Stalinization*, 21–40; on the significance of the July Plenum, see R. J. Service, 'The Road to the Twentieth Party Congress: An Analysis of the Events Surrounding the Central Committee Plenum of July 1953', *Soviet Studies* 33, no. 2 (April 1981): 232–45.
17 The article also reviewed Nikolai Okhlopkov's production of *The Storm* (1859) at the Theatre of Drama.
18 'Pravo i dolg teatra', *Pravda*, 27 November 1953, 3.
19 The play was also staged at the Bolshoi Dramatic Theatre in Leningrad that spring, directed by Vasilii Merkur'ev.
20 On Lobanov's production of *The Guests*, see 'Leonid Zorin', in *Andrei Mikhailovich Lobanov: Dokumenty, stat'i, vospominaniia*, ed. G. Zorina (Moscow: Iskusstvo, 1980), 318–30.
21 *Pravda*, 20 December 1954, 2.
22 Donald D. Egbert, 'The Idea of "Avant-Garde" in Art and Politics', *The American Historical Review* 73, no. 2 (December 1967): 339–66.
23 On Western support for avant-garde art during the Cold War, see Julia Bryan-Wilson, *Art Workers: Radical Practice in the Vietnam War Era* (Berkeley: University of California Press, 2009), 29.
24 Clement Greenberg, 'Avant-Garde and Kitsch', in *Art and Culture: Critical Essays* (Boston: Beacon Press, 1961), 3–21.
25 Jacques Rancière, *Aisthesis: Scenes from the Aesthetic Regime of Art*, trans. Zakir Paul (London: Verso, 2013), 262.
26 Ibid., 62.
27 Ibid.
28 A regime of art is defined as 'a mode of articulation between ways of doing and making, their corresponding forms of visibility, and possible ways of thinking about their relationships'. See 'Foreword' in Jacques Rancière, *The Politics of Aesthetics*, ed. and trans. Gabriel Rockhill (London: Bloomsbury Academic, 2013), 4.
29 Jacques Rancière, 'Artistic Regimes and the Shortcomings of the Notion of Modernity', in *The Politics of Aesthetics*, 15–26.
30 Jacques Rancière, 'Mechanical Arts and the Promotion of the Anonymous', in *The Politics of Aesthetics*, 28.
31 Rancière, 'Artistic Regimes and the Shortcomings of the Notion of Modernity', 17.

32 See George Kernodle, 'Open Stage: Elizabethan or Existentialist?', *Shakespeare Survey* 12 (1959): 1–7.
33 Rancière, *Aisthesis*, 68.
34 Ibid., 250.
35 Jacques Rancière, 'Prelude', in *Aisthesis*, x.
36 Rancière, 'Artistic Regimes and the Shortcomings of the Notion of Modernity', 18.
37 Peter Hallward, 'Staging Equality: On Rancière's Theatrocracy', *New Left Review* 37 (January 2006): 121.
38 Jacques Rancière, 'The Distribution of the Sensible: Politics and Aesthetics', in *The Politics of Aesthetics*, 8–14.
39 Jacques Rancière, 'The Paradoxes of Political Art', in *Dissensus: On Politics and Aesthetics*, trans. Steven Corcoran (London: Bloomsbury, 2015), 148.
40 Rancière, *Aisthesis*, 6.
41 John Wesley, 'Rhetorical Delivery for Renaissance English: Voice, Gesture, Emotion, and the Sixteenth-Century Vernacular Turn', *Renaissance Quarterly* 68, no. 4 (Winter 2015): 1265–96.
42 Earl. R. Wasserman, 'The Sympathetic Imagination in Eighteenth-Century Theories of Acting', *Journal of English and German Philology* 46 (1947): 265.
43 Although, for Diderot, the actor achieved this not by experiencing the emotions themself but through dispassionate, calculating imitation. Diderot's belief was in contrast to emotion-based theories of acting advocated at that time by Luigi Riccoboni and Remon Sainte-Albine.
44 Denise S. Sechelski, 'Garrick's Body and the Labor of Art in Eighteenth-Century Theater', *Eighteenth-Century Studies* 29, no. 4 (1996): 369–89.
45 On Maeterlinck's 'immobile theatre', see Rancière, *Aisthesis*, 111–20.
46 Rancière, *Aisthesis*, 115.
47 Ibid., 89–91.
48 For Meyerhold's discussion of the grotesque, see V. Meierkhol'd, 'Balagan' (1912), in *Meierkhol'd V. E. Stat'i, pis'ma, rechi, besedy*, ed. A. Fevral'skii, vol. 1 (Moscow: Iskusstvo, 1968), 224–7; for an English translation, see *Meyerhold on Theatre*, trans. Edward Braun (London: Methuen & Co., 1969), 119–42.
49 Meierkhol'd, 'Balagan', 229.
50 Rancière, *Aisthesis*, 171–90.
51 Ibid., 190.
52 The links between Shklovsky's concept of 'making strange' (*ostranenie*), Brechtian *Verfremdung* and Russian avant-garde theatre have been widely studied. See, for example, Silvija Jestrovic, 'Theatricality as Estrangement of Art and Life in the Russian Avant-Garde', *Substance* 31, no. 2/3, 98/99 (2002): 42–56; on the active nature of spectatorship in the theatre, see Jacques Rancière, *The Emancipated Spectator*, trans. Gregory Elliot (London: Verso, 2009), 17.

# Chapter 1

1. Mikhail Derza and Mervyn Matthews, 'Soviet Theatre Audiences', *Slavic Review* 34, no. 4 (December 1975): 719.
2. On Kerzhentsev's theory of theatre, see Lars Kleberg, *Theatre as Action: Soviet Russian Avant-Garde Aesthetics*, trans. Charles Rougle (London: Macmillan, 1993), 60–2.
3. On these trends in the early Soviet theatre, see E. D. Uvarova, 'Teatry Malykh Form', in *Russkaia sovetskaia estrada 1917–1929*, ed. E. D. Uvarova (Moscow: Iskusstvo, 1976), 302–72; Konstantin Rudnitsky, *Russian and Soviet Theatre: Tradition and the Avant-Garde*, trans. Roxane Permar (London: Thames and Hudson, 1988); Robert Leach, *Revolutionary Theatre* (London: Routledge, 1994); Christina Ezrahi, *Swans of the Kremlin: Ballet and Power in Soviet Russia* (Pittsburgh: University of Pittsburgh Press, 2012), 35.
4. V. Meierkhol'd, 'Akter budushchego i biomekhanika' (1922), in *Meierkhol'd V. E. Stat'i, pis'ma, rechi, besedy*, ed. A. Fevral'skii, vol. 2 (Moscow: Iskusstvo, 1968), 487.
5. Rancière, *Aisthesis*, 202.
6. Ibid., 228.
7. V. Meierkhol'd, 'Rekonstruktsiia teatra' (1929), in *Meierkhol'd V. E. Stat'i*, 206.
8. Cited in Chris Ward, *Stalin's Russia* (London: Edward Arnold, 1993), 15.
9. Ibid.
10. On Stalin's rise to power, see E. H. Carr, *The Russian Revolution from Lenin to Stalin 1917–1929* (London: Macmillan, 1980); Graeme Gill, *The Origins of the Stalinist Political System* (Cambridge: Cambridge University Press, 1990); Ward, *Stalin's Russia*, 7–38; Ronald Grigor Suny, *The Soviet Experiment: Russia, The USSR, and the Successor States* (Oxford: Oxford University Press, 1998), 157–68.
11. Walter Benjamin, 'Disputation bei Meyerhold', *Die literarische Welt* 3, no. 6 (11 February 1927): 3, cited in *The Soviet Theater: A Documentary History*, ed. Laurence Senelick and Sergei Ostrovsky (New Haven: Yale University Press, 2014), 268.
12. A. M. Smelianskii, *Mikhail Bulgakov v Khudozhestvennom Teatre* (Moscow: Iskusstvo, 1989), 112–13.
13. Nikolai Abalkin, *Sistema Stanislavskogo i sovetsky teatr* (Moscow: Iskusstvo, 1954), 205, cited in *The Soviet Theater*, 276.
14. *Vecherniaia Moskva*, 26 November, 1927, cited in *Moskovskii Khudozhestvennyi teatr v sovetskuiu epokhu: Materialy i dokumenty*, ed. A. V. Solodovnikova (Moscow: Iskusstvo, 1962), 272.
15. The 'imperial monopoly' was instituted by Tsar Nikolai I in 1827 and limited the right to stage theatrical performances in the two major Russian cities of St Petersburg and Moscow to the five imperial theatres: the Aleksandrinskii, Marinskii and Mikhailovskii in St Petersburg; and the Bolshoi and Malyi in Moscow.

16 On censorship in the Soviet Union, see Herman Ermolaev, *Censorship in Soviet Literature 1917–1991* (Lanham: Rowman & Littlefield, 1997); Sheila Fitzpatrick, *The Commissariat of Enlightenment: Soviet Organization of Education and the Arts Under Lunacharsky, October 1917–1921* (Cambridge: Cambridge University Press, 1970); *Enemies of the People: The Destruction of Soviet Literary, Theater, and Film Arts in the 1930s*, ed. Katherine Bliss Eaton (Evanston: Northwestern University Press, 2002).

17 See Sheila Fitzpatrick, *The Cultural Front: Power and Culture in Revolutionary Russia* (Ithaca: Cornell University Press, 1992), 117.

18 On the interplay between identity and mask in Stalinist culture, see 'Chapter 6: Face and Mask: Theatricality and Identity in the Era of the Show Trials (1936–1938)' in Katerina Clark, *Moscow, The Fourth Rome: Stalinism, Cosmopolitanism, and the Evolution of Soviet Culture, 1931–1941* (Cambridge, MA: Harvard University Press, 2011), 210–41; see also Sheila Fitzpatrick, *Tear off the Masks! Identity and Imposture in Twentieth-Century Russia* (Princeton: Princeton University Press, 2005).

19 J. V. Stalin, 'Reply to Bill-Belotserkovsky', 2 February 1929, in *Works*, vol. 11, January 1928–March 1929 (Moscow: Foreign Languages Publishing House, 1954), 341–4.

20 On RAPP's ambitions to take over the MAT, see I. N. Solov'eva, *Khudozhestvennyi teatr: Zhizn' i prikliucheniia idei* (Moscow: Moskovskii Khudozhestvennyi teatr, 2007), 532–3.

21 On RAPP's resolution, see *Literaturnaia gazeta*, 30 January 1931, 3; D. Zolotnitskii, 'Mnogoobrazie i sintez', in *Problemy teorii i praktiki russkoi sovetskoi rezhissury: 1925–1932*, ed. N. V. Zaitsev et al. (Leningrad: Leningradskii gosudarstvennyi institut teatra, muzyki i kinematografii, 1978), 14.

22 *Literaturnaia gazeta*, 12 December 1931, 1.

23 English translation by Charles Malamuth in *Six Soviet Plays*, ed. Eugene Lyons (London: Victor Gollancz ltd.,1935), 586; Russian original in A. Afinogenov, *Strakh* (Letchworth: Prideaux Press, 1976), 49.

24 Cited in Inna Solovyova, 'The Theatre and Socialist Realism, 1929–1953', trans. Jean Benedetti, in *A History of Russian Theatre*, ed. Robert Leach and Victor Borovsky (Cambridge: Cambridge University Press, 1999), 352.

25 See speech by Ivan Moskvin, 25 December 1936, in *Moskovskii Khudozhestvennyi teatr v sovetskuiu epokhu*, 77.

26 Ibid., 66–7.

27 For a discussion of how this return to nationalism was simultaneously combined with a flourishing cosmopolitanism, see Clark, *Moscow*, 7–12.

28 Leon Trotsky, *The Revolution Betrayed: What Is the Soviet Union and Where Is It Going?* (London: Faber & Faber, 1937).

29 See Sheila Fitzpatrick, 'The Russian Revolution and Social Mobility: A Re-examination of the Question of Social Support for the Soviet Regime in the 1920s and 1930s', *Politics & Society* 13, no. 2 (1984): 119–41.

30 Clark, *The Soviet Novel*, 141.
31 See Igal Halfin, 'The Demonization of the Opposition: Stalinist Memory and the Communist Archive of Leningrad Communist University', *Kritika* 2, no. 1 (2001): 48.
32 Michel Foucault, 'Truth and Power', in *Power/Knowledge: Selected Interviews and Other Writings 1972–1977*, ed. and trans. Colin Gordon (New York: Pantheon Books, 1980), 131.
33 For a discussion of Stalin's role as external arbiter of Marxist-Leninist ideology represented as 'objective truth', see Alexei Yurchak, *Everything was Forever, Until it was No More: The Last Soviet Generation* (Princeton: Princeton University Press, 2005), 10–14.
34 Clark, *Moscow*, 88.
35 It is thought that Stalin was, nevertheless, heavily involved in the invention of the term, even if the dates do not quite match up.
36 *Pravda*, 20 August 1934, 2.
37 Ibid.
38 Clark, *The Soviet Novel*, 37.
39 *Literaturnaia gazeta*, 29 August 1934, 1.
40 Clark, *The Soviet Novel*, 15–17.
41 Ibid., 18.
42 This return to a naturalistic style mirrored a similar trend in the theatres of Britain and America during the 1930s.
43 Similarly, authorities in the GDR pressurized Brecht's Berliner Ensemble to adopt the Stanislavsky system in the early 1950s.
44 Letter dated September 1909, in *Stanislavsky: A life in Letters*, ed. and trans. Laurence Senelick (Abingdon: Routledge, 2014), 265.
45 K. Stanislavskii, *Rabota aktera nad soboi, chasti I i II* (Moscow: Iskusstvo, 1951), 27.
46 Quoted in Dmitry Kalm, 'Problems of the Soviet Theatre', *International Literature* 10 (October 1939): 78, cited in *The Soviet Theater*, 394.
47 There were, however, still some fundamental differences between the two approaches. See Robert Leach, *Stanislavsky and Meyerhold* (Bern: Peter Lang, 2003), 158–89, 198–200; Edward Braun, *Meyerhold: A Revolution in Theatre*, 2nd edn. (1979; London: Methuen Drama, 1995), 291–2.
48 On Kedrov and the MPA, see Z. Vladimirovna, 'Kedrov', in *Portrety rezhisserov: kedrov, Akimov, Tovstonogov, Pluchek, Efremov*, vol. 1 (Moscow: Iskusstvo, 1972), 5–54.
49 One such student was Oleg Efremov who went on to employ the Method of Physical Actions at the Sovremennik Theatre-Studio in the late 1950s.
50 N. Volkov, 'Khudozhnik-myslitel'', *Pravda*, 17 January 1938, 4.
51 Shchepkin in turn had been inspired to reject the dominant declamatory style of French neoclassical theatre after watching a performance by Prince Prokopii Meshcherskii in the early 1800s.

52 The first was Ivan Moskvin who became a deputy to the first Supreme Soviet in 1937.
53 *Pravda*, 28 February 1936, 2.
54 A. Smelianksii, 'Drugoi MKhAT', in *MKhAT Vtoroi: Opyt vosstanovleniia biografii*, ed. A. M. Smelianskii (Moscow: Izdatel'stvo 'Moskovskii Khudozhestvennyi teatr', 2010), 11–15 (12).
55 'Sumbur vmesto muzyki', *Pravda*, 28 January 1936, 3.
56 Royal S. Brown, 'The Three Faces of Lady Macbeth', *Russian and Soviet Music: Essays for Boris Schwarz*, ed. Malcolm Hamrick Brown (Ann Arbor: UMI Research Press, 1984), 248.
57 Nine days later a second article was published denouncing Shostakovich's ballet *The Limpid Stream*, see 'Baletnaia falsh', *Pravda*, 6 February 1936, 3.
58 'Meierkhol'd protiv meierkhol'dovshchiny', in *V. E. Meierkhol'd stat'i, pis'ma...* Vol. 2, 330–47.
59 See for example Mikhail Kol'tsov, 'Obmanchivaia legkost', *Pravda*, 30 March 1936, 3; 'U teatral'nykh rabotnikov', *Pravda*, 4 April 1936, 4; 'Realizm, kul'tura, smelost'!', *Sovetskii teatr*, 4–5, 1936, 1–2.
60 On the Great Purges, see for example J. Arch Getty, *Origins of the Great Purges: The Soviet Communist Party Reconsidered 1933–1938* (Cambridge: Cambridge University Press, 1985); Vadim Rogovin, *1937: Stalin's Year of Terror* (Michigan: Mehring Books, 1998); William J. Chase, *Enemies within the Gates? The Comintern and the Stalinist Repression, 1934–1939* (New Haven: Yale University Press, 2001); Wendy Z. Goldman, *Inventing the Enemy: Denunciation and Terror in Stalin's Russia* (New York: Cambridge University Press, 2011).
61 P. Kerzhentsev, 'Fal'sifikatsiia narodnogo proshlogo', *Pravda*, 15 November 1936, 3.
62 Cited in M. Z. Levitan, *Tairov* (Moscow: Molodaia gvardiia, 2009), 294.
63 On the end of the TRAMs, see V. M. Mironova, *Tram: Agitatsionnyi molodezhnyi teatr 192–1930-kh godov* (Leningrad: Iskusstvo, 1977).
64 Platon Kerzhentsev, 'Chuzhoi teatr', *Pravda*, 17 December 1937, 4.
65 Stalin, 'Reply to Bill-Belotserkovsky'.
66 Emmanuel Levinas, *Otherwise Than Being or Beyond Essence*, trans. Alphonso Lingis (Pittsburgh: Duquesne University Press, 2000).
67 Michel Foucault, *The Archaeology of Knowledge*, trans. A. M. Sheridan Smith (New York: Pantheon Books, 1982), 79–87.
68 *Pravda*, 8 January 1938, 2.
69 A. Fadeev, 'Kommunisticheskoe vospitanie trudiashchikhsiia i sovetskoe iskusstvo', *Pravda*, 16 April 1939, 5.
70 Quoted in Braun, *Meyerhold*, 294.
71 Ibid., 298.
72 Ibid., 297.

73 The theory of 'socialist legality' stated that courts could convict on the basis of confession. See Eugene Huskey, 'Vyshinskii, Krylenko, and the Shaping of the Soviet Legal Order', *Slavic Review* 46, no. 3/4 (Autumn–Winter 1987): 414–28.
74 For an example of this argument, see Boris Groys, *The Total Art of Stalinism: Avant Garde, Aesthetic Dictatorship and Beyond*, trans. Charles Rougle (Princeton: Princeton University Press, 1992), 36.
75 The adjective 'conventional' (*uslovnyi*) is a commonplace in Soviet theatre criticism, used to describe theatre that embraces the artificiality of the medium and makes full use of stage conventions (e.g. chorus, masks, footlights) rather than conceal them behind an illusion of verisimilitude. See Patris Pavi, *Slovar' teatra*, trans. K. Razlogov (Moscow: Progress, 1991), 395–7.
76 Cited in Solovyova, 'The Theatre and Socialist Realism, 1929–1953', 330.
77 On the Stalin Prizes, see Sheila Fitzpatrick, *Everyday Stalinism: Ordinary Life in Extraordinary Times: Soviet Russia in the 1930s* (Oxford: Oxford University Press, 1999), 109; Kiril Tomoff, *Creative Union: The Professional Organization of Soviet Composers, 1939–1953* (Ithaca: Cornell University Press, 2006), 236–46.
78 On the similarity between the politicization of the Prix de Rome and the Stalin Prize, see Oliver Johnson, 'The Stalin Prize and the Soviet Artist: Status Symbol or Stigma?', *Slavic Review* 70, no. 4 (Winter 2011): 819–20.
79 For a discussion of the way in which the aesthetic regime and representative regime overlap and coexist with one another, including within specific works of art, see 'The Janus-face of Politicized Art: Jacques Rancière in Interview with Gabriel Rockhill', in *The Politics of Aesthetics*, 45–61 (47).
80 Y. Shiroky, 'The Theatre Serves the Navy', *Iskusstvo i zhizn'* 11 (1933): 15–17, cited in *The Soviet Theater*, 360.
81 Michael Glenny and William Lee Kinsolving, 'Soviet Theatre: 2 Views', *The Tulane Drama Review* 11, no. 3 (Spring 1967): 101.
82 The first resolution, issued on 14 August, condemned the recent publication of works by Mikhail Zoshchenko and Anna Akhmatova, while the third resolution, issued on 4 September, focused on cinema and criticized the pre-war film *A Great Life* (1939).
83 'O repertuare dramaticheskikh teatrov i merakh po ego uluchsheniiu: Postanovlenie TsK VKP(b) ot 26 Avgusta 1946', *Sovetskoe iskusstvo*, 20 September 1946, 1.
84 RGALI 2977/1/4/4/29.
85 For a detailed analysis of the theory of conflictlessness, see Jesse Gardiner, 'No Conflict on the Stage: The Theory of Beskonfliktnost'' in Postwar Soviet Drama', *The Russian Review* 77 (July 2018): 427–45.
86 N. Virta, 'Proizvedenie bol'shoi zhiznennoi pravdy', *Sovetskoe iskusstvo*, 16 January 1952.

87 K. S. Simonov, *Glazami cheloveka moego pokoleniia: razmyshleniia o I. V. Staline* (Moscow: Kniga, 1990), 203–4.
88 See for example K. Simonov, 'Iarche i polnee izobrazhat' nashu sovetskuiu zhizn', *Pravda*, 17 March 1952, 2; 'Preodolet' otstavanie dramaturgii', *Pravda*, 7 April 1952, 2; V. Frolov and V. Sitov, 'Bol'she zaboty o tvorcheskom roste pisatelei', *Pravda*, 21 July 1952, 2.
89 *Pravda*, 13 October 1952, 5.
90 'Ob odnoi antipatrioticheskoi gruppe teatral'nykh kritikov', *Pravda*, 28 January 1949, 3.
91 *Literaturnaia gazeta*, 4 December 1948, 4; *Literaturnaia gazeta*, 22 December, 1.
92 Gennadii Kostyrchenko, *Tainaia politika Stalina: vlast' i antisemitizm* (Moscow: Mezhdunarodnye otnosheniia, 2003), 305–6; Sheila Fitzpatrick, 'The Lady Macbeth Affair: Shostakovich and the Soviet Puritans', in *The Cultural Front: Power and Culture in Revolutionary Russia* (Ithaca: Cornell University Press, 1992), 210.
93 See for example Aleksandr Gerasimov, 'Za sovetskii patriotizm v iskusstve', *Pravda*, 10 February, 1949, 3; K. Zubkov, 'Gordost' russkogo iskusstva', *Pravda*, 19 October, 1949, 2; 'Ob odnoi antipatrioticheskoi gruppe teatral'nykh kritikov', 3.
94 'Do kontsa razoblachit' kosmopolitov-antipatriotov', *Pravda*, 26 February 1949, 3; 'Do kontsa razgromit' antipatrioticheskuiu gruppu kritikov', *Izvestiia*, 26 February 1949.
95 'Do kontsa razoblachit' kosmopolitov-antipatriotov', 3.
96 The first mention of Meyerhold in *Literaturnaia gazeta* was a few weeks earlier in an article by Anatolii Surov attacking the critic Iuzovskii for his previous support of Meyerhold. See A. Surov, 'Estetsvuiushchie klevetki', *Literaturnaia gazeta*, 9 February 1949, 3.
97 J. M. Symons, *Meyerhold's Theater of the Grotesque* (Cambridge: Cambridge University Press, 1973), 21.
98 On this history, see Gennadii Kostyrchenko, *Stalin protiv 'kosmopolitov': vlast' i evreiskaia intelligentsia v SSSR* (Moscow: ROSSPEN, 2009), 119–20.
99 Ibid., 131.
100 On the 'Doctor's Plot', see Iakov Etinger, 'The Doctors' Plot: Stalin's Solution to the Jewish Question', in *Jews and Jewish Life in Russia and the Soviet Union*, ed. Yaacov Ro'I (Ilford: Frank Cass & Co. ltd, 1995), 103–24; Alexander Lokshin, 'The Doctors' Plot: The Non-Jewish Response', 157–67, op cit; Kostyrchenko, *Stalin protiv 'kosmopolitov'*, 259–80.
101 Cited in Nikolai A. Gorchakov, *The Theater in Soviet Russia*, trans. Edgar Lehrman (New York: Columbia University Press, 1957), 398.
102 Boris Filippov, *Actors without Make-Up*, trans. Kathelene Cook (Moscow: Progress Publishers, 1977), 155.
103 Alisa Koonen (1889–1974) had been one of Stanislavsky's favourite actresses at the Moscow Art Theatre, before she left in 1913 to pursue greater creative independence.

## Chapter 2

1. 'Otchetnyi doklad Tsk VKP (b) XIX s"ezdu Partii', *Pravda*, 6 October 1952, 6.
2. On the theory of 'conflictlessness' in Soviet dramaturgy, see Chapter 1.
3. Simonov, *Glazami cheloveka moego pokoleniia*, 203–4.
4. 'Nikolai Vasil'evich Gogol'', *Pravda*, 4 March 1952, 1; 'Preodolet' otstavanie dramaturgii', *Pravda*, 7 April 1952, 2; Ia. El'sberg, 'Velikie traditsii Gogolia i Shchedrina', *Literaturnaia gazeta*, 24 June 1952, 3; Iurii Borev, 'Voprosy estetiki v "voprosakh filosofii"', *Literaturnaia gazeta*, 23 August 1952, 3.
5. See Richard L. Chapple, *Soviet Satire of the Twenties* (Gainesville: University of Florida Press, 1980).
6. See A. Lezhnev, 'Na puti k vozrozhdeniiu satiry', *Literaturnaia gazeta*, 22 April 1929, 2; V. Blium, 'Vozroditsia li satira', *Literaturnaia gazeta*, 27 May 1929, 2; G. Iakybovskii, 'O satire nashikh dnei', *Literaturnaia gazeta*, 8 July 1929, 3; M. Rogi, 'Puti sovetskoi satiry oshibka tov. Bliuma', *Literaturnaia gazeta*, 22 July 1929, 3.
7. On my use of the term 'Other', see Chapter 1.
8. 'Do kontsa razoblachit' kosmopolitov-antipatriotov', *Pravda*, 3.
9. On the Petersburg myth, see Solomon Volkov, *St Petersburg: A Cultural History*, trans. Antonina W. Bouis (New York: Simon & Schuster, 1995); On Moscow as the 'third Rome' see Judith E. Kalb, *Russia's Rome: Imperial Visions, Messianic Dreams, 1890–1940* (Wisconsin: University of Wisconsin Press, 2008).
10. See Chapter 1.
11. See Catriona Kelly, *St Petersburg: Shadows of the Past* (New Haven: Yale University Press, 2014), 224–5.
12. Other new satires included Semen Narin'iani's *Anonymous* (1952), Nikolai Pogodin's *When the Spears Break* (1953) and Leonid Lench's *Big Trouble* (1953).
13. 'V Komitete po delam iskusstv', *Sovetskoe iskusstvo*, 13 August 1949, 4.
14. Marina Zhezhelenko, 'Akimov', in *Portrety rezhisserov*, vol. 1, 62.
15. Nikolai Akimov, 'Put' Teatra Komedii', in *Akimov – eto Akimov*, ed. V. N. Zaitsev et al. (St Petersburg: Rossiiskaia natsional'naia biblioteka, 2006), 41; On Vakhtangov see Boris Zakhava, *Sovremenniki* (Moscow: Iskusstvo, 1969), 24, 163.
16. Marina Zabolotniaia, 'Gamlet v postanovke N. P. Akimova', in *Akimov – eto Akimov*, 96.
17. Nikolai Akimov, 'Vystuplenie na sobranii rabotnikov iskusstv, 9 Aprelia 1936', in *Akimov – eto Akimov*, 25.
18. Akimov, 'Put' Teatra Komedii', 37–8.
19. Gleb Grakov, 'Retsidivy formalizma. O gastroliakh Leningradskogo teatra komedii v Moskve', *Pravda*, 5 August 1949, 3.
20. Rancière, *Aisthesis*, 90–1.
21. Rancière, 'Artistic Regimes and the Shortcomings of the Notion of Modernity', 15–26.

22  On the links between the 'through action' and Aristotle's 'unity of action', see V. Volkenshtein, *Stanislavskii* (Moscow: Shipovnik, 1922).
23  Marina Zhezhelenko, 'Nikolai Akimov v novom teatre', in *Rezhisser i vremia: Sbornik nauchnykh trudov*, ed. V. M. Mironova et al. (Leningrad: Lgitmik, 1990), 64.
24  'V Komitete po delam iskusstv', 4.
25  'K novomu pod'emu teatral'nogo iskusstva!', *Pravda*, 29 September 1949, 1.
26  One of those who watched over Akimov was Vera Ivanovna, then secretary of the Party Obkom.
27  David Zolotnitskii, 'Pora nachinanii', in *Leningradskii gosudarstvennyi akademicheskii Teatr imeni Lensoveta 1933–1983*, ed. A. V. Lisitsyn (Leningrad: Iskusstvo, 1984), 24.
28  Nikolai Akimov, 'O teatral'no-dekoratsionnom iskusstve', in *Teatral'noe nasledie' tom 1*, ed. S. L. Tsimbal (Leningrad: Iskusstvo, 1978), 205.
29  Anatolii Smelianskii, *Nashi sobesedniki: Russkaia klassicheskaia dramaturgiia na stsene sovetskogo teatra 70-kh godov* (Moscow: Iskusstvo, 1981), 150.
30  Naum Berkovskii, 'Tsarstvo tenei i liricheskaia tema', in *Literatura i teatr: Stat'i raznykh let* (Moscow: Iskusstvo, 1969), 549.
31  Ibid., 538.
32  M. E. Saltykov-Shchedrin, *Sobranie sochinenii v 20 tomakh*, vol. 4 (Moscow: Khudozhestvennaia literatura, 1965), 376.
33  Moisei Iankovskii, *Leningradskii teatr komedii* (Leningrad: Iskusstvo, 1968), 105.
34  Vera Budreiko, 'Ol'ga Dmitrievna', in *Teni: Spektakl' Leningradskogo Gosudarstvennogo Teatra imeni Lensoveta*, ed. S. Tsimbal (Moscow: Iskusstvo, 1954), 100–1.
35  Saltykov-Shchedrin, *Sobranie sochinenii*, 387.
36  On this scene, see D. Zolotnistskii, 'Dramaticheskaia satira "Teni"', in *Teni: Spektakl'*, 29–30.
37  Aleksandr Tairov, *O teatre* (Moscow: VTO, 1970), 190.
38  S. Kara, 'Teni', *Vechernii Leningrad*, 20 January 1953, 2.
39  G. Kapralov, 'Satira shchedrina na stsene', *Pravda*, 24 January 1953, 3.
40  Ruben Simonov, 'Teni proshlogo', *Literaturnaia gazeta*, 28 February 1953, 3.
41  Ibid.
42  Budreiko, 'Ol'ga Dmitrievna', 100.
43  Brecht described Vakhtangov as the 'meeting point' between Stanislavsky and Meyerhold before the split. *Brecht on Theatre*, trans. John Willett (London: Methuen, 1964), 237–8.
44  A. Abramov, 'Svistikov', in *Teni: Spektakl'*, 88.
45  N. Akimov, 'Zametki rezhissera', in *Teni: Spektakl'*, 47.
46  Ibid., 46.
47  Galina Korotkevich, 'Sof'ia Aleksandrovna', in *Teni: Spektakl'*, 75.
48  Cited in Akimov, 'Zametki rezhissera', 52–54.
49  A. Sokol'skaia, 'Interesnyi spektakl', *Smena*, 18 January 1953, 2.

50  V. Ermilov, 'Satira Shchedrina na tsene', *Pravda*, 30 June 1953, 3.
51  Smelianskii, *Nashi sobesedniki*, 152; Boris Babochkin, *V teatre i kino* (Moscow: Iskusstvo, 1968), 101.
52  *The Case* was completed in 1861 but not staged until 1882 in a heavily censored version at the Malyi Theatre in Moscow. The uncensored play text was first staged in 1917 at the Aleksandrinskii Theatre by Meyerhold along with the other two plays in the trilogy.
53  Spencer Golub, *The Recurrence of Fate: Theatre and Memory in Twentieth-Century Russia* (Iowa City: University of Iowa Press, 1994), 130.
54  Edward Gordon Craig, *Towards a New Theatre: 40 Designs for Stage Scenes with Critical Notes by the Inventor* (London/Toronto: Dent & Sons, 1913), 41–7, cited in Rancière, *Aisthesis*, 177.
55  The Table of Ranks (Tabel' o rangakh) was introduced by Peter I in 1722 and replaced the old hereditary system of social hierarchy with a meritocratic one. It assigned faux-military ranks to fourteen civil service positions in a pyramidic structure but was known for its cronyism and inertia.
56  Zhezhelenko, 'Nikolai Akimov v novom teatre', 76.
57  Hannah Arendt, *Eichmann in Jerusalem: A Report on the Banality of Evil* (New York: The Viking Press, 1963).
58  Vera Shitova, 'Pravo na gnev', in *Spektakli etikh let: 1953–1956: Sbornik statei*, ed. I. N. Solov'eva (Moscow: Iskusstvo, 1957), 99.
59  Ibid.
60  Marc Elie, 'Khrushchev's Gulag: The Soviet Penitentiary System after Stalin's Death 1953–1964', in *The Thaw*, 114; Dobson, *Khrushchev's Cold Summer*, 52.
61  Zhores Medvedev and Roy Medvedev, *The Unknown Stalin*, trans. Ellen Dahrendorf (London: I.B. Tauris, 2003), 102.
62  Konstantin Rudnitskii, 'Delo', in *Spektakli i gody: Stat'i o spektakliakh russkogo sovetskogo teatra*, ed. A. N. Anastas'ev et al. (Moscow: Iskusstvo, 1969), 352.
63  English translation by Robert Chandler in Vasily Grossman, *Life and Fate* (London: Vintage, 2006), 667; Russian original in Vasilii Grossman, *Zhizn' i sud'ba* (Moscow: Knizhnaia Palata, 1988), 640.
64  Emmanuel Levinas, 'Peace and Proximity', in *Basic Philosophical Writings*, ed. Adriaan T. Peperzak et al. (Bloomington: Indiana University Press, 1996), 167, cited in Judith Butler, *Precarious Life: The Powers of Mourning and Violence* (London: Verso, 2004), 133–4.
65  Butler, *Precarious Life*, 133.
66  Ibid., 139.
67  The Comédie-Française performed in Moscow and Leningrad in April 1954.
68  Vladimir Sappak, 'Utverzhdenie samobytnosti', *Literaturnaia gazeta*, 1 September 1955, 2.
69  M. Petukhov, 'Bez repertuara, bez rezhissera', *Leningradskaia Pravda*, 27 August 1955.

70  E. K. Sokolinskii, fn.17, 'Pis'ma N. P. Akimova V. V. Ivanovnoi 1953–1955', in *Akimov – eto Akimov*, 261.
71  Nikolai Akimov, 'Rezhisser o spektakle "Revizor" N. Gogolia v teatre komedii', *Leningradskaia Pravda*, 29 November 1958.
72  Zhezhelenko, 'Akimov', 81.
73  David Zolotnitskii, 'Akimov i vremia', in *Akimov – eto Akimov*, 288.

# Chapter 3

1  *Pravda*, 30 July 1958, 1.
2  See Chapter 1.
3  Cited in V. Katanian, *Maiakovskii: Literaturnaia khronika* (Moscow: Sovetskii pisatel', 1948), 405. On the efforts to secure Mayakovsky's legacy, see Vahan D. Barooshian, *Brik and Mayakovsky* (The Hague: Mouton, 1978), 109–21.
4  RGALI 631/15/808.
5  *Mystery Bouffe* in 1918 and again in its second version in 1921, *The Bedbug* in 1929 and *The Bathhouse* in 1930.
6  On the relationship between Mayakovsky and Meyerhold, see Genrikh Shakhov, *Maksim Maksimovich Shtraukh* (Moscow: Vseros, 1964), 59; A. Fevral'skii, *Pervaia sovetskaia p'esa* (Moscow: Sovetsii pisatel', 1971), 153; Konstantin Rudnitskii, *Rezhisser Meierkhol'd* (Moscow: Nauka, 1969), 399; Aleksandr Gladkov, *Ne tak davno: Meierkhol'd, Pasternak i drugie* (Moscow: Vagrius, 2006), 317; Braun, *Meyerhold*, 166; Robert Leach, *Meyerhold* (Cambridge: Cambridge University Press, 1989), 152, 167.
7  Fevral'skii, *Pervaia sovetskaia p'esa*, 158.
8  Valentin Pluchek, *Na stsene – Maiakovskii* (Moscow: Iskusstvo, 1962), 6.
9  V. Meierkhol'd, 'O plane novoi postanovki "Klopa"', in *Meierkhol'd V. E. Stat'i*, vol. 2 (Moscow: Iskusstvo, 1968), 367; Gladkov, *Ne tak davno*, 175, 184; Fevral'skii, *Pervaia sovetskaia p'esa*, 221.
10  Pluchek, *Na stsene – Maiakovskii*, 6.
11  Vladimir Maiakovskii, 'Chto takoe "Bania"? Kogo ona moet?', *Ogonek* 47 (1929). Cited in V. V. Maiakovskii, *Teatr i kino*, vol. 2, ed. A. V. Fevral'skii (Moscow: Iskusstvo, 1954), 457–8.
12  'O "Bane" V. Maiakovskogo', in *Meierkhol'd V. E. Stat'i*, vol. 2, 219.
13  'Bania', *Rabochaia gazeta*, 21 March 1930 and V. B. 'Bania' v teatre im. Meierkhol'da, *Rabochii i teatr*, 18, 1930, cited in Shakhov, *Shtraukh*, 60–1.
14  Dmitrii Moldavskii, *S Maiakovskim v teatre i kino* (Moscow: VTO, 1975), 278.
15  Moldavskii, *S Maiakovskim*, 279; Pluchek, *Na stsene – Maiakovskii*, 57, 63.
16  Iutkevich, *Kontrapunkt rezhissera*, 192, cited in Moldavskii, *S Maiakovskim*, 279.
17  Pluchek, *Na stsene – Maiakovskii*, 52.

18  On Meyerhold's production of *The Bathhouse*, see A. Fevral'skii, *Desiat' let teatra Meierkhol'da* (Moscow: Federatsia, 1931), 79–81; Braun, *Meyerhold*, 256–9.
19  Pluchek, *Na stsene – Maiakovskii*, 65.
20  Iu. Ivashchenko, 'Natural'no, zhiznenno, pokhozhe', *Komsomol'skaia Pravda*, 12 December 1953, 3.
21  V. Ognev and Z. Papernyi, 'Maiakovskii na stsene', *Ogonek* 7 (1954): 23–4.
22  Ibid.
23  Vladimir Sappak, 'Boevoi satiricheskii spektakl'', *Sovetskaia kul'tura*, 6 February 1954.
24  V. Frolov, 'Satira Maiakovskogo na stsene', *Pravda*, 2 March 1954.
25  Nikolai Petrov, 'Vstrechi s Maiakovskom', *Teatr* 7 (1963): 13; Pluchek, *Na stsene – Maiakovskii*, 36.
26  V. V. Maiakovskii, *Sochineniia*, vol. 2 (Moscow: Khudozhestvennaia literatura, 1970), 96.
27  See Clark, *The Soviet Novel*, 15–17.
28  N. Zorkaia, 'Poiski novogo', *Teatr* 7 (1955): 38–54.
29  Iu. Ivashchenko, 'Groznoe oruzhie', *Komsomol'skaia Pravda*, 22 May 1955, 3.
30  Vladimir Sappak, 'Pered prem'eroi', *Sovetskaia kul'tura*, 14 April 1955.
31  On Meyerhold's production of *The Bedbug*, see Fevral'skii, *Desiat' let*, 67–8; Rudnitskii, *Rezhisser Meierkhol'd*, 400–6; Braun, *Meyerhold*, 248–51; Leach, *Meyerhold*, 157–63.
32  Pluchek, *Na stsene – Maiakovskii*, 119.
33  Author's own copy.
34  On jazz in the Soviet Union, see S. Frederick Starr, *Red and Hot: The Fate of Jazz in the Soviet Union* (New York: Oxford University Press, 1983).
35  Pluchek, *Na stsene – Maiakovskii*, 95.
36  Ibid., 107.
37  N. V. Gogol', *Revizor* (Letchworth: Bradda Books Ltd, 1964), 131.
38  Iutkevich, *Kontrapunkt rezhissera*, 202 cited in Moldavskii, *S Maiakovskim*, 294.
39  V. Frolov, 'Atakuiushchee slovo', *Pravda*, 29 June 1955, 2.
40  Yurii Khaniutin, 'Maiakovskii izdevaetsia', *Literaturnaia gazeta*, 17 May 1955, 3.
41  A. Kudriaev, 'Oruzhiem satiry', *Moskovskii komsomolets*, 19 May 1955, 3; Ivashchenko, 'Groznoe oruzhie', 3.
42  Frolov, 'Atakuiushchee slovo', 2; Kudriaev, 'Oruzhiem satiry', 3.
43  Museum Archive of the Moscow Satire Theatre.
44  Khaniutin, 'Maiakovskii izdevaetsia', 3.
45  Cited in E. Kolokolov, 'Prisypkin i emu podobnye', *Stalinskii Komsomol'sk*, 8 July 1956, 3. All further citations are from this source.
46  Marjorie L. Hoover, *Meyerhold: The Art of Conscious Theater* (Amherst: University of Massachusetts Press, 1974), 179.
47  The title suggests a mix of religious mystery play and comedy bouffe.

48  See Fevral'skii, *Pervaia Sovetskaia p'esa*.
49  Pluchek, *Na stsene – Maiakovskii*, 131–6.
50  Cited in *Ocherki istorii russkogo sovetskogo dramaticheskogo teatra*, vol. 3, ed. Iu. Kalashnikov et al. (Moscow: Izdatel'stvo Akademii nauk SSSR, 1961), 346.
51  On Meyerhold's production of *Mystery Bouffe* in 1921, see Fevral'skii, *Desiat' let teatra Meierkhol'da*, 28–9; Fevral'skii, *Pervaia sovetskaia p'esa*, 154–6; Rudnitsky, *Russian and Soviet Theatre*, 42, 62.
52  Pluchek, *Na stsene – Maiakovskii*, 151; *Ocherki istorii*, 347; Fevral'skii, *Pervaia sovetskaia p'esa*, 225–6.
53  A. Grebnev, 'Bessmertnyi dukh revoliutsii', *Sovetskaia kul'tura*, 5 November 1957, 3; K. Rudnitskii, 'Kak zhivoi s zhivym', *Moskovskaia Pravda*, 17 November 1957; B. Rostotskii, '"Misteriia-buff" na stsene', *Pravda*, 21 November 1957.
54  Pluchek, *Na stsene – Maiakovskii*, 141.
55  Timothy W. Ryback, *Rock Around the Bloc: A History of Rock Music in Eastern Europe and the Soviet Union* (Oxford: Oxford University Press, 1989), 30.
56  Ibid.
57  See Braun, *Meyerhold on Theatre*, 194; Katerina Clark, *Petersburg: Crucible of Cultural Revolution* (Cambridge, MA: Harvard University Press, 1995), 162.
58  G. Sviridov, 'Iskoreniat' poshlost' v muzyke', *Pravda*, 17 September 1958, 6.
59  Pluchek, *Na stsene – Maiakovskii*, 157.
60  Ibid., 158.
61  Rudnitskii, 'Kak zhivoi s zhivym'; Rostotskii, 'Misteriia-buff' na stsene'; *Ocherki istorii*, 348.
62  Vladimir Ognev, 'Doroga revoliutsii', *Teatr* 2 (1958): 87–93; V. Manuilov, 'Misteriia-buff', *Vechernii Leningrad*, 26 March 1958; I. Vishnevskaia, 'Dva spektaklia o revoliutsii', *Vecherniaia Moskva*, 16 November 1957; Rostotskii, 'Misteriia-buff' na stsene'.
63  Grebnev, 'Bessmertnyi dukh revoliutsii'.
64  Rostotskii, 'Misteriia-buff' na stsene'.
65  Pluchek, *Na stsene – Maiakovskii*, 145–6.
66  I. Vishnevskaia, 'Dva spektaklia o revoliutsii', *Vecherniaia Moskva*, 16 November 1957.
67  RGALI 2437/3/1009/1–51 (1–5). All further quotations from this event are from this source.
68  Iutkevich was no doubt referring here to Iurii Elagin, author of the now widely discredited book *Temnyi genii* (1955).
69  *Ocherki istorii*, 366.
70  Henry Glade, 'Brecht and the Soviet Theatre: A 1971 Overview', *Brecht Heute* 2 (1972): 173.
71  *Pravda*, 26 May 1955, 2.
72  Nina Velekhova, *Okhlopkov i teatr ulits* (Moscow: Iskusstvo, 1970), 120; Marjorie L. Hoover, 'Brecht's Soviet Connection Tretiakov', *Brecht Heute* 3 (1973): 48.

## Chapter 4

1. On the Twentieth Party Congress and Khrushchev's 'secret speech', see for example William Taubman, *Khrushchev: The Man and his Era* (New York: Norton, 2003); Donald Filtzer, *The Khrushchev Era: De-Stalinization and the Limits of Reform in the USSR 1953-1964* (London: Macmillan, 1993), 15-21; Zhores and Medvedev, *The Unknown Stalin*, 95-111; Polly Jones, 'From the Secret Speech to the Burial of Stalin: Real and Ideal Responses to De-Stalinization', in *The Dilemmas of De-Stalinization*, 41-63.
2. Medvedev and Medvedev, *The Unknown Stalin*, 105.
3. 'O preodolenii kul'ta lichnosti i ego posledstvii', *Pravda*, 2 July 1956, 1-2.
4. See Introduction.
5. Ibid.
6. For a definition of 'conventional' (*uslovnyi*) theatre, see Chapter 1.
7. The entire speech can be heard online at: http://theatrologia.su/audio/1740 (last accessed on 1 September 2021).
8. L. Viv'en, 'Chto takoe litso teatra?', *Teatr* 1 (1956): 49-58.
9. 'On the Party's Policy in the Field of Literature' Resolution of the Central Committee of the R. K. P. (b), 18 June 1925, Appendix iv in C. Vaughan James, *Soviet Socialist Realism: Origins and Theory* (London: Macmillan, 1973), 116-19.
10. *Iskusstvo*, 1-2, 1933, cited in Matthew Cullerne Bown, *Socialist Realist Painting* (New Haven: Yale University Press, 1998), 141; *Literaturnaia gazeta*, 29 August 1934, 1.
11. See Chapter 1 for the discussion of these terms.
12. The argument for a broader definition of realism in painting was advanced by a number of art critics. See for example Igor' Grabar', 'Zametki o zhivopisi', *Literaturnaia gazeta*, 27 September 1956, 2-3; A. Kamenskii, 'Razmyshleniia u poloten sovetskikh khudozhnikov', *Novyi mir* 7 (1956): 190-203.
13. 'K voprosu o tipicheskom v literature i iskusstve', *Kommunist* 18 (1955): 20.
14. R. Simonov, 'O teatrakh "perezhivaniia" i "predstavleniia"', *Teatr* 8 (1956): 58.
15. B. Zakhava, 'Za sintes teatra "predstavleniia" i "perezhivaniia"', *Teatr* 1 (1957): 45.
16. V. Bebutov, 'O teatre predstavleniia', *Teatr* 12 (1956): 66-72.
17. A. Popov, 'O sokrovennoi suti nashego iskusstva', *Teatr* 6 (1956): 47-58.
18. A. Efros, 'Bednyi Stanislavskii!', *Teatr* 10 (1956): 62-8.
19. M. Knebel, 'Universal'na li sistema Stanislavskogo?', *Teatr* 6 (1957): 11-19.
20. 'O svobode tvorchestva', *Izvestiia*, 25 November 1956.
21. Nikolai Gorchakov was a director at the MAT, Pavel Markov was head of the Meyerhold Heritage Commission and Igor Il'insky made his name as an actor at Meyerhold's Theatre.
22. Natalia Starosel'skaia, *Tovstonogov* (Moscow: Molodaia gvardiia, 2004), 116-17.

23 Tairov, *O teatre*, 144.
24 On Tairov's production of *An Optimistic Tragedy*, see B. Medvedev, 'Optimisticheskaia tragediia', in *Spektakli i gody: Stat'i o spektakliakh russkogo sovetskogo teatra*, ed. A. N. Anastas'ev et al. (Moscow: Iskusstvo, 1969), 161–73; Nick Worrall, *Modernism to Realism on the Soviet Stage: Tairov–Vakhtangov–Okhlopkov* (Cambridge: Cambridge University Press, 1989), 58–61; Starosel'skaia, *Tovstonogov*, 130–3.
25 R. Ben'iash, 'Optimisticheskaia tragediia', in *Spektakli i gody*, 374.
26 Ibid., 375.
27 Georgi Tovstonogov, *The Profession of the Stage-Director*, trans. Bryan Bean (Moscow: Progress Publishers, 1972), 202.
28 Ibid., 206.
29 Ibid., 268.
30 Ibid., 270.
31 Ibid.
32 Ben'iash, 'Optimisticheskaia tragediia', 378; Tovstonogov, *The Profession of the Stage-Director*, 272.
33 Konstantin Rudnitskii, 'O rezhisserskom iskusstve Tovstonogova', in G. A. Tovstonogov, *Zerkalo stseny*, ed. Iu Rybakov, vol. 1 (Moscow: Iskusstvo, 1984), 19.
34 O. Berggol'ts, 'Vystuplenie na obsuzhdenii spektaklia "Optimisticheskaia tragediia"', *Prem'ery Tovstonogova*, ed. E. I. Gorfunkel' (Moscow, 1994), 70.
35 Ben'iash, 'Optimisticheskaia tragediia', 378.
36 Anatoly Smeliansky, *The Russian Theatre after Stalin*, trans. Patrick Miles (Cambridge: Cambridge University Press, 1999), 50.
37 Tovstonogov, *The Profession of the Stage-Director*, 205.
38 Cited in Suny, *The Soviet Experiment*, 381.
39 A. Anastas'ev, 'Sila geroicheskogo', *Literaturnaia gazeta*, 21 January 1956, 3; Ol'ga Berggol'ts, 'Optimisticheskaia tragediia', *Pravda*, 5 February 1956, 4; B. Lvov-Anokhin, 'Masterstvo rezhissera' *Literaturnaia gazeta*, 26 April 1958, 3.
40 Anastas'ev, 'Sila geroicheskogo', 3.
41 Berggol'ts, 'Optimisticheskaia tragediia', 4.
42 Ibid.
43 Anastas'ev, 'Sila geroicheskogo', 3.
44 Boris Golubovsky, *Bol'shie malen'kie teatry* (Moscow: Izd. Im. Sabashnikovykh, 1998), 90, cited in *The Soviet Theater*, 493.
45 Tovstonogov, *The Profession of the Stage-Director*, 200.
46 Rancière, *Aisthesis*, 65.
47 B. Alpers, 'Razbeg v teatre Krasnoi Presni', *Sovetskii teatr* 5 (1932): 13–18, cited in Velekhova, *Okhlopkov i teatr ulits*, 92.
48 N. Okhlopkov, 'The Carnival Play: N. Pogodin's Aristocrats at the Realistic Theatre', *Izvestiia*, 16 January 1935, cited in *The Soviet Theater*, 417.

49 See Iu. Iuzovskii, 'Spektakl'-prazdnik: Aristokraty v realisticheskom teatre', *Literaturnaia Gazeta*, 5 February 1935, 4; Velekhova, *Okhlopkov i teatr ulits*, 120–3; Andre Van Gyseghem, *Theatre in Soviet Russia* (London: Faber and Faber, 1943), 199–204; Norris Houghton, 'Moscow Rehearsals', in *N. P. Okhlopkov: stat'I, vospominaniia*, ed. E. I. Zotova and T. A. Lukina (Moscow: VTO, 1986), 313–21; Worrall, *Modernism to Realism*, 161–5.
50 Iuzovskii, 'Spektakl'-prazdnik, 4.
51 N. P. Okhlopkov, 'Ob uslovnosti', in *Stat'i, vospominaniia*, 29–84.
52 Filippov, *Actors without Make-up*, 164–5.
53 S. Rozental, 'Aristokraty N. Pogodina: Realisticheskii teatr', *Pravda*, 11 March 1935, 4.
54 Iu. Zubkov, 'Aristokraty', *Sovetskaia kul'tura*, 3 January 1957.
55 V. Pomerantsev, 'Ob iskrennosti v literature', *Novyi mir* 12 (December 1953): 218–45.
56 Velekhova, *Okhlopkov i teatr ulits*, 119.
57 On the lack of psychological subtlety in *Aristocrats* and socialist realism more generally, see Cynthia A. Ruder, *Making History for Stalin: The Story of the Belomor Canal* (Florida: University of Florida Press, 1998), 170.
58 Van Gyseghem, *Theatre in Soviet Russia*, 201–2.
59 Elie, 'Khrushchev's Gulag', 109–42.
60 N. P. Okhlopkov, 'Ob uslovnosti', *Teatr* 11 (1959): 58–77; 12 (1959): 52–73.
61 Okhlopkov, 'Ob uslovnosti', in *Stat'i, vospominaniia*, 29–84. All further citations are from this version.
62 G. A. Tovstonogov, 'Otkrytoe pis'mo Nikolaiu Okhlopkovu', *Teatr* 2 (1960): 42–56.
63 G. A. Tovstonogov, 'Otkrytoe pis'mo Nikolaiu Okhlopkovu', in *Krug myslei: Stat'i, rezhisserskie kommentarii, zapisi repetitsii* (Leningrad: Iskusstvo, 1972), 86–109. All further citations are from this version.
64 'Vystavka Iaponskogo iskusstva', *Literaturnaia gazeta*, 23 October 1956, 3.
65 Tovstonogov, 'Otkrytoe pis'mo Nikolaiu Okhlopkovu', 109.
66 Okhlopkov, 'Ob uslovnosti', 83.

# Chapter 5

1 Derza and Matthews, 'Soviet Theatre Audiences', 720–1.
2 Quoted in Anatoli Smeliansky, *Oleg Yefremov: Masters of Soviet Art*, trans. Mikhail Nikolsky (Moscow: Novosti Press Agency Publishing House, 1988), 15.
3 Ibid., 30.
4 See for example Mikhail Kozakov, *Akterskaia kniga* (Moscow: Vagrius, 1999), 95; Anatolii Smelianskii, *Oleg Efremov. O teatre i o sebe* (Moscow: Moskovskii

khudozhestvennyi teatr, 1997), 58; RGALI 3152/4/1/1-36; RGALI 2329/6/394/124-125.
5 On Italian neorealism, see Mark Shiel, *Italian Neorealism: Rebuilding the Cinematic City* (London: Wallflower, 2006), 2-13; Saverino Giovacchini and Robert Sklar, 'Introduction: The Geography and History of Global Neorealism', in *Global Neorealism: The Transnational History of a Film Style*, ed. Giovacchini and Sklar (Jackson: University Press of Mississippi, 2011), 4; on links to Soviet cinema, see Josephine Woll, *Real Images: Soviet Cinema and the Thaw* (London: I.B. Tauris, 2000), 35; Masha Salazkina, 'Soviet-Italian Cinematic Exchanges, 1920s-1930s: From Early Soviet Film Theory to Neorealism', in *Global Neorealism*, 47.
6 On the establishment of the Sovremennik Theatre-Studio, see V. Ryzhova, 'Khochetsia, shtob tak i bylo!', *Moskovskii komsomolets*, 16 May 1956; Smelianskii, *Oleg Efremov*, 55-9; Viktor Rozov, *Udivlenie pered zhizn'iu* (Moscow: Vagrius, 2000), 403-4; Smeliansky, *Oleg Yefremov: Masters of Soviet Art*, 14-20; Aleksandr Svobodin, *Oleg Efremov* (Moscow: Soiuz teatr, 1992), 3-11.
7 'Programma deiatel'nosti studii molodykh akterov' (1956) in *Oleg Efremov Vse neprosto: Stat'i, vystupleniia, besedy, dokumenty* (Moscow: Artist. Rezhisser. Teatr, 1992), 264-8.
8 On Efremov's approach to directing, see Jesse Gardiner, 'Oleg Efremov: The Heir to Stanislavsky', in *Russian Theatre in Practice: The Director's Guide*, ed. Amy Skinner (London: Methuen, 2019), 179-92.
9 N. Volianskaia, 'V tvorcheskoi laboratorii rezhissera', *Teatr* 10 (1973): 51.
10 *Ocherki istorii*, vol. 3, 393.
11 English translation in *Contemporary Russian Drama*, ed. F. D. Reeve (New York: Pegasus, 1968), 32; Russian original in Viktor Rozov, *V dobryi chas: p'esy* (Moscow: Sovetskii pisatel', 1973), 544.
12 M. M. Kozakov, *Fragmenty* (Moscow: Iskusstvo, 1989), 141; Smeliansky, *The Russian Theatre after Stalin*, 19.
13 Ryzhova, 'Khochetsia, shtob tak i bylo!'; V. Berezkin, 'Kollektiv entuziastov', *Sovetskaia kul'tura*, 31 July 1956; Ia. Varshavskii, 'V dobryi put'!', *Vecherniaia Moskva*, 16 April 1957.
14 B. Babochkin, 'Tvorcheskaia zaiavka', *Moskovskaia pravda*, 25 April 1957.
15 RGALI 3152/4/1/1-36.
16 Ibid.
17 Aleksei Arbuzov, 'V zashchitu Malen'kogo Cheloveka', *Iskusstvo kino* 1 (January 1957): 132-4.
18 V. Berezkin, 'Kollektiv entuziaztov', *Sovetskaia kul'tura*, 31 July 1956. (N.B. the role of Boris was shared between Efremov and Gubanov).
19 RGALI 3152/4/188/1-2.
20 On the popularity of this poem, see Catherine Merridale, *Ivan's War: The Red Army 1939-1945* (London: Faber and Faber, 2005), 271.

21 See Woll, *Real Images*, 74–5.
22 Salazkina, 'Soviet-Italian Cinematic Exchanges', 48–9.
23 M. Kvasnetskaia, 'Imia emu – "Sovremennik"', *Komsomol'skaia Pravda*, 13 June 1958.
24 *Moskovskii teatr Sovremennik: 1956–2006*, ed. Evgeniia Kuznetsova (Moscow: Indeks Dizain & Pablishing, 2006), 31–2.
25 Aleksandr Galich, *General'naia repetitsiia* (Moscow: Sovetskii pisatel', 1991), 375.
26 *Literaturnaia gazeta*, 18 March 1958, 3.
27 Smelianskii, *Oleg Efremov*, 60.
28 On the production of *No one*, see A. V. Efros, *Izbrannye proizvedeniia*, vol. 1 (Moscow: Parnas, 1993), 102–4; Kozakov, *Fragmenty*, 144.
29 RGALI 2329/6/423/122.
30 Alexander Minchin, *20 Interv'iu* (Moscow: Eksmo-Press, 2001), 67.
31 RGALI 2325/6/423/101.
32 RGALI 2329/6/396/1-9.
33 RGALI 2325/6/423/86.
34 Clark, *The Soviet Novel*, 229.
35 RGALI 2325/6/423/85.
36 On reactions to *Not by Bread Alone*, see Denis Kozlov, 'Naming the Social Evil: The readers of Novyi mir and Vladimir Dudintsev's *Not by Bread Alone*, 1956–59 and beyond', in *The Dilemmas of De-Stalinization*, 80–98.
37 The first edition of the almanac was published in January 1956 and included Viktor Rozov's play *Alive Forever* and poetry by Evgenii Evtushenko.
38 Mark Shcheglov, 'Realizm sovremennoi dramy', *Literaturnaia Moskva II sbornik vtoroi*, ed. M. I. Aliger et al. (Moscow: Gosudarstvennoe izdatel'stvo khudozhestvennoi literatury, 1956), 685.
39 Aleksandr Kron, 'Zametki pisatelia', *Literaturnaia Moskva II sbornik vtoroi*, 782.
40 D. Eremin, 'Zametki o sbornike "Literaturnaia Moskva"', *Literaturnaia gazeta*, 5 March 1957, 3.
41 Quoted in Taubman, *Khrushchev*, 308.
42 On the Berliner Ensemble tour of Soviet Russia, see Jesse Gardiner, '*Mother Courage* and Political Pragmatism: Sovietizing Brecht during the Thaw', *Slavonic and East European Review* 93, no. 4 (2015): 626–54.
43 On the Moscow Festival of Youth and Students, see Kristin Roth-Ey, *Moscow Prime Time: How The Soviet Union Built the Media Empire that Lost the Cultural Cold War* (Ithaca: Cornell University Press, 2011), 163–5; Margaret Peacock, 'The Perils of Building Cold War Consensus at the 1957 Moscow World Festival of Youth and Students', *Cold War History* 12, no. 3 (2012): 515–35; Eleonory Gilburd, 'The Revival of Soviet Internationalism in the Mid to Late 1950s', in *The Thaw*, 362–401.
44 See Bittner, *The Many Lives of Khrushchev's Thaw*, 70.

45 Boris M. Poiurovskii, *Chto ostalos' na trube . . . Khroniki teatral'noi zhizni* (Moscow: Tsentroligraf, 2000), 16–18, cited in *The Soviet Theater*, 531–3.
46 N. Rabiniants, 'S veroi v cheloveke', *Leningradskaia pravda*, 13 April 1959.
47 Ibid.
48 V. M. Gaevskii, 'Peterburgskii kandid', in *Fleita Gamleta: Obrazy sovremennogo teatra* (Moscow: Soiuzteatr STD SSSR, 1990), 93.
49 See Elie, 'Khrushchev's Gulag', 125–6; Dobson, *Khrushchev's Cold Summer*, 51.
50 S. Kara, 'Shestoi vecher', *Sovetskaia kul'tura*, 11 July 1959.
51 Ibid.
52 Ibid.
53 K. Shcherbakov, 'Piat' vecherov', *Moskovskaia pravda*, 18 July 1959.
54 L. Zhukova, '"Sovremennik" i sovremennost'', *Sovetskaia kul'tura*, 13 August 1959.
55 RGALI 3152/2/191/1–36. All further quotations from the conference are taken from this source.
56 N. Okhlopkov, 'Geroi i epokha', *Literaturnaia gazeta*, 20 June 1959, 1.
57 Shcherbakov, 'Piat' vecherov'.
58 Ibid.
59 Zhukova, '"Sovremennik" i sovremennost'', 3.
60 Ibid.
61 RGALI 2329/6/423.
62 Quoted in Tat'iana Lanina, *Aleksandr Volodin* (Leningrad: Sovetskii pisatel', 1989), 114.
63 RGALI 2329/6/422.
64 RGALI 2329/6/423.
65 RGALI 2325/6/423/101.
66 RGALI 2329/6/394/124-5.
67 RGALI 2325/6/423/85.
68 RGALI 2329/6/423.
69 RGALI 2329/6/396.

# Chapter 6

1 Cited in Taubman, *Khrushchev*, 364.
2 On 'The Aviator's March', see for example Maria Enzensberger, 'We Were Born to Turn a Fairy Tale into Reality': Grigori Alexandrov's The Radiant Path, in *Stalinism and Soviet Cinema*, ed. Richard Taylor et al. (London: Routledge, 1993), 97.
3 On Evgenii Shvarts's work and career, see Amanda J. Metcalf, *Evgenii Shvarts and his Fairy-Tales for Adults* (Birmingham Slavonic Monographs No. 8, 1979);

J. Douglas Clayton, 'The Theatre of E.L. Shvarts: An Introduction', *Slavic and East-European Studies* 19 (1974): 23–43; Irina H. Corten, 'Evgenii Shvarts as an Adapter of Hans Christian and Charles Perrault', *The Russian Review* 37, no. 1 (January 1978): 51–67; Anja Tippner, 'Evgenii Shvarts's Fairy Tale Dramas: Theatre, Power and the Naked Truth', in *Russian Children's Literature and Culture*, ed. Marina Balina et al. (New York: Routledge, 2008), 307–24; *My Znali Evgeniia Shvartsa*, ed. S. L. Tsimbal (Leningrad: Iskusstvo, 1966); Evgenii Shvarts, *Obyknovennoe chudo: P'esy, stsenarii, skazki, avtobiograficheskaia proza, vospominaniia* (Kishinev: Literatura artistike, 1988).

4  On the fairy tale debate, see Marina Balina, 'Creativity through Restraint: The Beginnings of Soviet Children's Literature', in *Russian Children's Literature and Culture*, 1–18; Felix J. Oinas, 'The Political Uses and Themes of Folklore in the Soviet Union', in *Folklore, Nationalism and Politics*, ed. Oinas (Columbus: Slavica, 1978), 77–97.

5  'O sovetskoi Literature', *Literaturnaia gazeta*, 20 August 1934, 2–4.

6  *Pravda*, 20 August 1934, 3; *Literaturnaia gazeta*, 20 August 1934, 1.

7  See Clark, *The Soviet Novel*, 147.

8  Marina Balina, 'Introduction: Fairy Tales of Socialist Realism', *Politicizing Magic: An Anthology of Russian and Soviet Fairy Tales*, ed. Marina Balina et al. (Evanston: Northwestern University Press, 2005), 118.

9  This technique was the epitome of grotesque theatre for Meyerhold, see his essay 'The Fairground Booth' (1912), trans. Edward Braun in *Meyerhold on Theatre*, 137–40. On the grotesque in literature and culture more broadly, see Mikhail Bakhtin, *Rabelais and His World*, trans. Hélène Iswolsky (Bloomington: Indiana University Press, 1984); Wolfgang Kayser, *The Grotesque in Art and Literature*, trans. Ulrich Weisstein (New York: Columbia University Press, 1963).

10  Iankovskii, *Leningradskii teatr komedii*, 50–1.

11  For details, see Shvarts's diary entries for 1944 in *Zhivu bespokoino: Iz dnevnikov*, ed. K. N. Kirilenko (Leningrad: Sovetskii pisatel', 1990), 12–16.

12  N. Akimov, 'Nash Avtor Evgenii Shvarts', in *Ne tol'ko o teatre* (Leningrad: Iskusstvo, 1966), 274.

13  S. Borodin, 'Vrednaia skazka', *Literatura i iskusstvo*, 25 March 1944, 3, cited in Zhezhelenko, 'Akimov', 60.

14  Ibid.

15  See for example Ludmilla Alexeyeva and Paul Goldberg, *The Thaw Generation: Coming of Age in the Post-Stalin Era* (Pittsburgh: University of Pittsburgh Press, 1993), 1–5; On variations of public opinion following the 'secret speech', see Polly Jones, 'From the Secret Speech to the burial of Stalin', 53–7.

16  Iankovskii, *Leningradskii teatr komedii*, 141.

17  *My Znali Evgeniia Shvartsa*, 216–22.

18　Andrei Khrzhanovskii, 'Garin i Shvarts', in *Uchenik charodeia: Kniga ob Eraste Garine*, ed. A. Khrzhanovskii (Moscow: Iskusstvo, 2004), 319.
19　See Chapter 5.
20　RGALI 3152/4/9/1–2.
21　Ibid., 2.
22　Ibid.
23　RGALI 2329/6/423.
24　Margarita Mikaelian, *Golyi korol', Krasavets-muzhchina i...* (Moscow: Agraf, 2003), 40.
25　Ibid., 43.
26　RGALI 3152/4/10/1–6.
27　Ibid., 4.
28　Ibid., 2.
29　Ibid., 3.
30　Ibid.
31　Kozakov, *Akterskaia kniga*, 109.
32　See Efremov's interview in Minchin, *20 Interv'iu*, 68.
33　'Shest'desiat sovremennikov', *Smena*, 27 March 1960.
34　Ibid.
35　S. Vladimirov, 'Zdravstvui, "Sovremennik"!', *Leningradskaia Pravda*, 29 March 1960.
36　Grigori Svirski, *A History of Post-war Soviet Writing: The Literature of Moral Opposition*, trans. and ed. Robert Dessaix and Michael Ulman (Ardis: Ann Arbor, 1981), 136.
37　Mikaelian, *Golyi korol'*, 9, 12; 'Liudmila Ivanova', in *Evgenii Evstigneev. Narodnyi artist* (Nizhnii Novgorod: Dekom, 1998), 88.
38　Kozakov, *Akterskaia kniga*, 108.
39　Efim Dorosh, *Zhivoe derevo iskusstva* (Moscow: Iskusstvo, 1967), 29.
40　Mikaelian, *Golyi korol'*, 14.
41　Dorosh, *Zhivoe derevo iskusstva*, 45; Stanislav Rassadin, 'Teatr "Sovremennik" ishchet p'esu', *Iunost'* 8 (1962): 74.
42　Mikaelian, *Golyi korol'*, 14.
43　English translation by Elisaveta Fen in *The Naked King, The Shadow & The Dragon: Yevgheny Shvarts* (London: Marion Boyars, 1976), 58; Russian original in *Evgenii Shvarts: Antologia satiry i iumora Rossii XX veka* (Moscow: Eksmo-Press, 2001), 151.
44　Oleg Tabakov, *Moia nastoiashchaia zhizn'* (Moscow: Eksmo-Press, 2000), 201; Kozakov, *Akterskaia kniga*, 108.
45　Mikaelian, *Golyi korol'*, 25.
46　Bakhtin, *Rabelais and His World*, 10.
47　Ibid., 6.

48 Rancière, *The Emancipated Spectator*, 13.
49 Hallward, 'Staging Equality', 112–13; Rancière, 'The Distribution of the Sensible', 8.
50 Hallward, 'Staging Equality', 118.
51 Tabakov, *Moia nastoiashchaia zhizn'*, 203.
52 Ibid.
53 For details of this meeting, see Mikaelian, *Golyi korol'*, 7–8.
54 RGALI 2329/6/396/10.
55 Ibid., 10.
56 Ibid., 12–13.
57 RGALI 2325/6/423/86.
58 Gosudarstvennyi arkhiv Rossiiskoi federatsii [hereafter GARF] A501/1/3007.
59 GARF A501/1/3405.
60 Kozakov, *Akterskaia kniga*, 109.
61 I. Patrikeeva, 'Na pereput'e', *Teatral'naia zhizn'* 16 (1960): 8–10.
62 *Kapustniks* ('cabbage pie shows') were a tradition started at the MAT at the turn of the century during Lent, when people gave up meat and ate cabbage pies. Public performances were forbidden, so the MAT would put on in-house entertainments in which the actors sent up the management and themselves.
63 *Moskovskii teatr Sovremennik*, 49–51.
64 Metcalf, *Evgenii Shvarts*, 30–1.
65 A. Karaganov, 'Byt' vernym svoemu imeni', *Literaturnaia gazeta*, 5 July 1960, 3.
66 Ibid.
67 Kozakov, *Akterskaia kniga*, 110.
68 RGALI 2329/6/417.
69 RGALI 2329/6/423.
70 See for example Abram Mil', 'Zritelei', *Moskovskii teatr sovremennik*, 56; Kozakov, *Akterskaia kniga*, 227; Rassadin, 'Teatr "Sovremennik" ishchet p'esu', 68–75.
71 Cited in Taubman, *Khrushchev*, 514.
72 See Jones, 'From the Secret Speech to the burial of Stalin', 51.
73 RGALI 2329/6/438.
74 Quoted in Evgeny M. Binevich, 'Na puti k Drakonu', *Neva* 10 (1996): 178, in *The Soviet Theater*, 546.
75 English translation by Laurence Senelick in *The Dragon* (New York: Broadway Play Publishing Inc., 2012), 95.
76 Alla Mikhailova, 'How They Were Staged', in *Classic Soviet Plays*, ed. Alla Mikhailova (Moscow: Progress Publishers, 1979), 818.
77 On the Novocherkassk protest, see Erik Kulavig, *Dissent in the Years of Khrushchev: Nine Stories About Disobedient Russians* (Basingstoke: Palgrave, 2002), 123–54.
78 Bakhtin, *Rabelais and His World*, 11–12.
79 Hallward, 'Staging Equality', 111.

80  On the 'Manege Affair', see Susan E. Reid, 'In the Name of the People: The Manège Affair Revisited', in *Kritika: Explorations in Russian and Eurasian History* 6, no. 4 (Fall 2005): 673–716; Taubman, *Khrushchev*, 588–90.
81  Vladislav Zubok, *Zhivago's Children: The Last Russian Intelligentsia* (Cambridge, MA: Harvard University Press, 2009), 214.
82  Smelianskii, *Oleg Efremov*, 60.
83  Metcalf, *Evgenii Shvarts*, 64–5.
84  On this production, which premiered in the summer of 1962, see M. A. Zakharov, *Teatr bez vran'ia* (Moscow: AST, 2008), 85.
85  Taubman, *Khrushchev*, 11.
86  Ibid.
87  Ibid., 12.
88  Quoted in Smelianskii, *Oleg Efremov*, 34, 60.

# Epilogue

1  Quoted in Smelianskii, *Oleg Efremov*, 28.
2  On *The Master and Margarita*, see O. N. Mal'tseva, *Poeticheskii teatr Iuriia Liubimova: Spektakli Moskovskogo teatra dramy i komedii na Taganke: 1964–1998* (St Petersburg: Rossiiskii institut istorii iskusstv, 1999), 53–5, 77; Birgit Beumers, *Yury Lyubimov at the Taganka Theatre 1964–1994* (Amsterdam: Harwood Academic Publishers, 1997), 158–64; Smeliansky, *The Russian Theatre after Stalin*, 100–1.
3  On *The Good Person of Szechwan*, see R. Krechetova, 'Liubimov', in *Portrety rezhisserov: Zavadskii, Mil'tinis, Ravenskikh, Liubimov*, vol. 2 (Moscow: Iskusstvo, 1977), 123–5; Beumers, *Yury Lyubimov*, 14–17.
4  Tovstonogov, 'Otkrytoe pis'mo Nikolaiu Okhlopkovu', 95.
5  Mal'tseva, *Poeticheskii teatr Iuriia Liubimova*, 9; Beumers, *Yury Liubimov*, 8.
6  On *The Government Inspector*, see Starosel'skaia, *Tovstonogov*, 267–71; Smeliansky, *The Russian Theatre after Stalin*, 128–31.
7  On *The Traditional Reunion*, see R. Ben'iash, 'Efremov', in *Portrety rezhisserov*, vol. 1, 209–12; Birgit Beumers, 'The "Thaw" and after, 1953–1986', in *A History of Russian Theatre*, 362–3.
8  On *The Seagull*, see Anatolii Smelianskii, 'Kontsert dlia skripki s orkestrom', *Teatr Anatoliia Efrosa: Vospominaniia, stat'i*, ed. M. G. Zaionts (Moscow: Artist. Rezhisser. Teatr, 2000), 282–3; Beumers, 'The "Thaw" and after, 1953–1986', 367; Smeliansky, *The Russian Theatre after Stalin*, 63–6.
9  Andrei Siniavskii and Iulii Daniel were arrested in September 1965 for publishing satirical anti-Soviet works in foreign journals under the pen-names Abram Tertz

and Nikolai Arzhak. On 10 February 1966, Siniavskii was sentenced to seven years in a prison camp. Two days later Daniel was handed a five-year sentence.
10 Yurchak, *Everything was Forever*, 34.
11 On Liudmila Petrushevskaia, see Sergei Bavin, *Obyknovennye istorii: Liudmila Petrushevskaia, bibliograficheskii ocherk* (Moscow: Rossiiskaia gos. Biblioteka, 1995); Sally Dalton-Brown, *Voices from the Void: the genres of Liudmila Petrushevskaia* (Oxford: Berghahn, 2001).
12 On Aleksandr Vampilov, see Elena Gushanskaia, *Aleksandr Vampilov: ocherk tvorchestva* (Leningrad: Sovetskii pisatel', 1990); Vreneli Farber, *The Playwright Aleksandr Vampilov: An Ironic Observer* (New York: Peter Lang, 2001).
13 The term 'homo sovieticus' was popularized by the writer Alexander Zinoviev in his book of the same name published in 1982.
14 On *Duck Hunting*, see Smelianskii, *Oleg Efremov*, 73–4.
15 On *A Cabal of Hypocrites*, see A. Smelianskii, *Predlagaemye obstoiatel'stva: Iz zhizni russkogo teatra vtoroi poloviny XX veka* (Moscow: Artist. Rezhisser. Teatr, 1999), 201–3; Smeliansky, *The Russian Theatre after Stalin*, 149–50.
16 On *Batum*, see Smelianskii, *Predlagaemye obstoiatel'stva*, 194–5; Anatoly Smeliansky, 'Russian Theatre in the Post-Communist Era', trans. Stephen Holland, in *A History of Russian Theatre*, 388–9.
17 Aleksei Shishov, 'Pik Stalina', *Literaturnaia gazeta*, 11 November 1992, 2.

# Select Bibliography

Anastas'ev, A. N., and E. P. Peregudova, eds. *Spektakli i gody: Stat'i o spektakliakh russkogo sovetskogo teatra*. Moscow: Iskusstvo, 1969.
Bakhtin, Mikhail. *Rabelais and His World*, trans. Hélène Iswolsky. Bloomington: Indiana University Press, 1984.
Bastrakova, L. P., and D. I. Zolotnitskii, eds. *Leningradskii gosudarstvennyi akademicheskii Teatr imeni Lensoveta 1933–1983*. Leningrad: Iskusstvo, 1984.
Berkovskii, Naum. *Literatura i teatr: Stat'i raznykh let*. Moscow: Iskusstvo, 1969.
Bittner, Stephen V. *The Many Lives of Khrushchev's Thaw: Experience and Memory in Moscow's Arbat*. Ithaca: Cornell University Press, 2008.
Braun, Edward, ed. *Meyerhold on Theatre*. London: Methuen & Co., 1969.
Braun, Edward. *Meyerhold: A Revolution in Theatre*, 2nd edn. London: Methuen Drama, 1995.
Butler, Judith. *Precarious Life: The Powers of Mourning and Violence*. London: Verso, 2004.
Clark, Katerina. *The Soviet Novel: History as Ritual*, 3rd edn. Bloomington: Indiana University Press, 2000.
Clark, Katerina. *Moscow, The Fourth Rome: Stalinism, Cosmopolitanism, and the Evolution of Soviet Culture, 1931–1941*. Cambridge, MA: Harvard University Press, 2011.
Dobson, Miriam. *Khrushchev's Cold Summer: Gulag Returnees, Crime, and the Fate of Reform after Stalin*. Ithaca: Cornell University Press, 2009.
Dorosh, Efim. *Zhivoe derevo iskusstva*. Moscow: Iskusstvo, 1967.
Fevral'skii, A. *Desiat' let teatra Meierkhol'da*. Moscow: Federatsia, 1931.
Fevral'skii, A., ed. *V. E. Meierkhol'd Stat'i, pis'ma, rechi, besedy*, vol. 1 and vol. 2. Moscow: Iskusstvo, 1968.
Fevral'skii, A. *Pervaia sovetskaia p'esa*. Moscow: Sovetsii pisatel', 1971.
Filippov, Boris. *Actors Without Make-Up*, trans. Kathelene Cook. Moscow: Progress Publishers, 1977.
Fitzpatrick, Sheila. *Everyday Stalinism: Ordinary Life in Extraordinary Times: Soviet Russia in the 1930s*. Oxford: Oxford University Press, 1999.
Foucault, Michel. *Power/Knowledge: Selected Interviews and Other Writings 1972–1977*, ed. and trans. Colin Gordon. New York: Pantheon Books, 1980.
Gladkov, Aleksandr. *Ne tak davno: Meierkhol'd, Pasternak i drugie*. Moscow: Vagrius, 2006.

Golub, Spencer. *The Recurrence of Fate: Theatre and Memory in Twentieth-Century Russia*. Iowa City: University of Iowa Press, 1994.
Gorchakov, Nikolai A. *The Theater in Soviet Russia*, trans. Edgar Lehrman. New York: Columbia University Press, 1957.
Iankovskii, Moisei. *Leningradskii teatr komedii*. Leningrad: Iskusstvo, 1968.
Jones, Polly, ed. *The Dilemmas of De-Stalinization: Negotiating cultural and social change in the Khrushchev era*. Oxon: Routledge, 2006.
Kozakov, Mikhail. *Fragmenty*. Moscow: Iskusstvo, 1989.
Kozakov, Mikhail. *Akterskaia kniga*. Moscow: Vagrius, 1999.
Kozlov, Denis, and Eleonory Gilburd, eds. *The Thaw: Soviet Society and Culture during the 1950s and 1960s*. Toronto: University of Toronto Press, 2013.
Kuznetsova, Evgeniia, Anna Shalashova, and Ekaterina Voronova, eds. *Moskovskii teatr Sovremennik: 1956–2006*. Moscow: Indeks Dizain & Pablishing, 2006.
Leach, Robert, and Victor Borovsky, eds. *A History of Russian Theatre*. Cambridge: Cambridge University Press, 1999.
Levinas, Emmanuel. *Otherwise Than Being or Beyond Essence*, trans. Alphonso Lingis. Pittsburgh: Duquesne University Press, 2000.
Medvedev, Zhores, and Roy Medvedev. *The Unknown Stalin*, trans. Ellen Dahrendorf. London: I.B. Tauris, 2003.
Metcalf, Amanda J. *Evgenii Shvarts and his Fairy-Tales for Adults*. Birmingham Slavonic Monographs No. 8, 1979.
Mikaelian, Margarita. *Golyi korol', Krasavets-muzhchina i....* Moscow: Agraf, 2003.
Mironova, V. M., T. B. Zabozlaeva, and O. E. Skorochkina, eds. *Rezhisser i vremia: Sbornik nauchnykh trudov*. Leningrad: Lgitmik, 1990.
Moldavskii, Dmitrii. *S Maiakovskim v teatre i kino*. Moscow: VTO, 1975.
Pluchek, Valentin. *Na stsene – Maiakovskii*. Moscow: Iskusstvo, 1962.
Rancière, Jacques. *Aisthesis: Scenes from the Aesthetic Regime of Art*, trans. Zakir Paul. London: Verso, 2013a.
Rancière, Jacques. *The Politics of Aesthetics*, ed. and trans. Gabriel Rockhill. London: Bloomsbury Academic, 2013b.
Rancière, Jacques. *Dissensus: On Politics and Aesthetics*, trans. Steven Corcoran. London: Bloomsbury, 2015.
Rudnitskii, Konstantin. *Rezhisser Meierkhol'd*. Moscow: Nauka, 1969.
Rudnitsky, Konstantin. *Russian and Soviet Theatre: Tradition and the Avant-Garde*, trans. Roxane Permar. London: Thames and Hudson, 1988.
Senelick, Laurence, and Sergei Ostrovsky, eds. *The Soviet Theater: A Documentary History*. New Haven: Yale University Press, 2014.
Smeliansky, Anatoli. *Oleg Yefremov: Masters of Soviet Art*, trans. Mikhail Nikolsky. Moscow: Novosti Press Agency Publishing House, 1988.
Smelianskii, Anatolii. *Oleg Efremov. O teatre i o sebe*. Moscow: Moskovskii khudozhestvennyi teatr, 1997.
Smelianskii, Anatolii. *Predlagaemye obstoiatel'stva: Iz zhizni russkogo teatra vtoroi poloviny XX veka*. Moscow: Artist. Rezhisser. Teatr, 1999a.

Smeliansky, Anatoly. *The Russian Theatre after Stalin*, trans. Patrick Miles. Cambridge: Cambridge University Press, 1999b.
Solodovnikova, A. V., ed. *Moskovskii Khudozhestvennyi teatr v sovetskuiu epokhu: Materialy i dokumenty*. Moscow: Iskusstvo, 1962.
Starosel'skaia, Natalia. *Tovstonogov*. Moscow: Molodaia gvardiia, 2004.
Suny, Ronald Grigor. *The Soviet Experiment: Russia, The USSR, and the Successor States*. Oxford: Oxford University Press, 1998.
Tabakov, Oleg, *Moia nastoiashchaia zhizn'*. Moscow: Eksmo-press, 2000.
Tairov, Aleksandr. *O teatre*. Moscow: VTO, 1970.
Taubman, William, ed. *Nikita Khrushchev*. Yale: Yale University Press, 2000.
Taubman, William. *Khrushchev: The Man and His Era*. New York: Norton, 2003.
Tovstonogov, G. A. *Krug myslei: Stat'i, rezhisserskie kommentarii, zapisi repetitsii*. Leningrad: Iskusstvo, 1972.
Tovstonogov, Georgi. *The Profession of the Stage-Director*, trans. Bryan Bean. Moscow: Progress Publishers, 1972.
Tsimbal, S. L., ed. *Teni: Spektakl' Leningradskogo Gosudarstvennogo Teatra imeni Lensoveta*. Moscow: Iskusstvo, 1954.
Tsimbal, S. L., ed. *My Znali Evgeniia Shvartsa*. Leningrad: Iskusstvo, 1966.
Uvarova, E. D., ed. *Russkaia sovetskaia estrada 1917–1929*. Moscow: Iskusstvo, 1976.
Van Gyseghem, Andre. *Theatre in Soviet Russia*. London: Faber and Faber, 1943.
Velekhova, Nina. *Okhlopkov i teatr ulits*. Moscow: Iskusstvo, 1970.
Vladimirova, Z., ed. *Portrety rezhisserov: kedrov, Akimov, Tovstonogov, Pluchek, Efremov*, vol. 1. Moscow: Iskusstvo, 1972.
Ward, Chris. *Stalin's Russia*. London: Edward Arnold, 1993.
Worrall, Nick. *Modernism to Realism on the Soviet Stage: Tairov–Vakhtangov–Okhlopkov*. Cambridge: Cambridge University Press, 1989.
Yurchak, Alexei. *Everything was Forever, Until it was No More: The Last Soviet Generation*. Princeton: Princeton University Press, 2005.
Zaitsev, V. N., M. Iu. Liubimova and V. M. Mironova, eds. *Akimov – eto Akimov*. St Petersburg: Rossiiskaia natsional'naia biblioteka, 2006.
Zograf, N. G., and Iu. S. Kalashnikov, eds. *Ocherki istorii russkogo sovetskogo dramaticheskogo teatra*, vol. 3. Moscow: Izdatel'stvo Akademii nauk SSSR, 1961.
Zotova, E. I., and T. A. Lukina, eds. *N. P. Okhlopkov Stat'i, vospominaniia*. Moscow: VTO, 1986.

# Index

Note: Page numbers followed by 'n' refer notes; page numbers in italics refer figures.

Abramov, Anatolii   66
Adorno, Theodore, *Dialectic of Enlightenment*   10
aesthetic formalism   38, 123–4
*agitki*, one-act propaganda plays   23
Akimov, Nikolai   56–9, 151–3, 157
   *The Case*   8, 20, 55, 68–73, *70*, 188 n.52
   *The Dragon*   166–8
   *The Government Inspector*   74–5
   Lensovet Theatre   60–73
   return to Leningrad Comedy Theatre   73–5
   *Shadows* 7, 61–8, *67*
   *Springtime in Moscow*   60
Aleksander II, Tsar   4, 61–2
Aleksandrinskii Theatre (National Dramatic Theatre of Russia)   20, 56, 80, 86, 106, 107, 111, 116, 146
Aleksandrov, Grigorii, *The Radiant Path*   151
*alexandrine*   14
Al'kazar Variety Theatre   2, 19, 78, 164, 173
All-Russian Theatre Organization (VTO)   31, 106–7
All-Union Conference of Theatre Directors   36, 42
All-Union Conference of Theatre Workers, Dramatists and Critics   140
All-Union Festival of Drama Theatres   100
Al'tman, Iogan   49
Amaglobeli, Sergo, *The Good Life*   38
amateur theatre   23
Andersen, Hans Christian   150
   *The Shadow* (production)   152
anti-party group   140, 149
anti-Semitism   48–9, 53, 136, 163

Appia, Adolphe   17
Arbuzov, Aleksei   8, 9, 134, 139, 140
   'In Defence of the Little Man'   134
   *An Irkutsk Story*   8–9
   *Years of Wandering*   139
Ardov, Viktor   151
Arendt, Hannah   71
Aristotle   15, 58, 59
Arkhipova, Nina   81
Art Nouveau   13
Arts and Crafts   13
Arzhanov, Pavel   117
avant-garde   2–3, 10–12, 14, 17–19, 23–4, 39, 42–3, 58, 105, 124, 170
   aesthetics and politics   10–14
   art in aesthetic regime   12–14
   commodification of avant-garde culture   10
   fine arts and mechanical arts   13
   mise en scène   15–17
   modernism   11
   origins of   10
   Rancière on   11–12
'The Aviators' March' (1923)   150

Babel', Isaak   40
Babochkin, Boris   36, 68, 133
Bakhtin, Mikhail   160
   carnival laughter   21, 160, 169
*balagan*   95, 97
Barkin, Mikhail   2
Bauhaus   13
Bebutov, Valerii   105, 109
Belyi, Andrei   27
Beniaminov, Aleksandr   152
Ben'iash, Raisa   115
Benjamin, Walter   27
Bergel'son, David   49
Berggol'ts, Ol'ga   115, 116

Beria, Lavrentii   8, 42, 54
Bersenev, Ivan   38
biomechanics   25, 27, 30, 79, 96
Blok, Aleksandr, *The Little Fairground Booth*   16
Blue Blouse groups   24
Boiadzhiev, Grigorii   47
Boleslavskii, Richard   38
Borshchagovskii, Aleksandr   47
Bosulaev, Anatolii   112, 116
Brecht, Bertolt   5, 19, 23, 25, 101, 124–5, 139, 173
  *The Good Person of Szechwan*   19, 173–4
  'Verfremdungseffekt'   25, 124
Brezhnev, Leonid   4, 19, 54, 170, 175
Brik, Lilia   76
Bromlei, Nadezhda   60
Brook, Peter   5
Bubnov, Andrei   29
Buckner, Conrad   5
Budreiko, Vera   63
Bukharin, Nikolai   26, 27, 40
Bulgakov, Mikhail   27, 29–30, 173, 176
  *Batum*   176
  *A Cabal of Hypocrites*   176
  *The Crimson Island*   29
  *Days of the Turbins*   27–8, 31
  *Flight*   29
  *The Master and Margarita* (play)   173
  *The White Guard*   27
Bulganin, Nikolai   149
Burbage, Richard   14
Butler, Judith   73

cabaret   2, 24–5, 58, 173
Cannes Film Festival   135
canonization, process of   1, 28, 37, 76, 78, 85, 100
Castle, Hubert   5
Central Children's Theatre   1, 38, 109, 129
Chekhov, Anton
  *The Seagull*   50–1, 174, 201 n.8
Chekhov, Mikhail   38, 50, 174, 176
Cherkasov, Nikolai   86
Chronegk, Ludwig   35
Chukhrai, Grigorii   5
Chukovskii, Kornei   150

Cicero   14
circusization   24, 95
Clark, Katerina   32–4
  master plot   34, 85, 144, 150
collective leadership, principle of   104–5, 165
collectivization   29, 31–2
Commedia dell'arte   16, 119, 124
Committee for Artistic Affairs   32, 39–42, 44, 50, 57, 59, 60, 77, 150, 153
Communist International   27
Communist Party   10, 26, 71, 100
  Fifteenth Party Conference   26
  party line   6, 33, 41, 43, 46, 101, 104, 139, 165
  Twentieth Party Congress   102
  Twenty-Second Party Congress   165
conflictlessness, theory of   8, 38, 46–7, 84, 139, 184 n.85
constructivism   26, 43, 55, 80, 87, 95
conventionality (*uslovnost'*)   43, 81, 120–6, 130, 137, 146, 160, 164, 174, 184 n.75
Coquelin, Constant   36, 108
corruption   175
cosmopolitanism   45, 47–50, 53, 55, 57, 124
  anti-cosmopolitanism campaign   19–20, 45, 48–50, 53, 55, 57
Craig, Edward Gordon   17, 70, 71
  Übermarionette, concept of   71
Crommelynck, Fernand, *The Magnanimous Cuckold*   42–3
Crooked Mirror Theatre   56
Cuban Missile Crisis   170
cult of personality   7, 18, 33, 52, 72, 102, 104, 110, 115, 125, 139, 149, 152, 155–6, 158–9, 161, 165, 168, 169

Daniel, Iulii   175
De Filippo, Eduardo
  *My Family*   136
  *Vicenzo De Pretore* (*No One*)   136–7
Demichev, Petr   165
De Santis, Giuseppe   129
Descartes, *Traite des passions*   14
De Sica, Vittorio   129

De Vega, Lope, *The Dog in the Manger* 58
Diderot, Denis 15, 36, 108
Dikii, Aleksei 40, 46, 68, 117
distancing effect 25
Doronina, Tatiana 176
Doroshina, Nina 163
Dorrer, Valentin 157
Dudintsev, Vladimir, *Not by Bread Alone* 138
Duncan, Isadora 24

eccentrism 56, 74, 157
Efremov, Oleg 19, 127–34, 136–8, 143, 155–7, 161, 163, 170, 171, 173–6
  *Alive Forever* 129–35, *133*
  confessional principle 131
  *Five Evenings* 8, 138, 140–8, *142*
  *The Naked King* 148, 150–65, *159*, *161*
  *Tartuffe* 107
  'theatre house' 129–30
  through-action and use of études 130–1
  *The Traditional Reunion* 174
Efros, Anatolii 9, 109, 110, 130
  *No One* 136–7
  *The Seagull* 174
Ehrenburg, Ilia 4, 53, 148
Eichmann, Adolf 71
emotions
  experiencing 36, 108
  as passions 14
Erdman, Boris 154
Erdman, Nikolai 30, 154
Ermilov, Vladimir 80
Ermolova Theatre 8
*estrada* 2–3, 18–19, 88–9, 97
Estrada Theatre, Moscow 3, 18–19
Evstigneev, Evgenii 130, 157–8, *159*, 160, *161*, 164
expressionism 10, 55
expressive theatricalism 56, 59, 82
Ezhov, Nikolai 40, 41, 76
  *Ezhovshchina* 40, 72

Factory of the Eccentric Actor (FEKS) 24, 56
Fadeev, Aleksandr 31, 37, 41

fairy-tale play 150–72, 198 n.4
  children's literature 150
  fairy tale debate 150–1
Fedotov, Aleksandr 37
Fefer, Itsik 49
Five-Year Plan 29, 32, 118, 134, 136
Flaubert, Gustave 13
Fokin, Mikhail 24
Foregger, Nikolai 24
formalism 10–11, 17, 20, 23, 28, 30, 37, 39–43, 48, 53, 55–9, 68, 76–8, 84, 108–10, 122, 124, 140
  anti-formalism campaign 22, 37, 38–9, 47, 57, 60, 105, 108, 152
Foucault, Michel 33, 41
Free Comedy Theatre 56
Furtseva, Elena 163
Futurism 76, 78, 87, 94–5, 174

Gaevskii, Vadim 141
Galich, Aleksandr 136
Garin, Erast 152
Garrick, David 15
Gerasimov, Sergei, *The Village Doctor* 47
Giul'tsen, Aleksandr 66
Gladkov, Aleksandr 100
*glasnost'* 19, 171
Glaviskusstvo 28–9
Glavlit 29
Glavrepertkom 29
Gofshtein, David 49
Gogol, Nikolai 27, 52, 55, 64, 70, 74, 90–1, 174
  *The Government Inspector* 27, 55, 64, 70, 74–5, 90, 152, 174
Golovanovism 29
Gomulka, Wladyslaw 104
Gorbachev, Igor 113
Gorchakov, Nikolai 111
Goriunov, Anatolii 57
Gorky, Maksim 31, 33, 138, 151
  *Egor Bulychev and Others* 31
  *The Lower Depths* 138
  speech at the First Soviet Writers' Congress 151
Great Purges 22, 30, 38–42, 48–9, 77, 90, 102, 105, 114, 120, 136, 183 n.60
Greenberg, Clement 10, 11
Gronskii, Ivan 33

Grossman, Vasilii
    *Black Book* 53
    *Life and Fate* 53, 73
grotesque 8, 16, 21, 55, 56, 62, 65–6, 70, 74, 84, 86, 90–2, 150–2, 157, 160, 164, 169, 198 n.9
Gulag 5, 7, 40, 54, 68, 72, 118, 121–2
Gurvich, Abram 47
Gusev, Viktor, *Springtime in Moscow* 60

*Hamlet* 5, 7, 57, 125
Harunobu, Suzuki 125
Hikmet, Nazim 94
Hill, Aaron 15
Hitler, Adolf 152–3, 162
Hokusai, Katsushika 125
homogenization, of theatre 7, 23, 41–2, 45, 50–1, 107–8, 110, 121
'homo sovieticus' 175, 202 n.13
Horkheimer, Max, *Dialectic of Enlightenment* 10
House of Culture in the Humanities Faculty of Moscow State University 100
Hungarian Revolution (1956) 104, 169

Iachnitskii, Apollon 101
Il'insky, Igor 111
imperial monopoly 28, 180 n.15
Inber, Vera 115
industrialization 31–2
Industrial Party Trial (1930) 29
internationalism 124–5
    Soviet internationalism 139
Iutkevich, Sergei 20, 56, 78, 79, 81, 86, 87, 91, 100, 146
Iuzovskii, Iosif 47
Ivanov, Viacheslav 16
Ivanov, Vsevolod 27
    *Armoured Train 14-69* (1927) 27
Ivanovna, Vera 74

Jewish Anti-Fascist Committee (JAC) 49, 53
Jewish State Theatre 49

Kabuki theatre 119, 125
Kachalov, Vasilii 44
Kaganovich, Lazar 103, 165

Kalatozov, Mikhail, *The Cranes Are Flying* 135
Kamenev, Lev 26, 39, 48, 54
Kamernyi Theatre 25, 29, 40, 44, 50–1, 59, 68, 77, 105, 111, 113
    attacks on 29, 40, 50, 59
Kant, Immanuel 12
*kapustniks* 163, 200 n.62
Karaganov, Aleksandr 164
Karayev, Kara 113
Karpova, Tat'iana 121
Katanian, Vasili, *They Knew Mayakovsky* 86, 94
Kedrov, Mikhail 36, 106–8, 110, 123, 125, 130
    *The Winter's Tale* 123
Kerzhentsev, Platon 23, 40
Khanzel', Iosif 167
Khmelev, Nikolai 27
Kholodov, Efim 48
Khrushchev, Nikita 4–6, 8, 10, 18, 20, 21, 72, 102–6, 115, 122, 125, 127, 131, 138–40, 149, 150, 157, 161, 163, 165, 167, 169–71, *see also* secret speech
    attack on avant-garde art 6, 169–70
    collective leadership 104–5, 165
    *Our Nikita Sergeevich* 157
    secret speech 8, 72, 102–4
    Third Party Programme 165
Kirichenko, Aleksei 149
Kirpotin, Valerii 34, 76, 108
Kirsanov, Semen 94
Kirshon, Vladimir 40
Knebel', Maria 46, 109, 110, 130
Kolesov, Lev 167, *168*
*kolkhoz* 29, 46
Kolmanovskii, Edik 157
*komsomol* 27–8, 81, 132, 170
Koonen, Alisa 50, 51, 113
Kopelian, Efim 142
Korneichuk, Aleksandr
    *Platon Krechet* 35
    *Truth* 35
Korneva, Nelli 167, *168*
Korotkevich, Galina 61, 67–8, *67*
Kosygin, Aleksei 175
Kozakov, Mikhail 163–4
Kozintsev, Grigori 56, 157

Kron, Aleksandr  139
Krupskaia, Nadezhda  26, 150
Kumanin, Vladimir  155
Kurbas, Les'  40
Kurginian, Sergei  176
Kuznetsov, Anatolii  21, 129, 137, 155
  *Sequel to a Legend*  137–8, 155–6
Kuznetsov, Isai, *Two Colours*  138, 156
Kuznetsov, Vsevolod  142
Kvasha, Igor  130, 155, 158, *159*
Kvitko, Lev  49

Labiche, Eugène, *The Journey of Mr. Perrichon*  57–8
Lazarenko, Vitalii  95
Lebedev, Valentin  61, *67*
Le Brun, Charles  14
Lebzak, Ol'ga  113, 116
Legouvé, Ernest  51
  *Adrienne Lecouvreur*  51
Lenin, Vladimir  31, 33, 35, 37, 50, 53, 54, 92, 99, 165
Leningrad Affair  54
Leningrad Bolshoi Dramatic Theatre  1, 3, 8–9, 39, 56, 140, 142, *142*, 146, *146*, 174
Leningrad Comedy Theatre  9, 21, 55, 59, 149, 151–2, 166–9
Leningrad Satire Theatre  60
Lenin Komsomol Theatre  9, 40, 111, 174, 175
Lensovet Theatre  56–73
Leonidov, Leonid  30
Lepko, Vladimir  88, *91*, 96, 101
Levin, Moisei  56
Levinas, Emmanuel  41, 73
*Literaturnaia Moskva II* almanac  138–9
Liubimov, Iurii  5, 9, 19, 173, 174
Lokshina, Khesia  154
Lunacharskii, Anatolii  28, 107

Macklin, Charles  15
Maeterlinck, Maurice  15–16
Malenkov, Georgii  52, 54, 55, 100
Maliugin, Leonid  47
Malyi Theatre  1, 3, 35, 37, 46
Manege Affair  169–70, 201 n.80
Marinskii Theatre  61
Markov, Pavel  99, 111

Marshak, Samuil  151
Mayakovsky, Vladimir  1, 7, 30, 34, 75, 76
  *The Bathhouse* (1953 production)  7, 77, 79–86, *83*
  *The Bedbug* (1955 production)  77, 86–93, *89*, *91*
  canonization  76–9
  Futurism  76
  'A Letter to Maksim Gorky'  85
  Mayakovsky Metro station  76
  *Mystery Bouffe* (1957 production)  77, 93–101, *96*, *98*
  *plakatnost'*  77
  relationship with Meyerhold  77
Mayakovsky Theatre  9, 20, 86, 101, 106, 117, 120, 142, 144
Mei Lanfang  124
Meiningen Company  35, 108
  Meiningen approach  58, 65
Menglet, Georgii  82, 92
Meyerhold, Vsevolod  2, 26, 27, 34, 53, 57, 76, 118–19, 122, 124, 127, 130, 157
  arrest and execution  41–2
  *The Bathhouse*  80–2
  *The Bedbug*  87, 90
  biomechanics  25, 27, 30, 96
  *Bubus the Teacher*  117
  *Don Juan*  79
  *The Government Inspector*  27, 64, 70, 74
  *The Little Fairground Booth*  16
  *The Magnanimous Cuckold*  42–3
  *Masquerade*  79
  Meyerhold as 'Other'  41, 53, 101
  'Meyerholdism'  39, 75
  *Mystery Bouffe*  95, 97
  pre-acting  25
  rehabilitation  75, 79, 99–101, 110, 166
  relationship with Mayakovsky  77
  rhythm  56
  *The Trust D. E*  97
  *Woe to wit*  90, 152
Meyerhold State Higher Theatre Workshop  79
Meyerhold State Theatre (GOSTIM)  2, 27, 79

Mikaelian, Margarita   137, 155–8, 161
  *The Naked King*   148, 150–65, *159*, *161*
Mikhailov, Nikolai   161, 163
Mikhalkov, Sergei, *Crayfish*   55
Mikhoels, Solomon   49, 111, 166
Mikoyan, Anastas   163
Milinder, Lev   154
*mimesis*, principle of   12, 15, 58
Mizeri, Svetlana   130, 134
Molotov, Viacheslav   39, 103, 165
Morozova, Tanya   151
Moscow Art Theatre (MAT)   1, 3, 17, 19, 23, 27, 30–1, 35, 37–8, 41, 44, 46, 57, 59, 65, 78, 85–6, 105, 106–8, 110, 123–4, 126, 128, 130, 132, 135, 137, 138, 145–6, 162, 164, 173, 175–6
  canonization as model theatre   28, 37–8, 42, 45, 47, 50
  as Chekhov Moscow Art Theatre   1, 176
  division of   176
  First Studio   2
  Fourth Studio   2, 117
  as Gorky Moscow Art Theatre   31, 131, 176
  MAT realism   42, 169, 173
  MAT tradition   65, 146
  Order of Lenin   37
  Order of the Red Banner of Labour   37
  Second MAT   38, 60
  Subsidiary Stage   57, 127, 135, 137
  Third Studio   25
Moscow Art Theatre School   20, 51, 127, 129
Moscow Drama Theatre   86
Moscow Linguistic Circle   76
Moscow Regional Professional Union Theatre   37
Moscow Satire Theatre   2, 7, 9, 20, 78–93, 95–101, 148
  productions, 1953–7   76–101
Moskvin, Ivan   44
Mosolova, Elizaveta   60
Mossovet Theatre   46
Muradeli, Vano   48, 140
  *The Great Friendship*   48
music-hallization   24

naturalism   15–16, 39, 45, 50, 55, 82
  naturalistic style   35, 182 n.42
Nazarov, Ivan   70
Nemirovich-Danchenko, Vladimir   21, 30, 35, 37, 44, 108, 124, 126, 128, 130
neo-Platonism   32–3
neorealism   21, 128–9, 134, 135, 137, 147, 195 n.5
New Economic Policy (NEP)   29, 87, 88, 90
Nikitin Brothers' Circus   2
Nikolai I, Tsar   4, 62
*nomenklatura*   175
*Novyi mir* journal   6, 138, 140

Offenbach, Jacques   63, 64
Okhlopkov, Nikolai   2, 9, 39, 40, 44, 101, 105–7, 109, 110, 117–26, 144, 145, 174
  *Aristocrats* (1934 production)   44, 101, 118–19
  *Aristocrats* (1956 production)   106, 119–22
  *Hamlet*   125
  realistic conventionality   120, 122–4
  *Running Start*   118
  spectator's imagination   120, 122–3, 126
Omon Theatre of Buffonade and Miniatures   2
Opera Theatre   36, 41
operetta-mania   63–4
Operetta Theatre   1–2, 63–4, 152
Order of Lenin   37, 50, 54
Order of the Red Banner of Labour   37
Orlova, Liubov'   151
Osborne, John, *Look Back in Anger*   175
the 'Other'   20, 41–2, 53–4, 84, *see also* Meyerhold, Vsevolod
Ovechkin, Valentin   8

Pankov, Pavel   71
Parnakh, Valentin   97
Pasolini, Pier Paolo   135
Pasternak, Boris, *Dr Zhivago*   6
patriotism, Soviet   45, 132
Paulus, Vladlen   155
Pegasus Electro-Theatre   2

*perezhivanie* (emotion-experiencing)   36, 58, 82, 108–10, 121, 123, 128, 130, 164
Perm Regional Drama Theatre   40
Perrault, Charles   150
Perventsev, Arkadii, *Southern Liaison*   35
Petrov, Nikolai   79, 85, 86
Petrov, Vladimir   61
Petrushevskaia, Liudmila, *Three Girls in Blue*   175
Piatakov, Iurii   40
Pimenov, Iurii   68
Plato   160
Pluchek, Valentin   9, 20, 75, 77–9, 82, 85–8, 90, 91, 93–5, 97–100, 146, 148
   *The Bathhouse*   7, 77, 79–86, *83*
   *The Bedbug*   77, 86–93, *89*, *91*
   *Mystery Bouffe*   77, 93–101, *96*, *98*
Pogodin, Nikolai   20, 35, 47, 101, 104, 105, 117, 119, 120, 121, 138
   *Aristocrats*   20, 35, 44, 101
   *Man with a Gun*   35
   *A Petrarchan Sonnet*   104, 138–9
Pokarzhevskii, Boris   155, 161, 162
Pomerantsev, Vladimir   121, 126, 140
Popov, Aleksei   109–11
*Porgy and Bess*   5
*predstavlenie* (representation)   36, 108–10, 126, 130
Prokofiev, Sergei   140
Proletkult (Proletarian Cultural Organization)   23
Pugacheva, Kapitolina   *120*
Puppet Theatre   2–3
Pushkin, Aleksandr
   *Boris Godunov*   57
   *The Tales of Belkin*   60
Pushkin Drama Theatre   50, 68, 162–3
Pushkin Museum of Fine Art   125
Pustynin, Mikhail   24
Pyzhova, Ol'ga   129

Quintilian   14

Radek, Karl   40
Radlov, Sergei   24, 39
Raikin, Arkadii   54

Rancière, Jacques   11–15, 17, 23–6, 43, 58, 160, 169
   aesthetic regime of the arts   12–14, 16, 23–4, 43–4, 58, 178 n.28
   art, concept of   13–14
   *dissensus* (disruption)   14, 160, 169
   *mimesis*, principle of   12, 15, 58
   modernism   11
   representative regime of the arts   12, 15, 43, 44
Ravenskikh, Boris   109–10
Realistic Theatre   2, 40, 44, 105–6, 117, 120
Red Army Theatre   109, 136
Red Theatre   40
Reisner, Larissa   112
*remeslo* (stock-in-trade)   16, 36, 108–9
Revolution of 1917   23, 94, 98
Ribot, Théodule-Armand   35
Rodchenko, Aleksandr   87
Rodin, Auguste   13, 30, 77
Romashov, Boris   35, 48
   *Fighters*   35
Rossellini, Roberto   129
Rozov, Viktor   21, 138–40, 148, 151, 164, 174
   *Alive Forever*   129–35, *133*
   *Good Luck*   130, 138–9
   *Her Friends*   129
   *In Search of Happiness*   135
Rudnitskii, Konstantin   72, 114
Runge, Boris   84
Russian Association of Proletarian Writers (RAPP)   29–31, 83
Russian telegraph agency (ROSTA)   24
Russian-language theatre, first   3
Ryndin, Vadim   112

Saint-Simon, Henri de   10
Saltykov-Shchedrin, M. E.   7, 20, 52, 55, 61–3, 65–8, 100
   *Shadows*   7, 55, 61–8, *67*
   'Shchedrin style'   66
Samoilov, Evgenii   121
Samoilova, Tatiana   135
Sappak, Vladimir   156
Sats, Natalia   40
Schiller, Friedrich   12
Scribe, Eugène   51
   *Adrienne Lecouvreur*   51

Second All-Union Soviet Writers'
    Congress  8
secret speech  6, 8, 20, 72, 102–6,
    115, 127, 131, 150, 160, 163,
    192 n.1
Sergachev, Viktor  157
Serov, Vladimir  169–70
Sharko, Zinaida  *142*
Shcheglov, Mark  139
Shchepkin, Mikhail  37
Shelepin, Aleksandr  170
Shepilov, Dmitrii  96, 171
Shklovsky, Viktor  179 n.52
Sholokhov, Mikhail  8
Shostakovich, Dmitrii  38–9, 48, 87, 100,
    140
    *Lady Macbeth of the Mtsensk
        District*  38, 48
Shvarts, Evgenii  18, 21, 75, 148–54,
    158, 160, 162, 164, 166–9, 171,
    197 n.3
    *The Dragon*  21, 75, 149, 152–3,
        165–8, *168*, 170
    *Little Red Riding Hood*  150
    *The Naked King*  148, 150–65,
        *159*, *161*
    *An Ordinary Miracle*  153–4
    *The Princess and the Swineherd*  151–2,
        155
    *The Snow Queen*  150
    *The Story of a Young Couple*  153–4
Simonov, Konstantin  6, 8, 134
Simonov, Ruben  40, 65, 99, 108, 109,
    121, 148, 163
    *Kirill the Great*  99
Siniavskii, Andrei  174–5
Sino-Soviet split  170
Sixth World Festival of Youth and
    Students  88, 96, 139
Skachkov, Oleg, *Breakers of the
    Silence*  138, 148
Smelianskii, Anatolii  38, 115
socialist realism  7–8, 10, 17, 20, 33–4,
    74, 78, 84–6, 122, 126, 129, 132–4,
    147, 150–1, 166
    acting methodology  35–7, 58
    contrasted with formalism  10, 39, 59
    criticism of  121
    definition  33–4

dramaturgy  34–5
mise en scène  35, 43
origin  33
socialist realism in theatre,
    debate  105–10
spontaneity-consciousness
    dialectic  34, 85, 89, 112, 119
Society for the Study of Poetic Language
    (OPOYAZ)  76
Sofronov, Anatolii  46–8, 140
    *In One Town*  46
    *Moscow Character*  46
Sokolov, Aleksandr  113
Sokolovsky, Mikhail  23
Solodovnikov, Aleksandr  127, 136–7
Solzhenitsyn, Aleksandr, *One Day in
    the Life of Ivan Denisovich*  140,
    169
Sovremennik Theatre-Studio  2, 126–38,
    142–8, 169, 171, 173–6
    *Alive Forever*  129–35
    *Five Evenings*  142–8
    manifesto of 1956  130
    *The Naked King*  152, 154–65
    neorealism  128–9
    'whispering realism'  132
Sputnik 1  97–8
Stalin, Joseph  3–7, 19, 22, 23, 28, 31, 33,
    44, 47, 49, 50, 52, 53, 61, 76, 78–80,
    102–4, 114, 115, 125, 126, 140,
    149–52, 159, 163, 165, 176
    consolidates power  26–9
    cult of personality  33, 52, 102–4
    de-Stalinization  3, 18, 20, 72, 106,
        125–6, 140, 160–1, 165, 166, 169,
        171
    letter to Bill-Belotserkovsky  29
    'Stalin' Constitution  32
Stalinism as return to representative
    regime  42–5, 79, 105, 124, 126
Stalinist aesthetic system  3, 18, 43,
    75, 106, 126
Stalinist epistemology  32–3
Stalinist anti-Jewish repression  49–50
Stalin Peace Prize  101
Stalin Prize  44–6, 128, 184 n.77
Stanislavsky, Konstantin  16, 19, 21, 30,
    31, 34–8, 41, 44–6, 60, 100, 105–11,
    126–8, 130, 131, 138, 174

Stanislavsky system   19, 30, 31, 34, 36,
    45–6, 60, 65, 105, 107, 109–11, 128,
    130, 174
  affective memory or emotional
    memory   35–6, 44, 108
  'Method of Physical Actions'   36–7,
    108, 130
  'through-action'   36, 58, 112, 130
Stanitsyna, Ol'ga   157
Stavskii, Vladimir   118
Stepanova, Angelina   37
Stepanova, Galina   88
Stevens, Rise   5
Sukhanov, Pavel   149, 167
Sukhovo-Kobylin, Aleksandr   8, 20, 55,
    68, 100
  *The Case*   8, 20, 55, 68–73, *70*, 188 n.52
  *Krechinsky's Wedding*   68
  *Tarelkin's Death*   117
Sullivan, Ed   5
Surkov, Aleksei   8
Surov, Anatolii   46–8
  *Dawn over Moscow*   46
Sushkevich, Boris   60
Suslov, Mikhail   47, 50
Svetlov, Mikhail   157
Sviridov, Georgii   97
symbolism   15–16

Tabakov, Oleg   130, 135, 138, 160
Table of Ranks   71, 140, 188 n.55
Taganka Theatre   5, 9, 173–4
Tairov, Aleksandr   19, 25, 40, 44,
    45, 50–1, 56, 59, 64, 68, 75,
    77, 105
  *Lady Windermere's Fan*   50
  'master-actor'   25
  *An Optimistic Tragedy*   44, 105,
    111–12, 117
  Order of Lenin   50
  *The Seagull*   50–1
  synthetic theatre   25, 56
Tarasova, Alla   37
Taylor, Frederick Winslow   25
Tchaikovsky, Petr   50
Tchaikovsky Concert Hall   2
Terent'ev, Igor   40, 174
Terevsat (Theatre of Revolutionary
    Satire)   24

The Thaw   4–7, 55, 61, 93, 128–9,
    138–40, 153, 165–6, 169–71, 173
  definition   4
  Thaw in Soviet theatre   7–10
  theatre debate   106–11
Theatre of Cinema Actors   163
Theatre of Operetta   2
Theatre of Popular Comedy   24
Theatre Square   1–2
theory of socialist legality   42, 184 n.73
Third Party Programme   165
'Thirty Years of the Moscow Artist's
    Union' exhibition   169–70
Tiutchev, Fedor   4
Tolmacheva, Lilia   130, 136, 143, *144*,
    156
Tolstikov, Vasilii   170
Tolstoy, Leo, *Anna Karenina* (1937
    play)   37
Tolubeev, Iurii   114–17
Toporkov, Vasilii   36, 107, 108, 130
Tovstonogov, Georgii   9, 106, 109,
    111–17, 122–6, 142, 146, 157, 174
  *Five Evenings*   140–2
  'Open Letter to Nikolai
    Okhlopkov'   123–4
  *An Optimistic Tragedy* (1955
    production)   105–6, 111–17,
    *116*, 146
TRAM movement (Theatre of Young
    Workers)   7, 23–4, 30
transnational   124, 129
Treaty of Nystad   1
Trenev, Konstantin, *On the Bank of the
    Neva*   35
Tretiakov, Sergei   30, 40
Triumfal'naia Square   19, 76, 78, 118,
    165, 173
  history of   1–2
Trofimov, Nikolai   74
Trotsky, Leon   26–7, 32, 42, 49
  'Soviet Thermidor'   32
  Trotskyite-Zinovievite bloc   54
Tsvetaeva, Marina   138
Turovskaia, Maiia   156
Tvardovskii, Aleksandr   6, 140
Tyshler, Aleksandr   95

Ustinov, Vladimir   148

Vakhtangov, Evgenii   25, 30, 38, 56, 75, 100, 109
  *Princess Turandot*   25
  Vakhtangov method, 'compromise'   65, 74, 85, 146, 164, 187 n.43
Vakhtangov, Sergei   2, 80
Vakhtangov Theatre   5, 50, 57, 65, 99–100, 109, 121, 128, 163, 173
Vampilov, Aleksandr, *Duck Hunting*   175
van Gogh, Vincent   59
Virta, Nikolai   46, 47
  *Our Daily Bread*   46
Vishnevskaia, Irina   99
Vishnevskii, Vsevolod   35, 105, 111, 116
  at the Kamernyi Theatre   105, 112
  *An Optimistic Tragedy*   35, 44, 111–12
  *The Unforgettable 1919*   35
Viv'en, Leonid   107, 111
Volchek, Galina   130, 137
Volodin, Aleksandr   8, 21, 104, 129, 138, 140, 142, 146, 147
  *The Factory Girl*   104, 140
  *Five Evenings*   8, 138, 140–8, *142*
Voronov, Gennady   170
Voropaev, Gennadii   167
Voroshilov, Kliment   165
Vovsi, Miron   49

*vydvyzhensty*   32
Vyshinskii, Andrei   120

Wagner, Richard   17, 25
  'total work of art'   25
Whitman, Walt   13, 118
Winckelmann, Johann, *History of the Art of Antiquity*   12

youth novel   137–8
Yurchak, Alexei   175

Zagarov, Aleksandr   61
Zak, Avenir, *Two Colours*   138
Zakharchenko, Vasilii   157
Zakharov, Mark   170
Zakhava, Boris   109, 121
  *Aristocrats*   121
Zavadskii, Iurii   46
Zbarskii, Lev-Feliks   137
Zhdanov, Andrei   22, 45, 48, 54, 88
  Zhdanovism   45, 50
Zhezhelenko, Marina   74
Zhukov, Aleksandr   60
Zhukov, Georgii   171
Zinoviev, Grigorii   26, 39, 48, 54
Zionism   49
Zolotnitskii, David   75
Zorin, Leonid, *The Guests*   8, 104
Zorkaia, Neia   85, 86
Zuskin, Benjamin   49

www.ingramcontent.com/pod-product-compliance
Lightning Source LLC
Chambersburg PA
CBHW062224300426
44115CB00012BA/2205